BOTTOM LINE
COMPETITIVE
INTELLIGENCE

BOTTOM LINE COMPETITIVE INTELLIGENCE

John J. McGonagle
Carolyn M. Vella

QUORUM BOOKS
Westport, Connecticut • London

Library of Congress Cataloging-in-Publication Data

McGonagle, John J.
    Bottom line competitive intelligence / John J. McGonagle and Carolyn M. Vella.
        p.   cm.
    Includes bibliographical references and index.
    ISBN 1–56720–505–4 (alk. paper)
        1. Business intelligence.   I. Vella, Carolyn M.   II. Title.
    HD38.7.M385   2002
    658.4'7—dc21   2002017766

British Library Cataloguing in Publication Data is available.

Library of Congress Catalog Card Number: 2002017766
ISBN: 1–56720–505–4

First published in 2002

Quorum Books, 88 Post Road West, Westport, CT 06881
An imprint of Greenwood Publishing Group, Inc.
www.quorumbooks.com

Printed in the United States of America

The paper used in this book complies with the
Permanent Paper Standard issued by the National
Information Standards Organization (Z39.48–1984).

10   9   8   7   6   5   4   3   2   1

Contents

Preface

Almost two decades after it emerged on the world business scene, Competitive Intelligence (CI) is still trying to find its footing. While its importance is clearly recognized, in too many situations, those in businesses seeking to use CI are still frustrated. They do not get the CI they need, and/or they cannot measure how and where CI has contributed to the firm's successes. In fact, the failure to be able to show the bottom line impact of CI is continually cited by CI professionals and their customers, or end-users, as a major problem or concern.

There are three fundamental, intertwined, reasons for this constant complaint:

1. Firms that seek to measure CI may use the wrong metrics for the CI they are actually collecting and using.
2. Firms may be collecting the right type of CI, but they are not providing it to end-users in the right form and at the right time.
3. Firms are not collecting the right type(s) of CI for their unique competitive environment.

All a firm has to do is to make one of these fundamental errors to assure that its efforts to measure the impact of CI on the firm will fail. In other words, you can select and apply the proper metrics only after you make sure you are using the right type of CI and that it is being given to the end-users in the right form at the right time.

The only way to untangle this knot is first to provide a way for a firm to determine which form(s) of CI it should be using, and how it should be communicated, and then to provide a way for that firm to select the proper metrics for those form(s) of CI as the firm uses them. Without going through this process, there is no way for providers and/or end-users of any type of a CI to honestly evaluate the performance of CI unit and then to honestly assess and measure its impact on the enterprise's overall financial operations.

This book provides CI professionals and the end-users with the tools to help them to understand what CI they should use, and then to demonstrate where and how CI contributes to the bottom line. That means, to get to the bottom line of this problem, we must first start from the very top. This involves taking the CI professionals and end-users through the following steps:

First, we dissect CI today, showing that it has evolved into five different, but overlapping types of CI. Each of these types of CI has differing characteristics, including turn-around times for finished intelligence, identities and roles of the end-users, as well as the mix of raw data versus refined analysis in the final product(s). And these differing characteristics demand the use of different metrics by management.

We then develop a framework for the CI professionals and end-users to determine which type(s) of CI are best for the particular competitive landscape faced by their firm. For example, a firm in an industry where technical innovation can quickly change the landscape should probably be seeking technology-oriented CI, supplemented by strategy-oriented CI. On the other hand, a firm in a commodity-type market, such as chemicals, or direct mail insurance, needs CI on new initiatives and prices, plus a sense of the direction that each key competitor is being driven by its owners/investors, as well as future investments in new capacity. That set of tasks is most likely to be the realm of tactics-oriented CI, perhaps supplemented by strategy-oriented CI. A firm operating in an industry where competitors compete across similar product lines, like food, may profit from target-oriented CI, supplemented with a defensive CI program. That would allow it to develop critical information on competing firms' visions for product line positioning and underlying distribution issues, while protecting their own competitively sensitive data.

Second, for each of the types of CI, we show the best ways of communicating that CI (reports on capital investment versus news flashes on price changes pending), and what ways are most likely to produce unsatisfactory results. Communicating the right CI in the right way at the right time is integral to providing the end-user with actionable CI.

Third, we then quickly review the most common broad categories of sources for the raw data that are used to support CI analyses. This is important because there are situations where the types of sources used by a CI professional may impact the selection of the most appropriate metrics.

Fourth, we then face the issue of how metrics in general can work, why they can fail, and what the key characteristics are of various types of metrics. Following that, we list and then evaluate the myriad of metrics currently used by CI professionals and end-users to demonstrate and measure the impact of CI on a firm's bottom line.

"You can talk all you want to about articles, books and theories, but what good is it if there is no CI in action piece?" Flynt Tuller, Manager of Competitive Intelligence, MetLife.

Fifth, we then develop and provide CI professionals and end-users with a process that will enable them to select the most appropriate metrics for their unique competitive and CI context from among all of those available.

To paraphrase Mary Harris, getting to the bottom line of CI is a journey, not a destination.[1]

NOTE

1. "Reformation, like education, is a journey, not a destination." Attributed to Mary B. Harris (U.S. prison administrator 1874–1957), *I Knew Them in Prison*, (1936), ch. 34. Available at http://www.bartleby.com/66/76/26876.html (October 23, 2001).

PART I

OVERVIEW

Introduction

—1

Competitive Intelligence involves the use of public sources to develop data on competition, competitors, and the market environment. It then transforms, by analysis, that data into information. Public, in CI, means all information you can legally and ethically identify, locate, and then access.[1]

This book is not intended to be a basic primer on CI. Since Competitive Intelligence has been a part of the business environment, those of us dealing with CI have been struggling to measure its precise impact on businesses. Intuitively, we understand that effective CI must contribute to the performance of a business. If you now know more about your competition and the competitive environment than you did before, it only makes sense that you will make better decisions. But CI usually has only an indirect impact on the bottom line of any business. That makes its contribution hard to measure. It has an additional characteristic that makes measuring its impact more difficult.

That characteristic is that we cannot always determine when, or even if, an individual or firm has made use of that CI, much less how and when it was used. That means that CI's impact on businesses has to date been largely a matter of speculation, of approximation, and of faith. We seek in this book to provide CI professionals, their clients and customers with tools to help them understand, to determine, and to measure where and how CI has contributed to the bottom line.

To do that, we have first to reverse engineer CI. That is, we must see what CI includes and what it does not, how it should and should not be used, and how it is best communicated, before we can determine how to measure the way it has been used. A word of caution: the categories to which we have assigned various types of CI, the ways of collecting data and reporting results, as well as the appropriateness of particular metrics are based on the authors' experiences and those of the studies and articles noted here. We would hope that, before using this system, you understand why such assignments were made. If the environment, whether corporate or competitive, in which you operate makes some of these less accurate, feel free to adapt what we have provided to help you produce your own adapted system.

Originally, CI emerged as a process to be undertaken to support the development of competitive strategy.[2] Its initial place in business management was to link the development of a competitive strategy with achieving competitive advantage.[3] And for many highly respected CI practitioners, that still is and should be its primary, or even sole, mission.[4] However, the reality is that numerous profiles of the CI teams and of the end-users of CI shows that is not the case.[5]

TO WHOM DO CI TEAMS REPORT?

Senior Level Executives	26 percent
Sales and Marketing	23 percent
Strategic Planning	19 percent
Global Marketing	13 percent
Vice President, Market Research	6 percent
Director of CI	5 percent
Other[6]	8 percent

WHAT ARE THEIR JOB FUNCTIONS OR AREAS OF ANALYSIS?

CI/Analysis	38 percent
Market Planning, Research or Analysis	25 percent
Information Center or Services	11 percent
Business Development/Product Planning/ Research & Development	10 percent
Strategic Planning	8 percent
Financial Planning/Counterintelligence/Other[7]	8 percent

WHO USES CI MOST SIGNIFICANTLY
IN DECISION MAKING?

(1 = To No Extent, 5 = To a Significant Extent)

Strategic Planning	4.57
Product Development	4.00
Product Marketing	3.71
Business Development	3.57
Customer Targeting	3.43
Technology Forecasts	3.29
Resource Planning	2.86
Manufacturing Forecasts[8]	2.71

WHICH DEPARTMENTS PRODUCE THE
MAJORITY OF CI REQUESTS?

Marketing	37 percent
Sales	35 percent
Senior Management/Special Projects	13 percent
Mergers and Acquisitions/Finance	9 percent
International Marketing[9]	6 percent

In the past, we,[10] as well as others,[11] have been urging CI professionals to view CI as having evolved into several different types of intelligence. We have previously categorized these as defensive intelligence, or cloaking, strategic intelligence, competitor intelligence, and market intelligence. We then added to that list competitive technical intelligence. In addition, we have shown how other functions, that is benchmarking, reverse engineering, and crisis management, have very strong links to CI.[12]

As we approached the problem of measuring the impact of CI on the bottom line of a business enterprise, we realized that as CI has continued to evolve, we had to revisit this model. In addition, the terms that we had used, taken from those in use for twenty years by CI professionals, caused some confusion, as they were so similar. Also, to generate a valid approach to determining how to measure the value of CI in a particular context, we essentially had to produce a value-chain type methodology for those reading this book to use in analyzing their own situations. That means understanding what types of CI are practiced, determining which one(s) are best for your particular competitive landscape, understanding where the raw data for that intelligence are gathered, and seeing the best ways in which the finished CI is delivered. Then, and only then, after reviewing the types of measures available, can you hope to select the small number of metrics that really enable you to measure the value of CI to you in your particular context.

Also, we have seen that, as it is now practiced, CI units often provide some of more than one type of intelligence, whether the unit's title, or even its mission, allows for that. Finally, there will continue to be changes and developments in what CI is and what it means to its end-users. For all of these reasons, we now feel that, for analytical purposes, we should revisit the way we look at CI and now divide the types of CI practiced into two separate categories, and from there, into four broad divisions based on the type of intelligence actually being provided.

As we see it now, CI has now become, at the first level, divided into two separate disciplines: active and defensive. This is in part because active CI is most often actually managed and conducted by CI professionals. But CI professionals guide a defensive CI program. It is actually conducted by all employees.

"Not only are the two activities, offensive [active] and defensive, linked, but they also offer the competitive intelligence staff yet another avenue of opportunity to meet the intelligence user's needs and wants."[13]

And active CI, in turn, is dividing into four separate, but somewhat overlapping, types of intelligence processes. These each reflect the mission of the CI professionals providing the CI and the needs of their clients, which are, in turn, determined by the overall competitive environment. For that reason, we have chosen to describe them in terms of their orientation, and not as is often done today, by the location of the unit, such as marketing or strategy departments. The four types of active CI are

1. Strategy-oriented Competitive Intelligence
2. Target-oriented Competitive Intelligence
3. Tactics-oriented Competitive Intelligence
4. Technology-oriented Competitive Intelligence

While these terms seem to differ only slightly from those we have used in the past, they actually mark a significant change. As you will shortly see, they each encompass a set of priorities that are not designed to be completely separate from all others, but rather to overlap, as they do in the real world. For that reason, we find them significantly more realistic and useful from an analytical position than our previous efforts.

Each of these four divisions has certain elements in common. They include the following:

- First, its reliance on the use of public sources to develop data, or raw facts, on competition, competitors, and the market environment. These sources may be primary or secondary or both.
- Second, access to the broad variety of analytical tools available to CI professionals to transform that data.
- Third, the transformation, by analysis, of that data into intelligence, or usable results.
- Fourth, the communication of the intelligence in a timely and understandable manner to the end-user. Or, if the end-user is also the CI professional, the incorporation of the intelligence into his or her decision making.

However, each of these four divisions has significant differences from the others. The key differences lie primarily in these areas:

- Subject matter, or focus, of the intelligence efforts
- Relative balance of raw data with completed analysis
- Typical responsibilities of those supported by these intelligence efforts
- The time line with which the intelligence output typically deals

These differences in turn result in differences among these divisions in terms of the following:

- Most common data sources utilized
- Typical methods of delivering the intelligence outputs
- Frequency of delivery of intelligence outputs

That means it is critical to understand which types of CI are those that are needed by a business at any point in time. To that end, we have developed a methodology, indirectly based on the concepts included in Michael Porter's classic forces model, to help CI professionals determine which types of CI are best for their firm's particular situation.[14]

"Analyzing competitors is too important to handle haphazardly."[15]

Finally, as we show you, understanding the differences among the broad divisions in intelligence allows CI professionals and others to begin to determine what measurements (or metrics) they can and should apply to their own intelligence operations, as well as to identify which ones are inappropriate—and why. To put it simply, at present, most efforts to measure the performance of CI operations use tools best applied to strategy-oriented CI processes only.

NOTES

1. See John J. McGonagle and Carolyn M. Vella, *The Internet Age of Competitive Intelligence* (Westport, Conn.: Quorum Books, 1999), ch. 1.

2. Michael E. Porter, *Competitive Strategy: Techniques for Analyzing Industries and Competitors* (New York: The Free Press, 1980). Porter described "how to conduct an industry analysis" as an appendix to his "framework for competitor analysis." See ch. 3 and Appendix B. See also Carolyn M. Vella and John J. McGonagle, *Improved Business Planning Using Competitive Intelligence* (Westport, Conn.: Quorum Books, 1988), and Kirk W. M. Tyson, *Business Intelligence: Putting It All Together* (Lombard, Ill.: Leading Edge Publications, 1986).

3. See Porter, *Competitive Strategy*, and Michael E. Porter, *Competitive Advantage: Creating and Sustaining Superior Performance* (New York: The Free Press, 1985).

4. See, for example, "Understanding the Competition: The CEOs Perspective," in John E. Prescott and Stephen H. Miller, eds., *Proven Strategies in Competitive Intelligence: Lessons from the Trenches* (New York: John Wiley & Sons, 2001), 133–147, and Ben Gilad, "Strategic Intent and Strategic Intelligence," Gary E. Costly, "An Executive Perspective of Competitive Analysis," and Max C. Downham, "Risk, Trust, and Corporate Vision: Linking Business Intelligence and the CEO" in Ben Gilad and Jan P. Herring, eds., *Advances in Applied Business Strategy, Supplement 2A* (Greenwich, Conn.: JAI Press, 1996).

5. See Jerry Miller and the Business Intelligence Braintrust, *Millennium Intelligence: Understanding and Conducting Competitive Intelligence in the Digital Age* (CyberAge Books: Medford, N.J., 2000), 18: "The scope of the intelligence process is quite broad and can be applied to various issues within a firm. . . . [T]he intelligence process can support key decisions within numerous departments of a firm."

6. Shelia Greco Associates, Inc., "2001 Competitive Intelligence Survey," 2, reprinted as "By the Numbers," available at http://www.scip.org/news/cimagazine_article.asp?id_147.

7. Society of Competitive Intelligence Professionals, *2000/'01 Competitive Intelligence Professionals Salary Survey Report and Reference Guide on Analyst Job Descriptions* (Alexandria, Va.: Society of Competitive Intelligence Professionals, 2001), 47.

8. APQC International Benchmarking Clearinghouse, *Competitive and Business Intelligence: Leveraging Information for Action* (Houston, Tex.: American Productivity & Quality Center, 1997), 33.

9. Greco, "Competitive Intelligence Survey," 3.

10. See John J. McGonagle and Carolyn M. Vella, *A New Archetype of Competitive Intelligence* (Westport, Conn.: Quorum Books, 1998), chs. 5–11, and McGonagle and Vella, *Internet Age*, 17–24.

11. See, for example, Tyson, *Business Intelligence*, 9, Sheena Sharp, "Truth or Consequences: 10 Myths that Cripple Competitive Intelligence," *Competitive Intelligence Magazine* 3, 1 (January–March 2000): 37–40, and Constance Thomas Ward, "Real Life CI: Alphabet Soup for Lunch, Anyone?" *Competitive Intelligence Magazine* 2, 4 (October–December 1999): 42. Cf. Victoria Turner Shoemaker, "Using a Marketing Framework to Communicate Competitive Intelligence," in Craig S. Fleisher and David L. Blenkhorn, eds., *Managing Frontiers in Competitive Intelligence* (Westport, Conn.: Quorum Books, 2001), 100–109; Jennifer Swanson, "The Morphing of CI," in *Fifth Annual SCIP European Conference, Conference Proceedings: Competitive Advantage: How to Get It and Maintain It* (Alexandria, Va.: Society of Competitive Intelligence Professionals, 2000), 127–146; and Michael Belkine, ed., "Corporate CI—Tactical or Strategic?" *Competitive Intelligence Magazine* 4, 5 (September–October 2001): 27–31.

12. See McGonagle and Vella, *A New Archetype*, chs. 8–10.

13. Walter D. Barndt, Jr., *User-Directed Competitive Intelligence: Closing the Gap Between Supply and Demand* (Westport, Conn.: Quorum Books, 1994), 71.

14. We have adopted this model in an effort to echo the analytical framework first developed by Professor Michael Porter. Over time, he has himself adapted and revised this. Compare Porter, *Competitive Strategy*, ch. 1 with Porter, *Competitive Advantage*, ch. 1. So have others involved in CI. See Liam Fahey, *Competitors: Outwitting, Outmaneuvering, and Outperforming* (New York: John Wiley & Sons, 1999), 55–59. In any case, it is also a comfortable fit for the reason that this book is widely regarded as one of the first that described the CI process. See Porter, *Competitve Strategy*, Appendix B.

15. Porter, *Competitve Strategy*, 48.

2

Does CI Impact the Bottom Line?

"The Competitive Intelligence activity has identified objectives, or measures, by which it determines if the activity is effective. Examples might be

. . . Changes in market share;

. . . Employee awareness of competitor strategies, performance or product features;

. . . Competitive win rates; and

. . . Impact on related business objectives (e.g., financial performance or customer satisfaction)."[1]

WHERE ARE WE STARTING FROM?

Anecdotal Data

There has always been a general belief, almost a matter of faith, that CI functions are economically justifiable, particularly at the macro level.[2] For example, in a 1993 study of packaged food, telecommunications, and pharmaceutical industries, two academic researchers reported the following findings, based on research surveys:

• Organizations that engage in high levels of CI activity show 37 percent higher levels of product quality, which is, in turn associated with a 68 percent increase in business performance. This is in comparison with organizations reporting low levels of product quality.

- Organizations that engage in high levels of CI activity show 36 percent higher levels of quality in strategic planning. And high confidence levels in strategic plans are, in turn, associated with a 48 percent increase in business performance.
- Organizations that engage in high levels of CI activity show 50 percent higher levels of market knowledge. This is associated with a 36 percent increase in business performance.
- The lack of a formal, sanctioned CI structure leads to "less collection, analysis and use of competitive intelligence."[3]

In 1994, NutraSweet's CEO publicly valued CI to NutraSweet at $50 million. That figure, he said, was based on a combination of revenues gained and revenues which were "not lost" to competitive activity.[4]

In 1995, another study concluded that companies that emphasize CI on average outperformed other companies in three important financial measures.[5] Several years after that study, it was asserted that CI's participation in the value extraction process of intellectual asset management alone has financial impacts ranging from millions of dollars (patent maintenance and filings), to tens of millions of dollars (licensing), to hundreds of millions of dollars (research and development [R&D]) to billions of dollars (mergers and acquisitions [M&A]).[6]

Thus, through the mid-1990s we have a continuing stream of indirect and anecdotal evidence for what we all believe—CI (and thus all CI efforts) has a positive "bottom line" impact on companies.[7] However, this does not tell us which is the case:

- Companies that use CI usually work smarter because of that decision.
- Companies that work smarter will eventually decide to use CI.
- Both of the above.

And, more important, it does not tell us how to measure and to show to what extent and where CI contributed to a firm's bottom line.

The goal of this book is to show you both that all types of CI impact the bottom line and how you can see and show that. The key here is to understand the CI process, as it is working in your enterprise, and then select those available metrics which best demonstrate and measure where and how the CI that you conduct benefits your firm's bottom line.

TYPICAL EFFORTS TO MEASURE CI EFFECTIVENESS

Companies do not have a tested, consistent set of metrics to which they can point that measure the effectiveness of and/or justify the existence of CI functions. A 1997 survey reported on the most common measures of effectiveness of CI systems used by U.S. companies:[8]

Actions taken	67 percent
Market share changes	49 percent
Financial goals met	49 percent
Leads generated	48 percent
New products developed	44 percent

Nothing material has changed since then.[9] To date, we have no single process or set of processes for measuring CI's performance that has achieved any widespread acceptance. Rather, there have been a variety of approaches that have been suggested, each of which has some appeal, but each of which also has severe limitations. And the measures are often used for different purposes, ranging from determining growth and development of the unit to budget justification. These have fallen into four broad, somewhat overlapping categories:

- Mission Statements
- Worth to the Business
- Intelligence Asset Building
- Recording Contributions

Mission Statements

One suggestion has been made that a CI unit's performance should be measured against its stated mission.[10] However, the ability of the unit to be so measured depends, in large part, on the specificity of that mission statement. And unfortunately, most mission statements are like the composite one that follows, lacking any real criteria that can be quantified and then measured:[11]

COMPOSITE CI UNIT MISSION STATEMENT

The CI unit's mission is to develop and to communicate an in-depth and current understanding of the following areas to senior management on both a regular and as-needed basis:

Current and future products/services of major competitors.
Current technologies underlying the activities of major competitors.
Current market activities of major competitors.
Current and future business strategies employed by major competitors.

Identity of potential new competitors.

Officers and managers of this corporation will use this CI in setting over-all business strategies and making decisions on marketing, manufacturing, and distribution tactics.

As absent, agreed-on metrics for CI, it is unlikely that mission statements with measurable goals in them can really be drafted.

Worth to the Business

Another option for measuring CI's impact has been to try to appraise its worth to the business. One suggested approach entails dealing with three separate questions, focusing on the costs of missing or underutilizing a business opportunity, as well as avoiding or minimizing a threat to the business:[12]

- What would happen to the business if the CI disappeared altogether?
- What would happen if we doubled the amount of key CI we have?
- How does the value of this CI change—after a day, week, month, or year?

This type of measurement can be both subjective and erratic. Take, for example a press release announcing a major corporation's appointment of a new president:

Conseco Inc.'s (NYSE:CNC) shares jumped as much as 30 percent on Tuesday after the troubled insurance and loan company said it hired a turnaround specialist as president and chief financial officer.[13]

In essence, this says that the projected worth of this individual to Conseco is 30 percent of the market value of the firm the day before, based on the stock market's evaluation. However, experience shows that such estimates of implicit worth may not be justified, and/or of long duration. In fact, the same article quoted one analyst as saying that "the stock's jump was probably a 'knee-jerk reaction' to the appointment." He may have been correct, as the stock then fell almost 5 percent the next day. The article also noted that a similar increase had occurred in June 2001 with the appointment of a new CEO at Conseco. At that time, it peaked at over $23 per share and then gradually fell to about $18.50 per share by the end of August 2001.

So, if a firm announced the creation of a CI unit, and its stock then jumped 5 percent, is that 5 percent increase in the market value of the underlying stock the worth of the CI unit to the firm? Given the volatile nature of these valuations, which do reflect what is economically regarded as the fairest measure, fair market value, how then can internal, nonmarket valuations be given any real credibility? This does not mean that a CI unit's worth cannot be estimated. Rather, it means that we must understand what we are measuring and why.

A similar approach is to suggest that CI merely adapt measures of effectiveness (MOEs) used by other corporate functions to determine their worth. This would, it is suggested, produce MOEs for CI, such as

- Time savings
- Cost savings or avoidance
- Revenue increase or enhancements
- Investment maximization
- Value added or creation[14]

Not all of these are even in widespread use. In fact, the most common of these being used now appear to be cost savings, responsiveness, and whether the CI process helps support specific business activities, such as new product development and launches.[15] However, this approach still does not come to grips with the underlying problem of how to link CI to such measurable changes.

"There's been quite a lot of sage advice about how failing to quantify the value of a project in terms of ROI . . . or ROCE . . . will doom you to the netherworld of obsolete management practices. . . . [M]y difficulty centers on the hidden assumption. . . . [It] is that somehow IT should undertake the role of demonstrating the benefits of its projects. But if we're building a system for the benefit of a business unit, why should we be the ones burdened with proving its worth?

[A survival strategy is to] do your best to find the holes in the benefits [if someone comes to you with a project]. Approach it with these two viewpoints: 1) I believe in you and want to help you convince all of the nay sayers who want to trash your great idea; and 2) I need to make sure I understand the value so that I can do a better job in building it for you."[16]

Intelligence Asset Building

A similar approach is to seek to identify intelligence asset building. This entails both providers and end-users of CI determining how the CI is being used, and how well intelligence needs are met by current systems and procedures. Among the wide variety of targets that this can focus on are four of interest:

- New business development.[17] Identify how well and how often the new business development and CI units are working together.

- Cost savings from matching the CI function to professional assets. For example, are CI professionals (mis)used to develop information from online sources alone, or conversely, do the CI professionals task an information center with basic background research and studies better handled by them alone?[18]

- Treating CI as if it were a form of insurance. That is, you calculate the potential financial impact of critical, pending decisions and then compare the cost of the CI against the potential exposure without such protection against competitive surprise.[19]

- Surveying the end-users of the CI on their relative satisfaction with the CI process. This can be used to generate numeric values or ratings.[20]

Recording Contributions

Another way that has been suggested to demonstrate, without necessarily quantifying, the benefits of a CI function is to keep a running record, even a chart, of corporate actions which have been impacted by CI—and how. For example, such a record could note that the CI function helped identify a better acquisition target, or, conversely, provided an analysis that indicated that a planned acquisition was not prudent. The key is to identify every possible deliverable from the CI function that was acted upon and valued by your firm's executives.[21]

A variation is to view CI as providing a service assisting the achievement of success, and to affirmatively note the impact that CI has on the overall process, such as noting how your firm can play the game better as well as how it plays the game differently.[22] But, as with so many other suggestions, this process is also focused on strategic uses of CI.

Pros and Cons

While each of these approaches have value, each has significant limitations as well. And not the least of the limitations is the fact that most people trying to measure CI's impact assume that there is only one style of CI, strategy-oriented, and apply what they feel would be appropriate measures. Rather than merely try to refit these suggestions to the problem, we will look at the process of measurement, as it is used and applied in business today. We will then take the lessons from this body of experience and apply them to each type of CI, strategy-oriented, tactics-oriented, target-oriented, and technology-oriented, taking into account the differences in mission, audiences, and deliverables.

To use a sports analogy, it as if we have been seeking to determine the winners at the every event at the Olympic games using only a tape measure and a stop watch. That would certainly work for the marathon and ski jumping, but it would not let us determine the winners in the decathlon, basketball, or figure skating. In those events, success is not measured by speed or distance alone.

WHY EVEN TRY TO MEASURE CI?

There are several reasons, of varying validity, for seeking to find ways to measure CI's impact on the bottom line.[23] The most evident ones include

- All, or at least most, other processes within the firm are also being measured.
- Measurements are integral to a greater, firm-wide initiative, such as TQM, 6 Sigma, Balanced Scorecard, and so forth.
- The CI unit needs to measure its operations and impact to justify an increased budget, or protect against a decrease in it.
- Measurement serves to demonstrate to management that the CI unit and CI as a discipline are in fact impacting the firm in some positive way(s).
- The process of measuring CI's impact serves to introduce CI's role to other potential end-users.
- Involving current end-users in a measurement process serves to improve the way in which they view and use CI in the future.
- Assisting in selling the concept of CI to management by showing (1) that CI's contribution can be measured and (2) that there are areas where CI's impact in the past might have made a difference.

What we must keep in mind, as well, is that the very act of trying to measure an element of the CI process, or of any business process at all, will always cause a change of some sort in the way in which the process is conducted.[24]

What all of these have in common is that the actual purpose of using one or more measurement encompasses more than merely determining that the CI unit is working well. By being able to make some showing of the bottom line impact of CI, CI units and CI professionals can avoid the "flavor of the month" syndrome. That is where management adopts a new management theory or system, but soon drops it because it fails to show it is making a positive impact on the firm.

To overcome these problems, we have to first understand exactly what CI means today, and then determine which type or types of CI are best for firms in a bewildering variety of competitive contexts.

Then, we have to learn how each type of CI delivers its message, and where its analysts go to get the data supporting their analyses. From there, we will look at analytical issues underlying the entire process of metrics. Then, taking the variety of metrics being used by CI units, we can determine which metrics are best for which types of CI, given the predominant sources of raw data and the ways in which the CI findings are communicated to end-users.

NOTES

1. TEA Booklet, 14.
2. See Jerry P. Miller, "The Education of Intelligence Professional: A Surmountable Challenge," *Competitive Intelligence Review* 6, 3 (Fall 1995): 20–28; Roger Q. Kerr, "Are Your CI Skills Valued?" *Competitive Intelligence Review* 6, 3 (Fall 1995): 61–63.
3. Bernard Jaworski and Liang Chee Wee, *Competitive Intelligence: Creating Value for the Organization—Final Report on SCIP Sponsored Research* (Vienna, Va.: Society of Competitive Intelligence Professionals, 1993).
4. Robert Flynn, "NutraSweet Faces Competition: The Critical Role of Competitive Intelligence," *Competitive Intelligence Review* 5, 4 (Winter 1994): 4–7.
5. James J. Cappel and Jeffrey P. Boone, "A Look at the Link between Competitive Intelligence and Performance," *Competitive Intelligence Review* 6, 2 (Summer 1995): 15–23.
6. Paul Germeraad, "Intellectual Asset Management: The New Strategic Weapon of Corporate America," in Society of Competitive Intelligence Professionals, *14th Annual International Conference and Exhibit—Proceedings* (SCIP, April–May 1999): 347–362.
7. See, for example, Ben Gilad, "What Do You Tell Management When They Ask: What Is the Value of CI?" in SCIP, *2000 Annual International Conference and Exhibit—Conference Proceedings* (SCIP, March–April, 2000): 39–60. Gilad uses case studies to show the cost of operating without CI (failures of companies and the loss of executive positions) and the benefits, again by the overall success of the company and executives.
8. The Futures Group, "Ostriches & Eagles 1997," Available at http://www.tfg.com/pubs/docs/O_EIII-97.html (Ostriches & Eagles, 1997).
9. See, for example, International Benchmarking Clearinghouse (APQC), *Developing a Successful Competitive Intelligence Program: Enabling Action, Realizing Results* (Houston, Tex.: American Productivity & Quality Center, 2000), 103 et seq.
10. McGonagle and Vella, *Internet Age*, 199 and APQC, *Developing a Successful Competitive Intelligence Program*, 97 et seq.
11. For other examples, see APQC, *Developing a Successful Competitive Intelligence Program*, 102–103.
12. Jean L. Graef, *Executive Briefing: CFO's Guide to Intellectual Capital* (Montague, Mass.: Limited Edition Publishing, 1997), 45.
13. "Conseco shares jump after new CFO hired." Available at http://biz.yahoo.com/rf/010925/n25340712_1.html (September 25, 2001, Reuters).

14. Jan P. Herring, *Measuring the Effectiveness of Competitive Intelligence—Assessing & Communicating CI's Value to Your Organization* (Alexandria, Va.: Society of Competitive Intelligence Professionals, 1996), 29; Kenneth Sawka, "The Analyst's Corner: Are We Valuable?" *Competitive Intelligence Magazine* 3, 2 (April–June 2000): 53–54.

15. Nick Wreden, "Business Intelligence—Turning on Success," *Beyond Computing* (September 1997): 19, 24.

16. Herbert W. Lovelace, "Secret CIO: The Hidden Assumption," *InformationWeek* 16 (February 1998): 148.

17. See, for example, Paul Germeraad, "Intellectual Asset Management," 351. He identifies CI's participation in the value extraction process of intellectual asset management. They include improve returns from patent maintenance fees, improve return from foreign licensing of patents, and obtain revenues from licensing unused intellectual property.

18. Marc Solomon, "The Intelligence Asset-Building Process," *Competitive Intelligence Review* 7, 4 (Winter 1996): 69–76.

19. Kenneth Sawka, "The Analyst's Corner: Drills and Holes," *Competitive Intelligence Magazine* 4, 1 (January–March 2000): 36–37. Cf. Ben Gilad, "Industry Risk Management: CI's Next Step," *Competitive Intelligence Magazine* 4, 3 (May–June 2000): 21–27.

20. See James Russell, "Measuring the Value of Competitive Intelligence (CI) Activities: A Pilot Study," in Society of Competitive Intelligence Professionals, *Conference Proceedings—2000 Annual International Conference and Exhibit* (Alexandria, Va: SCIP, 2000), 263; and Leigh Davison, "Measuring CI Effectiveness: Insights from the Advertising Industry," in *Proceedings—2001 Annual International Conference and Exhibit* (Alexandria, Va.: SCIP, 2000), 387–391.

21. Dick Klavans, "So, What Is the Value of Technical Intelligence?" *Actionable Intelligence* (December 1997): 4.

22. John H. Hovis, "CI at Avnet: A Bottom-Line Impact," *Competitive Intelligence Review* 11, 3 (Third Quarter 2000): 5–15.

23. For a very useful look at the analogous issues of measuring the bottom line impact of science and technology on businesses, see Eliezer Geisler, *The Metrics of Science and Technology* (Westport, Conn.: Quorum Books, 2000).

24. See, for example, John J. McGonagle, Jr., "The Uncertainty Principle and Regulation," in Benjamin Gilad and Stanley Kaish, eds., *Handbook of Behavioral Economics: Volume B (Behavioral Macroeconomics)* (Greenwich, Conn.: JAI Press, 1986), 123–132.

3

Two Significant Categories of Competitive Intelligence

When CI was first becoming popular in the mid-1980s and early 1990s, there was virtually no discussion of anything except actions and programs aimed at collecting data on competitors. As CI became more widespread and sophisticated, its practitioners and their clients began to realize that what they were doing would be done to them, if it were not already being done. The result was a rise in interest in activities aimed at protecting companies from the CI activities of other companies.

At first, defensive activities were merely discussed among CI professionals. Over time, their existence and application became of interest to CI's internal clients, as well as other corporate interests. Today we have a formal division between them based on several key elements. In essence, CI professionals teach defensive CI, but practice active CI.

"Keeping a little ahead of conditions is one of the secrets of business."[1]

ACTIVE

Active CI processes are those aimed at collecting raw data as well as analyzing those data to provide finished intelligence. The intelligence may be prepared by a CI unit for use by an internal corporate client, by an external consultant or a research firm as an input to a CI unit's reports, or developed by the same person who will use it. In each case, the production of the intelligence is conducted following a formal, commonly understood process, commonly known as the CI cycle. It is then to be used as an input to improve decision making.

Basics of an Active CI Program

"• Direction is more important than position.

• Flow is more important than stick.

• Magnitude is more important than precision.

Determining the magnitude and direction of a flow is more important than ascertaining the position of a stock with precision. Decision-making is always geared to the future, not the present nor the past."[2]

The CI process is usually divided into five basic phases, each linked to the others by a feedback loop (see Figure 3.1). These phases, making up the CI cycle, are as follows:

- *Establishing your CI needs.* This means that you both recognize the need for CI and define what kind of CI you or your end-user, if you are providing the CI for someone else, need. It also means considering what type of issue (strategic, tactical, marketing, etc.) is motivating the assignment, what questions you want to answer with the CI, who else may be using the CI, and how, by whom, and when the CI will ultimately be used.[3]

- *Collecting the raw data you need.* First you must translate your end-user's needs into an action plan. This involves either formally or informally identifying what questions need to be answered and where it is likely that you can collect the data needed to answer these questions.[4] You may also have to decide who should be collecting the raw data that will be turned into intelligence through the CI process. This can be one or more of the following: the end-user, an internal CI professional, other employees such as sales personnel, and/or an external CI firm. You should by this point have a realistic understanding of any significant constraints you face in carrying out this assignment, such as time, finances, organization, information, and legal issues, to develop the specific CI you are seeking. Thus, you can now identify the data sources that are most likely to produce reliable, useful data and proceed to acquire them.

- *Evaluating and analyzing the raw data.* In this phase, the data you have collected are evaluated and analyzed and thus transformed into CI.[5] This might involve comparing the data you found with data from other sources, integrating your conclusions from the data with other CI, or measuring the results of your CI against predetermined benchmarks. It can involve the application of experience or involve the use of sophisticated CI ana-

Figure 3.1
The CI Cycle

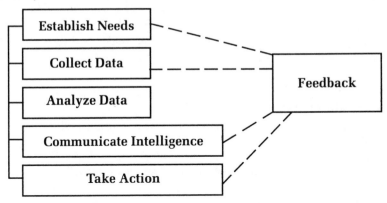

lytical tools and models. It should be kept in mind that there are at least two ways in which analysis is applied. The first is the use of analysis to make a selection, such as deciding which of a dozen news articles is important. The second is the use of analysis to add value to one or more pieces of data. That would mean, for example, adding a statement to an article indicating why and how its contents are important to the end-user. While CI analysts provide both types of analysis, end-users most frequently only regard the latter process as analysis.

- *Communicating the finished intelligence.* This phase involves preparing and presenting the results to the end-user in a usable format and in a timely manner. The CI may have to be distributed to those who asked for it and, in some cases, to others who might also profit from having it. A recent study sadly notes "More than 70 percent of employees report knowledge is not reused across the company."[6] In other cases, the CI is simply made available to potential users. In any case, the final form of the CI, as well as its timeliness and its security, are important considerations.

- *Taking Action.* This involves using the CI in decision making. The CI may be used as an input to decision making, or it may be the first of several steps in an overall assessment of, for example, a new market.[7] If the end-user also does the analysis, then this is just a part of the previous stage.

"Despite their importance, individual facts and data do not usually provide an effective basis for actions or setting priorities. Actions depend on an understanding of relationships, derived from analysis of facts and data."[8]

The feature that runs through and directly links all the phases of the CI cycle is the need to monitor, on a continuous basis, what you have done and how well you have done it. The goal is to provide feedback from each phase to the other three (or four) phases of the CI cycle. By doing this, you will improve both the product of an individual assignment as well as the entire CI process as you are using it.

Feedback to and from each phase to all others is essential. That feedback generates a constant review that seeks to raise and then answer questions like these:

- Are the targets still correct?
- Are the areas of interest still correct?
- Should the CI unit add or delete targets, areas, internal customers, and so forth?

But the feedback process must go further. For example,

- A change in the job description of the end-user to whom you are providing the CI could mean that you have to change the kind of data you are collecting and/or the way in which you are presenting your intelligence.
- Similarly, difficulty in collecting important data, if identified in time, may mean that you have to reconsider the type of data you are seeking or even reconsider the specific target, despite the fact that you may be in the middle of an assignment.
- If you find out that regular updates of a CI report you are now preparing might be needed in the future, you should think about changing the way you are collecting data now. That means, given a choice, you should leave open, rather than close, routes to potential data sources for the future work. This may mean making sure you identify and capture sources of data that might have key data in the future, even if they do not now have anything you can use.

The CI Process: A Checklist

Phase I. Establishing Your CI Needs

- Identify your targets.
- Determine what specific information you need.
- Establish who will get and use the finished CI.
- Decide which of several assignments are most important and which must be done first.
- Decide when you need the CI for it to be useful.
- Review what your CI needs are in light of the results of the other phases.

Phase II. Collecting the Raw Data You Need

- Identify the most likely sources for those raw data.

- Develop research strategies and techniques.
- Arrange to get the raw data, either on a regular basis or on a one-time basis.
- Conduct supplemental data collection efforts, if necessary.
- Review your data collection efforts in light of results of the other phases.

Phase III. Evaluating and Analyzing the Raw Data

- Establish the reliability of the sources of the raw data you obtained.
- Estimate the accuracy of the raw data you have.
- Make sure the data are relevant to your CI needs.
- Analyze the raw data.
- Draw conclusions, such as anticipating how your competitor thinks, based on what it has done.
- Conduct analysis of supplemental data collection efforts, if necessary.
- Review your evaluation and analysis in light of results of the other phases.

Phase IV. Preparing, and Presenting Your Resulting CI

- Format the results so the CI is readable, understandable, and useful.
- Deliver the results in the right manner and in a timely fashion.
- Make sure the CI is kept secure.
- Review the way you prepare and distribute the CI in light of results of the other phases.

Phase V. Using the CI

- Integrate the CI into your business decision making.
- Keep the CI secure.
- Review the way you use the CI in light of results of the other phases.

Which Phases Are More Important?

It should be intuitively obvious that analysis is a vital component in providing CI that the end-user will find effective. In fact, in 1996, a consultant took a hard look at CI. He tried to evaluate if, where, and how CI could contribute to generating a sustainable competitive advantage (SCA). He concluded the following:

- Analysis had the highest probability to generate an SCA.
- Gathering and dissemination of data had a lower probability of generating an SCA.

• Merely storing and protecting raw data probably would not provide an SCA, but might help prolong one.[9]

There appears to be an optimal balance among the four stages of CI that the typical CI unit is involved with: needs, collection, analysis, and communication.

Phase	Percentage of Overall Effort
Needs	15–20 percent
Collection	25–30 percent
Analysis	40–45 percent
Communication	10–15 percent
TOTAL	100 percent

DEFENSIVE

Defensive CI processes are also dependant on a working knowledge of CI techniques.[10] However, when properly conducted, defensive CI involves CI professionals in an educational or advisory role only. That is, CI professionals use their skills and experience to help their firm determine what kinds of raw data competitors will probably try to capture, to teach all company employees to understand what is competitively sensitive information that they should protect, and to understand how to protect that data.[11]

What Is a Cloaked Competitor?

Companies that successfully protect themselves from the intelligence-gathering efforts of their competitors can be called cloaked competitors. The term is used deliberately instead of more military-associated terms: Cloaked competitors don't operate by stealth or clandestine methods. Instead, they take some fundamental steps to control the flow of information into the public domain, without trying to stop the flow or taint it with false information.

A cloaked competitor is one that protects its competitively sensitive information to develop, maintain, and improve its competitive advantage.

Six Keys to Becoming an Effective Cloaked Competitor

The goal of a defensive CI program is to make life more difficult for your competitors' intelligence analysts, so as to give your firm more operating flexibility. While you cannot try to hide everything, you can and should make it as difficult as possible for others to see what you're doing.

There are six keys to becoming an effective cloaked competitor:

1. Determine what areas of your activities are of greatest interest to your competitors.
2. Focus on protecting those areas.
3. Understand the channels through which your competitors collect raw data on your firm.[12]
4. Control what goes into those channels with a view to protecting key bits of competitive information.
5. Discern what techniques your competitor probably uses to analyze the data.
6. Work to deprive competitors of a few key pieces of data that are vitally necessary to complete the analysis.

NOTES

1. Charles Schwab quoted in Wynn Davis, *The Best of Success* (Lombard, Ill.: Celebrating Excellence Publishing, 1992), 6.

2. Kent Ridge Digital Labs, *Charting Your Course in the Digital Age—An IT Perspective* (Singapore: Kent Ridge Digital Labs, 1999), 111.

3. See, for example, Richard Telofski, *Dangerous Competition: Critical Issues in eCompetitive Intelligence Analysis* (New York: Writers Club Press, 2001), 8. He states, "So why doesn't management get from the competitive intelligence analyst the intelligence that they crave? Because, say it with me: *The analyst doesn't know what's in management's head.*"

4. For a description of the issues involved in managing the collection effort, see Anthony M. Page, "The Art and Science of Collection Management," in Ben Gilad and Jan P. Herring, eds., *Advances in Applied Business Strategy, Supplement 2B* (Greenwich, Conn.: JAI Press, 1996), 181–206.

5. For a look at some of the issues involved in managing CI analysis, see Craig S. Fleisher, "A Farout Way to Manage CI Analysis," *Competitive Intelligence Magazine* 3, 2 (April–June 2000): 37–40.

6. Korn/Ferry International and the University of Southern California's Center for Effective Organizations at the Marshall School of Business, *Strategies for the Knowledge Economy: From Rhetoric to Reality*, as reported in "Employees in Dark about Competitors, Study Shows." Available at http://www.scip.org/news/cimagazine_articleasp?id=170.

7. See, for example, Chuck Klein, "The 7 Gates of Export Marketing Intelligence," *Competitive Intelligence Magazine* 3, 2 (April–June 2000): 34–36.

8. Baldrige National Quality Program, *2001 Criteria for Performance Excellence* (Milwaukee, Wisc.: American Society for Quality, 2000), 29.

9. Kenneth D. Cory, "Can Competitive Intelligence Lead to a Sustainable Competitive Advantage," *Competitive Intelligence Review* 7, 3 (Fall 1996): 45–55.

10. We cannot cover all of the aspects of creating and managing a defensive CI program here. For additional information on that, see McGonagle and Vella, *Protecting Your Company*.

11. See Mark Robinson, "Competitive Information Security: Lessons from Los Alamos," *Competitive Intelligence Magazine* 4, 4 (July–August 2001): 14–16.

12. These channels can include your own (disgruntled) employees. Deborah C. Sawyer, "Defining Your Competition: Trojan Horses, Fifth Columns, and Other Threats," *Competitive Intelligence Magazine* 3, 2 (April–June 2000): 45–46.

PART II

ACTIVE COMPETITIVE INTELLIGENCE

In this part, we look at active CI only. First, we will dissect each of them to understand how they are similar, and more important, where they differ. Then we will develop an analytical system to help you to determine which type or types are most likely to contribute to your firm's bottom line.

From there, we will work our way through data sources for CI and the ways in which CI can be delivered. Moving into the issues underlying efforts to measure a process like CI, we will look at the options available to you to measure active CI's impact on your firm. From there, we will show you how to select from among the wide variety of options to use those metrics which best suit your particular situation.

4

Active CI: The Four Divisions

As we noted earlier, as it is now practiced, CI can now be seen as divided into four separate divisions:

1. Strategy-oriented CI
2. Tactics-oriented CI
3. Technology-oriented CI
4. Target-oriented CI

FOUR DIVISIONS—AN OVERVIEW

Strategy-Oriented Competitive Intelligence

Strategy-oriented Competitive Intelligence is CI provided in support of strategic-level, as distinguished from tactical, decision making. This means providing the higher levels of management information on the competitive, economic, legal, and political environment in which your firm and its competitors now operate as well as that in which they will operate in the future.[1] In practice, this may even include information on products and services that differentiate one competitor from another,[2] or even an assessment of a criminal environment in which a firm may find it is involuntarily operating.[3]

It also can involve developing CI on candidates for potential mergers and acquisitions as well as for alliances and partnerships.[4] Most CI as practiced in the 1980s and early 1990s, including much of what fell within the category of "business intelligence," can be considered as strategy-oriented CI.

Tactics-Oriented Competitive Intelligence

Tactics-oriented Competitive Intelligence is CI developed on the very current activities and near-term plans in the marketplace. In a real sense, tactics-oriented Competitive Intelligence is a child of the computer age's support for the detailed analysis of retail consumer goods sales. It encompasses much of what has previously been called "market" or "sales and marketing" intelligence. However, it can also be a critical component in mergers and acquisitions.[5]

Firms are increasingly tracking what is going on in the trenches; that is, where competitors face off for customers and consumers, with tactics-oriented Competitive Intelligence. This, in turn, permits them to fine tune marketing efforts, including field force support, to respond faster and faster.[6] The faster and deeper the data are received, the more they permit a firm to do the following:

- Find out that a product promotion is less successful than anticipated, and immediately respond to change a promotion that is not working or to intensify one that is working.
- Determine what other promotions competitors are running against yours— and where—and respond appropriately.
- Test product linkages by seeing if customers buying your products also buy another one very frequently and cross-promote your products.
- Get early warnings of competitor moves and market vulnerabilities.
- Improve product and service development as well as the targeting of messages to consumers.

Technology-Oriented Competitive Intelligence

Technology-oriented CI permits a firm to respond to threats and to identify and exploit opportunities resulting from technical and scientific change.[7] Technology-oriented Competitive Intelligence, as we use the term, encompasses much of what has been referred to as TI (Technology Intelligence), or CTI (Competitive Technical Intelligence).

While this intelligence did not make an appearance until the mid-1990s, the import links between technology and competitive advantage have been known longer.[8] Technology-oriented CI, supporting technology strategies as well as research and development, has become a growth area within CI.[9] Practitioners of technology-oriented CI are also providing their own valuable insights on organizational and management issues through technology-oriented CI. One of these is that TI is a function that, if executed properly, should result in a saving of from 10 to 100 times the investment in the function.

Target-Oriented Competitive Intelligence

Target-oriented Competitive Intelligence is intelligence about competitors, their capabilities, current activities, plans, and intentions. It is most often used when CI efforts are best focused on a small number of competitors that a firm faces in several market niches. It encompasses elements of what is sometimes called "business intelligence" or "competitor intelligence."

COMMON ELEMENTS

The four major divisions of active CI, as would be expected, have many critical elements in common. The most important commonalities are these:

- Common sources of raw data
- Access to a common CI toolbox
- Government by the CI cycle

Sources of Raw Data

"Success is the sum of detail."[10]

A key maxim common to each of the four active CI divisions is that 90 percent of all information that a firm needs to make key decisions and to understand its market and competitors is already public or can be systematically, legally, and ethically developed from public data. Public, in each type of CI, means all information you can legally and ethically identify, locate, and then access. It ranges from a document released by a competitor as a part of a local zoning application to the text of a press release issued by a competitor's advertising agency describing its client's proposed marketing strategy, while the advertising firm extols the virtues of a new product and the related opening of a new plant.

It is the common principle of the use and analysis of public information to assist in the effective management of a company that link these four critical divisions within CI.

Common Toolbox

The entries of doubts are as so many suckers or sponges to draw use of knowledge. . . . If a man will begin with certainties he shall end in doubts, but if he will be content to begin with doubts, he shall end in certainties.[11]

Over the past twenty years, the CI profession has developed a significant toolbox, consisting of analytical techniques and tools that can be applied to CI. Some of these, such as SWOT analysis, have been adopted from other business disciples.[12] Its practitioners developed others, such as patent mapping for CI.[13] Still others, such as psychological profiling, were developed by the behavioral sciences and adapted to CI.[14]

Some Common CI Analysis Techniques are the following:[15]

Competitor analysis
SWOT analysis[16]
Portfolio analysis
Plans and intentions
Benchmarking, competitive and shadow
Gap analysis
Response modeling
Market analysis
Win or loss analysis
Value chain analysis
Supply chain analysis
Financial analysis
Cash flow and conversion analysis
Cost analysis
Ratio analyses
Asset turns
Credit and debt analysis
Sustainable growth analysis
Organizational analysis
Organization assessment
Cultural assessment
Individual assessment (profiling)

Technology assessment
    Patent mapping and analysis
    Research and development, product and manufacturing process analysis
    Technology forecasting
    Reverse engineering
    Benchmarking
Environmental assessment
    Legislative and regulatory analysis
    Political and economic assessment
    Country and area risk analysis
    Crisis management assessment
Forecasting
    Statistical and econometric analysis
    Trend analysis and projections
    Scenario development and analysis
    Modeling and simulations
    Qualitative, quantitative, and other analyses
Industry analysis
    "Five Forces" Model
    Structural and trend analyses
    Critical success factors
    Relationship mapping
    Distribution strategy analysis
    Share and growth matrices (also known as BCG matrices[17])

The maturation of the development of the CI toolbox can be seen in the fact that government and political intelligence services now are seen to avail themselves of the techniques and tools being developed or refined by their business-sector equivalents, CI professionals.

All Follow the CI Cycle

"Developing an effective intelligence program requires several basic activities including: identification of user needs; collection and screening of basic source materials; analysis of data and information; presentation and dissemination of analysis results; and use of the resulting intelligence in company planning, decision making, and/or operations."[18]

As discussed in Chapter 2, the CI cycle has the following phases:

- Establish need
- Collect data
- Apply analysis
- Communicate results
- Utilize results
- Feedback

All four divisions of active CI are governed by this cycle. Any CI processes that deviate from this cycle do so at their own risk.

Key Issues Involved In Setting Up and Running an Active CI Unit

While there are many ways to set up and run a CI unit, there are some core issues that have to be dealt with to assure success and that are common to all. Among the more critical are the following:[19]

- Selecting the right staff
- Dealing with internal customers
- Integrating the CI process in the unit or firm
- The key role of training

Selecting the Right Staff

Best practice studies have shown that having the right staff with the right skills is critical to start up any CI unit. What skills do the CI staff need at the start-up of a CI unit? These studies indicate that there are two sets of "must have" skills for a CI unit at the beginning:[20]

- Strategic and analytical thinking
- Communication and interpersonal abilities

The need for strategic and analytical thinking skills is possibly a surrogate for requiring education and formal training in CI. As yet, there are not sufficient numbers of graduates from post-Bachelor of Arts level programs emphasizing CI to staff business CI units. As time passes and that changes, this need may be able to be filled by using such graduates.

The need for communication and interpersonal skills is due to the fact that world-class CI units have found that regular, intensive face-to-face communication with internal customers throughout CI projects is vital to effective operation of the CI process.[21] This continuous and two-way feedback is a vital part of the job.

What attitudes do the start-up CI staff need? Again, best practice studies show that the CI staff must be

- Risk-takers
- Committed to the CI profession[22]

The need for a risk-accepting attitude is due to the fact that, in successful CI units, CI managers and end-users must allow for, and in fact even support, differing opinions among the staff. In addition, as professionals, the CI staff must openly identify CI failures so they can learn from them. The commitment to the CI profession both inside and outside of the firm gives the staff the opportunity to improve its CI skills to meet the growing demands and needs of the current and future internal clients.

What is interesting is that these same studies have shown what many might intuit is not the case. *That is, in start-up CI units, knowledge of the company or even of the industry is not a critical qualification.* Rather it is only "moderately important."[23] The reason is that knowledge of the company and of the industry is easier to learn than are analytical skills.[24]

Dealing with Internal Customers

The first and most important step in managing any CI unit is to establish who the customers are for the CI, and what they would or should use the CI for. This is because experience shows that there is no point in spending resources to collect complete information on every target for everyone. When a firm does that, it is really running a newsletter, not a CI function.

The key here is to determine what CI will make a difference with the firm's key decision makers.[25] One proven way to accomplish this is through internal interviews, and that is really the best way to do this. A quick way to start this process is to ask key decision makers questions designed to elicit real needs, based on experience. For example, "What has happened in the past one to two years with respect to key competitors that had an impact on our firm? Of those events, which ones do you think that our firm might have avoided and/or exploited had it only had some early warning of the events?" Then, those involved with creating the CI function could do some quick retrospective research. That research would seek to determine if CI could actually have given your firm that desired early warning. If so, then you have identified one critical area for the new CI function.

What a new or established CI unit does not want is to receive a mission or even an assignment that says, in essence, "We want to know everything about this target or targets." Frankly, given the easy availability of raw data, sometimes in vast quantities, your internal clients do not really want this, because they would then spend all of their time digesting the data the CI unit could accumulate, without ever having the time to act on that small portion of it that needs action. All this means that, as a part of this effort, one must get to the real decision makers at a firm, the ones we call the internal clients and end-users.

Those managing a CI function also have to determine when their internal clients need intelligence, as well as what they need it for. For example, if your firm has formal planning cycles, are there key dates for introducing CI into that process? If your firm is launching a new product or service, and the CI function is directed to check on potential new products hitting the market, when is your own go or no go date?

Intelligence about a new launch by a competitor provides no benefit if it arrives after your own firm has made an irrevocable decision.

Integrating the CI Process

Integrating CI in a business firm takes a lot of time, and is a continuous process, independent of any individual. It requires that the CI personnel continuously identify the firm's strategic goals and changes in them, and then create and maintain links to them.[26] A critical element to institutionalizing CI, according to the experience of best-practice CI firms, is to affirmatively develop the CI process. That means that all CI personnel must have, and then follow, an underlying affirmative promotional plan.

For example, institutionalizing CI can be aided by seeding the firm with a variety of products, services, and practices. These range from holding road show presentations illustrating a CI unit's capabilities to conduct ongoing training of all employees in CI techniques. But to be accomplished effectively, they must be planned.

For the firm that has formal CI units, affirmatively developing the CI process means a formally planned evolution, planned from the first day of operation, if not earlier. The experience of best-practice firms is that CI units evolve or dissolve, or put another way, they either "Grow or Go."

A critical element in this is the ongoing affirmative development and maintenance of a high level of awareness of the role of CI. And experience shows that this is best accomplished through internal training.

Another element in the institutionalization process is to integrate across the entire CI cycle. In particular, best-practice CI programs affirmative work to integrate three of the CI cycle processes:

1. Needs assessment
2. Taking action
3. Feedback and evaluation

The reason for this integration effort is that, if this is not done, there is an almost inevitable series of events that lead to the demise of the CI unit. First, poorly defined intelligence requests, which are the result of problems in the area of needs assessment and feedback, eventually result in unfulfilled end-user expectations. The end-users did not get what they needed; they got what they asked for.

Regardless of the cause, these internal customers then implement few, if any, CI project deliverables. Over time, less and less action by the firm is based on the efforts of the CI unit. Finally, the CI unit then loses its credibility and influence, first gradually and then rapidly, as end-users see no value in the process. The final step is that the CI unit ultimately ceases to exist.

The Key Role of Training

The experience of the best-practice CI firms shows that an ongoing training program is absolutely vital.[27] This is training that is not limited to the CI professionals; there must also be training for end-users of CI as well as for all other employees.

For CI professionals, an ongoing training process should concentrate on several key areas:

- Analytical techniques
- Legal and ethical issues
- Communications and management

For the end-users of CI, the training process must not only be ongoing, but it should actually widen over time. For the end-users, experience shows that the key areas to be covered are CI techniques, and ethical and legal issues. Here, the explicit goal is to make these users of CI into better customers by controlling and eventually eliminating unreasonable client expectations, and also by preventing improper, that is, unethical or even illegal, intelligence requests.

For all other employees, the best-practice companies offer training on CI basics as well as on the firm's CI needs. The goal is to enable all employees to help in collecting CI. But the experience of the best-practice firms shows that such ongoing training also has several key implicit goals that are linked to the process of institutionalizing CI. They are to

- Generate and support organizationwide knowledge of and participation in CI
- Link customer successes with CI activity through training connections

In other words, in the context of CI, training is not merely training—it is also marketing.

CRITICAL DIFFERENCES

"Different organizations institutionalize the CI process in different ways: from a separate, formal, structured CI department to an individual CI professional handling all the organization's CI needs. Each method can be effective so long as the intelligence personnel understand the CI process and manage it proficiently."[28]

The four divisions of active CI differ among themselves in a number of important ways:

- What and who is served
- Primary focus
- Time horizon
- Balance between raw data and finished analysis
- Intelligence-related processes typically used
- Typical topics of importance

Each of these divisions may, in one of these areas, show very little, if any variation from another, but, when all of the differences are combined, they show a very distinct set of CI processes.

Who and What Is Served?

Strategy-Oriented Competitive Intelligence

"Management uses CI at all levels of decision making (i.e. strategic, tactical, planning, etc.). . . . The CI activity has clearly understood objectives and consciously identified the target audience it aims to serve (e.g., sales force or top executives)."[29]

Strategy-oriented Competitive Intelligence typically supports senior managers, the individuals who make and execute a firm's overall strategy. Its more common applications are in the development of the following:

- Strategic (three- to five-year) plans
- Capital investment plans
- Political risk assessment
- Merger and acquisition, joint venture, and corporate alliance policies and plans
- Long-term research and development planning

Target-Oriented Competitive Intelligence

Target-oriented Competitive Intelligence is most often found providing assistance to strategic planning operations as well as to the operating managers within strategic business units (SBUs). It may also be provided to product managers, as well as to those involved with product development, new business development, and mergers and acquisitions.

Tactics-Oriented Competitive Intelligence

The primary customers of tactics-oriented Competitive Intelligence are usually, but not always, the marketing department and the sales force. To a lesser degree, tactics-oriented CI can serve marketing planning by providing retrospective data on the success and failure of your own sales efforts.

Technology-Oriented Competitive Intelligence

Competitive Intelligence itself has always had a particular relevance and linkage to research and development activities. Using

CI techniques in areas of technology and research, those practicing technology-oriented CI can now determine the following:

- Current manufacturing methods and processes in use
- Key patents and proprietary technology being used by or being acquired by competitors
- A competitor's access to, use of, and dependence on outside technology, as well as its need for new technology
- The size and capabilities of competitors' research staff
- Types and levels of research and development being conducted by competitors, as well as estimates of current and future expenditures for research and development

While those in research and development are clearly major end-users of technology-oriented CI, it is also used to support other initiatives, such as capital investments plans, productivity and production improvement, business development, and the creation of strategic alliances.[30] It appears that such programs are "most effective in organizations that strategically focus on technology."[31]

What Is its Primary Focus?

Strategy-Oriented Competitive Intelligence

Strategy-oriented CI usually focuses on the overall strategic environment. A firm's immediate competitive environment and its direct competitors are, of course, included in that focus, as should be the most important indirect competitors. In addition, strategy-oriented Competitive Intelligence should provide CI on the long-run changes caused by, as well as affecting, all of the forces driving industry competition. In each marketplace, these include:

- Suppliers
- Customers
- Substitute products or services[32]
- Potential competitors

To develop the appropriate strategy-oriented Competitive Intelligence, analysts must necessarily factor in many critical, potential events, such as technology trends, regulatory changes and even potential political risks that, in turn affect these market forces.[33] In addition, they must factor in the strategies, goals, and underlying assumptions of key competitors.[34]

Strategy-oriented CI seeks to collect and analyze data so that a firm can evaluate the actual success, or failure, of its strategies and those of its competitors. This in turn permits the firm to better weigh its own options for the future. In addition, the firm looks to the past to help learn what may happen in the future.

The major focus of strategy-oriented CI is, however, on the future, not on the past. Its primary goal is to give a firm an understanding of its total business environment—competitive, regulatory, and political. It has historically been compared with radar, and as with radar, its aim is to warn the firm of impending major problems, and alert it to upcoming opportunities—always in time to take necessary action.[35]

Target-Oriented Competitive Intelligence

Target-oriented Competitive Intelligence usually helps answer a wide variety of key business questions, including ones such as these:

- Who are our current competitors and who are our potential competitors?

- How do our competitors see themselves? How do they see us? Are they right?

- What are the track records of the key people at our competitors? What are their personalities? What difference do these people make in terms of our ability to predict how competitors will react to our competitive strategy?

- What are the short-term and long-term trends in our industry? How have our competitors responded to them in the past? How are they likely to respond to them in the future?

- What patents or technologies have our competitors or potential competitors recently obtained or developed? What do those innovations mean to us?

- How and where are our competitors marketing their products and services? What is their rate of success? What new directions will they probably take?

- What markets or geographic areas will our competitors tap in the near future? Which will they abandon?

- What are our competitors' overall plans and goals for the next two to five years for the companies or divisions that currently compete with us? What are their plans and goals for their other companies or divisions, and how will those affect the way they run our competitors?

Tactics-Oriented Competitive Intelligence

Tactics-oriented Competitive Intelligence's focus is on what occurs in the marketplace. That includes current and future changes in a competitor's products and services, its sales, pricing, payment and financing terms, as well as promotions it is offering and their effectiveness.[36] In some firms, that may also include what is happening with your own product or service.

OBJECTIVES OF SALES AND MARKETING INTELLIGENCE (1998)

Develop marketing strategies

Anticipate change/Market monitoring

Identify new opportunities

Identify new sources of advantage

Help sales win business[37]

Technology-Oriented Competitive Intelligence

Technology-oriented CI practitioners see it as having a slight overlap with both target- and tactics-oriented Competitive Intelligence, particularly with respect to its interest in key suppliers and customers. However, instead of dealing with market trends, technology-oriented CI is usually more focused on technology trends and scientific breakthroughs, as well as the protection of technologies.[38] Some technology-oriented CI practitioners have argued that technology-oriented CI should in fact focus more on opportunities such as the acquisition of technologies and leveraging technologies for the firm than it should on threats to the firm.[39]

What Is Its Time Horizon?

Strategy-Oriented Competitive Intelligence

Strategy-oriented CI interest is significantly less on the present than it is on the past and on the future. The time horizon of interest typically runs from up to two years in the past to five to ten years in the future.

Target-Oriented Competitive Intelligence

Target-oriented CI time horizon typically runs from six to twelve months in the past to one to two years in the future.

Tactics-Oriented Competitive Intelligence

Tactics-oriented CI time horizon typically runs from three to six months in the past to no more than six months in the future. Most of the time, however, the horizon is actually measured in terms of weeks past and future rather than months.

Technology-Oriented Competitive Intelligence

Technology-oriented CI time horizon typically runs from twelve months in the past to five or more years in the future.

What Is the Relative Balance between Raw Data and Finished Analysis?

Strategy-Oriented Competitive Intelligence

Given the long time frames involved for the end-users of strategy-oriented CI, the analysts providing it tend to have a significant amount of time to prepare their analyses. In addition, given the nature of the decisions being made based on this CI, its end-users logically expect that they will receive finished, polished, thorough, and digestible analytical pieces, answering the specific questions that they have posed. Thus, it can be said that, for strategy-oriented CI, the final work product tends to be largely, that is more than 90 percent, analysis.

Target-Oriented Competitive Intelligence

Target-oriented CI is used for many purposes. For some end-users, there is a need to stay abreast of changes in the structure, management, and so forth of a particular competitor, the target. For them, the emphasis tends to be on receiving somewhat digested data fairly rapidly.

Other end-users of the target-oriented CI tend to have a more strategic view of the individual target. For them, it is less critical to have a bit of news than it is to have that news digested and its significance explained.

Thus, it may be said that for target-oriented CI, the final work product can range from as low as 20 percent to as high as 90 percent analysis.

Tactics-Oriented Competitive Intelligence

The end-users of tactics-oriented CI are most often in the marketing or sales arenas. These end-users function in a world of very short deadlines, short time horizons, and rapid turn-around times. For that reason, CI is of greatest value to them when it is fresh. This, in turn, puts a premium on having the analyst identify a critical event or change from the blizzard of raw data, extract that, and get it to the end-user as quickly as possible. While it may be said that there is significant analysis applied in doing this, in that the analyst must decide which fact is important and why, the amount of traditional analysis applied in such contexts is typically quite low. Thus it may be said that, for tactics-oriented CI, the final work product is usually low, that is from 5 to 25 percent, in the amount of analysis added.

Technology-Oriented Competitive Intelligence

The end-users of technology-oriented CI are most often persons already deeply involved with the technology in question, such as researchers, and production and materials specialists. As such, they tend to want to have provided to them the actual data, and are very often reluctant to accept what an intermediary, even one as well trained as a CI analyst, has to say about the data. They will, of course accept both.

As with the tactics-oriented CI, the value of the analyst to the end-user often lies in his or her ability to weed out irrelevant data. However, experience also shows that the end-users of technology-oriented CI who are not deeply involved with the technology itself appreciate and can utilize some analysis in addition to the raw data.

Thus it can be said that, for technology-oriented CI, the final work product incorporates a low to moderate range of analysis, from 20 to 50 percent.

"Fundamentally, a company's intelligence operation provides information . . . and analysis is the activity that makes the raw materials useful for these purposes."[40]

What Intelligence-Related Processes Are Typically Used?

Each of these variants of CI also has a tendency to adopt other tools that are indirectly related to CI.[41] These tools are crisis management, shadowing, reverse engineering, and benchmarking.[42] As with other characteristics, while each may have its own unique purpose in adopting such tools, such tools also provide value to at least one other variant:

- Strategy-oriented CI: Crisis management
- Target-oriented CI: Shadowing, reverse engineering, crisis management, and benchmarking

- Tactics-oriented CI: Shadowing and benchmarking
- Technology-oriented CI: Reverse engineering and benchmarking

Typical Topics of Importance

What follows is a master list of CI topics, reflecting the experiences of the authors and their clients. On it we have indicated which topics are usually of significant interest to each variant of CI. This list is not inclusive, but rather illustrative of the typical areas of interest to the end-users of CI.

For the Industry and Market

	Orientation			
	Strategy	Target	Tactics	Technology
Industry involved	•	•	•	•
Industry structure	•	•	•	•
Number of competitors, their product lines (or range of services), and locations	•	•	•	•
Market shares, gross sales, and net profitability of all competitors	•	•	•	
Expansion potentialities of all competitors	•	•		
Important differences among all competitors	•	•	•	•
Industry marketing, distribution, and pricing practices	•	•	•	
Rate of technological change in this niche	•	•	•	•
Need for new technology	•	•	•	•
Barriers to entry and exit	•	•	•	•
Regulatory constraints	•	•	•	•
Potential entrants and future competitors	•	•		•
Indirect competition	•	•	•	•

For Individual Competitive Target(s)

Identity

	Orientation			
	Strategy	Target	Tactics	Technology
Full name	•	•	•	•
Name or acronym commonly used	•	•	•	•
Ultimate parent	•	•	•	•
Major shareholders or partners	•	•		•

	Strategy	Target	Tactics	Technology
Directors and officers, their backgrounds, and other business relationships	•	•		
Corporate and management organization: formal and informal	•	•	•	
Ownership history	•	•		•

Decision Making

	Orientation			
	Strategy	Target	Tactics	Technology
Management styles, abilities, and emphases	•	•	•	•
Depth, capabilities, and weaknesses of management in key functional areas	•	•	•	•
New personnel and recent restructuring	•	•	•	•
Corporate politics	•	•	•	•

Products and Services

	Orientation			
	Strategy	Target	Tactics	Technology
Product lines and services currently offered	•	•	•	•
Current and future applications of products and services	•	•	•	•
Depth and breadth of products and services currently offered	•	•	•	•
Analysis of new products and services, including impact on the market and on competition	•	•	•	•
Who makes decisions on new products and services and on what basis?	•	•	•	•
Customer service policies and performance	•	•	•	
History of key products and services	•			
Products and services likely to be introduced, changed, or eliminated in the near future	•	•	•	•
Channels of distribution, including strengths and weaknesses	•	•	•	
Possible changes in distribution channels	•	•	•	

Sales and Pricing

	Orientation			
	Strategy	Target	Tactics	Technology
Commercial, nonprofit, and government sales		•	•	

	Strategy	Target	Tactics	Technology
Domestic versus foreign sales		•	•	
Seasonal and cyclical patterns and problems		•	•	
Pricing strategy: who prices products and services and how	•	•	•	
Price levels and flexibility		•	•	
Credit, discounts, incentives, consignments, any other special pricing policies		•	•	
Type of sales force: in-house versus independent sales agents		•	•	
Organization of sales force: by product and service line, by geographic market, or by end-user	•	•	•	
Training, capability, and compensation of sales force		•	•	
Number of customers	•	•	•	
Distribution and concentration of customers	•	•	•	
Analysis of largest and most important customers	•	•	•	

Marketing

	Strategy	Target	Tactics	Technology
Market shares by product and service line, by geographic area, and by industry segment	•	•	•	
Marketing approaches and their current effectiveness	•	•	•	
Samples of advertising, product literature, and other promotional materials		•	•	
Samples of products and services		•	•	•
Probable future changes in marketing direction and timing	•	•	•	
History of any questionable marketing practices	•	•	•	

Financial and Legal Positions

	Strategy	Target	Tactics	Technology
Long-term borrowing capacities and ability to secure equity financing	•			•
Short-term borrowing capacities		•	•	

	Strategy	Target	Tactics	Technology
Sources of financing, including duration and strength of the relationship	•	•		
Sales margin, return on assets, and return on equity	•	•	•	•
Profitability of key divisions, products, or services	•	•	•	•
Projections of financial position, margins, and profitability over next two to five years	•			
Comparison of profitability, cash flow, and other key ratios with those of major competitors	•	•		
Major liabilities	•	•		
Regulation of company or unit		•	•	
Major lawsuits and regulatory enforcement or rule-making actions: probable impacts on unit	•	•	•	•

Technology, Research, and Development

	Orientation		
	Strategy	Target	Tactics	Technology
---	---	---	---	---
Current manufacturing methods and processes	•	•	•	•
Key patents and proprietary technology	•	•	•	•
Access to, use of, and dependence on outside technology	•	•	•	•
Need for new technology	•	•	•	•
Potential changes in manufacturing methods and processes	•	•		•
Size and capabilities of research staff	•	•	•	•
Usual lead-time between a research and development breakthrough and the delivery of a product or service to market	•	•	•	•
Types and levels of research and development, including current and future expenditures	•	•	•	•

Personnel, Resources, and Facilities

	Orientation		
	Strategy	Target	Tactics	Technology
---	---	---	---	---
Labor force: cost, availability, turnover, and quality	•	•	•	
Union status, contracts	•	•	•	

	Strategy	Target	Tactics	Technology
Raw materials: prices, sources, and availability	•	•	•	•
Quality control programs in place or planned	•	•	•	•
Level and consistency of quality control	•	•	•	•
Manufacturing and operating costs	•	•	•	•
Facilities: locations, current performance, and potential		•	•	•
Planned improvements to existing facilities or new facilities	•	•		•
Facilities closing or divestitures planned	•	•		•
Productivity programs	•	•	•	•
Joint ventures, minority interests, and other investments or ownership interests	•	•		•
Make or buy policies	•	•	•	•

Strategies, Objectives, and Perception of Self — Orientation

	Strategy	Target	Tactics	Technology
Business philosophy and corporate strategy	•	•		•
How strategy is made and implemented	•	•		
Targeted markets and market shares	•	•	•	
Target growth rates and other financial objectives	•	•	•	
Technological trends and objectives	•	•	•	•
IT strategy	•	•	•	•
Recent improvement and restructuring initiatives and their results	•	•	•	•
Supply chain management structure and strategies	•	•	•	
How the company sees itself	•	•	•	

Perceptions about Competitors and Customers — Orientation

	Strategy	Target	Tactics	Technology
Quality of product or service	•	•	•	•
Pricing	•	•	•	
Marketing and service capabilities and reliability	•	•	•	
Management and organization	•	•		
Technological base and capabilities	•	•	•	•

CI Capabilities	Orientation			
	Strategy	Target	Tactics	Technology
Separate CI (or other intelligence) unit	•			
Number of Society of Competitive Intelligence Professional (SCIP) members	•			
Outside intelligence consultants used	•			
Level of intelligence efforts	•			
Targets of intelligence efforts	•	•		
Defensive activities	•	•	•	•

CONFLICT AND COOPERATION AMONG THOSE INVOLVED WITH THESE FOUR DIVISIONS

The American Productivity and Quality Center/Society of Competitive Intelligence Professionals (APQC/SCIP; see the Bibliography) CI best-practice studies support what experience and intuition suggests: There are conflicts that arise among CI units with different orientations. As we have shown, each CI orientation tends to have its own different

- Internal markets
- Time horizons
- Balances of raw data with analysis
- Cycle times

These differences immediately impact how CI units with differing orientations and different end-users work. The differences in the environments, including in the location and identity of the end-users, in which each orientation of CI operations occurs, thus create natural tensions among the units.[43] Experience shows that this is unavoidable.

However, this conflict does not necessarily have to be destructive. Each of these CI units must have the same skills, and each uses, or at least can select from, the same analytical tools. This creates commonalities, which can then be exploited and developed through affirmative networking among these groups.

In fact, to achieve the true potential of CI, all these types of CI should be coordinated, whether formally or informally. And, as the APQC/SCIP CI best-practice studies show, that coordination must be at the staff not just at the manager level. The goal is to see that each of these CI units is in a circular relationship with all of the others. That is, they feed, challenge, and reinforce each other.[44] The experience of the CI best-practice firms indicates that one key to this is to force and support the ongoing communication of the firm's overall intelligence needs among the analysts and researchers to help them coordinate and integrate the firm's intelligence production.

APPENDIX: PROCESSES RELATED TO COMPETITIVE INTELLIGENCE—SHADOWING, REVERSE ENGINEERING, BENCHMARKING, AND CRISIS MANAGEMENT

Shadowing

Shadowing actually has four differing aspects:

1. Shadowing of specific markets
2. Developing a shadow market plan
3. Shadow planning, as an ongoing process
4. Shadow benchmarking[45]

Shadowing Markets

This involves just what it seems—watching, without disclosing your interest, a market or competitor(s) on a long-term basis. That means regular, even daily, review of raw data and communication of findings to end-users. This is actually more radical than it seems, since the majority of CI assignments are still one-time studies. Thus, the existence of a shadowing program implies that a CI end-user realizes the importance of critical intelligence so much that it must be available on a current and continuous basis. Some CI practitioners call this process "surveillance."[46]

Developing a Shadow Market Plan

In contrast with shadowing, this is most usually a one-time assignment. The goal is to produce a document that is as close to your competitor's real marketing plan as possible. The point is to use it to analyze what the competitor will do, even if your competitor does not have a specific, written document. How individual products, campaigns, and departments are arranged, developed, and operated by the target's management can be strong and useful indicators of the general marketing strategy the target company employs.

First try to learn whether any details of that plan have been made public. After capturing those data, legally and ethically, you must then immerse yourself in that competitor, its philosophy, operations, and its history. From these data, you try to construct a picture of what your competitor is probably doing and why. Based on that, you then estimate what that competitor will be doing over the next several years under certain sets of facts. This analysis of your competitor is a shadow market plan. It is a critical component of what some, inaccurately, call "war gaming."[47]

Engaging in Shadow Market Planning

This involves the regular monitoring of the elements that contribute to the competitor's marketing and market planning. The goal is to enable one or two persons to act as if they were the specific competitor or competitors so they can respond to "what if" competitive questions on a current basis.

Shadow market planning requires you to estimate what your competitor is planning in its marketing efforts and to estimate its capabilities to carry out that plan. This is, of course, based on CI that you develop about that competitor. Typically, if you are producing a shadow market plan you have to put yourself in the place of the competitor you are shadowing and try to duplicate what that competitor's market plan would be. A shadow market plan differs from shadow market planning in that the former is a project-oriented operation and the latter is a process.

While this is sometimes called "war gaming," interestingly enough, the most common nonmilitary application of this technique is found in football. In many sports, the second team's players have to learn to duplicate the look of an opponent's offense or defense. That lets the first team and coaches practice against that opponent before a game.

Reverse Engineering

Reverse engineering involves acquiring, usually buying at retail, and then dismantling a product to identify how it was designed and constructed.[48] This process enables an investigator to estimate costs and evaluate the quality of the product. In the case of nonpatentable processes and devices, it can also provide information on how to produce a competitive, a compatible, or a substitute product.

The concept of reverse engineering is routinely applied to services as well as products. In the case of services, it is essentially deconstructing a service. Investment instruments or insurance products are examples of services and intangible goods that can be reverse engineered. In those cases, you determine what components go into providing the service, and then cost them out.

Reverse engineering primarily supports new product development by disclosing the costs involved in making products that do not now manufacture. However, reverse-engineering products can often provide assistance to other functions:

- It may show you how to pack and ship your products at a lower cost or with less damage for the same cost.
- It may show you that there are less costly ways to accomplish similar ends, in terms of the costs of raw materials or the manufacturing techniques used.
- It can also be used to convince your own personnel that a particular innovation or modification really is possible.[49]

Benchmarking

Benchmarking involves analyzing what you do, quantifying it, and then finding ways that other firms do it better, or better and differently, or not at all.[50] Then you adapt, not just adopt, what you have learned to your own firm.[51]

Benchmarking, of course can and should be used to analyze your firm's efficiencies by comparing its performance against performance levels of a number of different firms. Another application of benchmarking is to compare your firm's standards of operation with those of its competitors.[52] In this case, the goal is not to determine the most efficient cost levels of each component of an activity. Instead, you undertake a process that enables you to compare your performance with that of another firm.

Those in planning and marketing most often use one form of benchmarking, competitive benchmarking. That form focuses on what the competition does better and how your firm can catch up or even overtake those competitors.

Other forms of benchmarking are designed to have your firm learn from dissimilar industries and companies through the exchange of information on techniques and practices. Here, the focus is more often on manufacturing, engineering, and distribution practices, with the customers being the owners of those processes in your own firm. And, as with competitive benchmarking, the time horizon is the present.

As experience with benchmarking continues to grow, we now find that there are in fact several different types of benchmarking, each of which has its appropriate place in the ongoing efforts to make modern businesses more competitive. The result is that businesses that wish to engage in benchmarking have a varied menu from which to select:

- Internal Benchmarking—In this type, a firm looks within, often to other divisions or even branches for ideas for improvements. Typically, the focus is on operational matters, those that are lower level, often repetitive operations, lacking in a strategic focus.
- Competitive Benchmarking—This involves specific competitor-to-competitor comparison, typically stressing a key product or process. In some firms, this may not be a function of the benchmarking team but rather assigned to a CI unit.
- Shadow Benchmarking—In this type, competitor-to-competitor comparisons are made with the partner unaware that they have a shadow. If a firm has a shadow team in the CI unit, that team may be involved in this process.
- Industrial Benchmarking—This entails a comparison with similar, but not identical, functions within the same industry. This is often, but not always, against industry leaders.
- Transnational Benchmarking—This involves the comparison of specific processes that are the virtually identical, regardless of industry, such as handling order entry, preparing marketing proposals, managing telephone sales systems. The comparisons are typically made outside of one's industry, preferably against firms that are world class for that process.
- Failure Benchmarking—This forces you to understand why a process or even a firm failed to perform. From this understanding, you identify new options. These may be ways to avoid problems unseen by your target. It can also be things that were done well by them, but that were lost in the overall failure.

Crisis Management

Crisis management involves preparing a firm for those shocks which can do significant, sudden damage to its operations or to its reputation.[53] The classic cases studied by crisis managers range from how firms handled the Tylenol tampering case, the Bhopal disaster, and the rumors that some hamburgers were made with worms.

A Crisis Management Program (CMP) seeks to serve middle and senior management by developing a crisis management plan. It also involves creating systems that permit rapid response by a company to an external threat where swift reaction is critical. The goal is to avoid damage to the company and, when damage is unavoidable, to minimize that damage as quickly as possible.

The primary focus of a CMP is an internal, well-designed program that looks to the past experience of competitors, as well as other firms, to try and anticipate probable crises. An effective CMP considers not only a crisis which may exist within your own company, but also takes into account the crisis that could impact your company if one of your suppliers should have a major crisis of its own.

NOTES

1. See, for example, Craig S. Fleisher, "Public Policy Competitive Intelligence," *Competitive Intelligence Review* 10, 2 (Second Quarter 1999): 23–36.

2. Kenneth Sawka, "The Analyst's Corner: Are We Strategic?" *Competitive Intelligence Magazine* 3, 3 (July–September 2000): 57–58.

3. Phil Williams, "Criminal Risk Assessment: A New Dimension of Competitive Intelligence," *Competitive Intelligence Review* 10, 2 (Second Quarter 1999): 37–45.

4. See Louis-Jacques Darveau, "Forecasting an Acquisition: 5 Steps to Help You See it Coming," *Competitive Intelligence Magazine* 4, 1 (January–February 2001): 13–17; and Michelle Cook and Curtis Cook, "Anticipating Unconventional M&As: The Case of DaimlerChrysler," *Competitive Intelligence Magazine* 4, 1 (January–February 2001): 19–22.

5. "CTI = M&A Success of DuPont," *Competitive Intelligence Magazine* 4, 1 (January–February 2001): 7. See also "CI at Cisco Systems: An Acquisitions Success Story," *Competitive Intelligence Magazine* 4, 1 (January–February 2001): 5–6.

6. John Cain, "Supporting Field Force Sales with Competitive Intelligence," *Competitive Intelligence Magazine* 1, 1 (April–June 1998): 16–18.

7. See, for example, Tim Budd, "Competitive Technical Intelligence at Applied Biosystems: Attracting, Monitoring, and Exploiting Technology-Based Opportunities," *Competitive Intelligence Review* 11, 4 (Fourth Quarter 2000): 5–11. On using this to identify new competitors, see F. Michael Hruby, "Scramble Competition: New Tools for Confronting New Competitors," *Competitive Intelligence Magazine* 2, 3 (July–September 1999): 15–18.

8. See Porter, *Competitive Advantage*, ch. 5.

9. See Fahey, *Competitors*, ch. 13 on technology strategy and CI.

10. Harvey S. Firestone quoted in Wynn Davis, *The Best of Success* (Lomard: Ill.: Celebrating Excellence Publishing, 1992).

11. Sir Francis Bacon, quoted in Catherine Drinker Bowen, *Francis Bacon: The Temper of a Man* (Boston: Little, Brown, 1963), 109.

12. For a good example of how this is applied in CI, see Paul Dishman, "Two Tools for M&A Analysis," *Competitive Intelligence Magazine* 4, 1 (January–February 2001): 23–26.

13. For an example of how such results can be effectively presented, see Susan E. Cullen, "Communicating Complex Issues to Decision Makers," *Competitive Intelligence Magazine*, 3, 3 (July–September 2000): 23–30.

14. See, for example, Carolyn M. Vella and John J. McGonagle, "Profiling in Competitive Analysis," *Competitive Intelligence Review* 11, 2 (Second Quarter 2000): 20–30; Cheryl Ann Wells, "Analyzing Corporate Personalities: A New Method for Your CI Toolkit," *Competitive Intelligence Magazine* 4, 4 (July–August 2001): 17–20.

15. Adapted from Jan P. Herring, "Creating the Intelligence System that Produces Analytical Intelligence," in Gilad and Herring, *Applied Business Strategy 2A*, 71.

16. SWOT stands for strength, weakness, opportunity, threat.

17. BCG stands for Boston Consulting Group.

18. Society of Competitive Intelligence Professionals, *CI Team Excellence Award: 2001 SCIP World-Class Competitive Intelligence Award—Application and Instruction Booklet* (Alexandria, Va: SCIP, 2000), 9.

19. These issues will be covered in much greater detail in the forthcoming book, McGonagle and Vella, *A Manager's Guide to Competitive Intelligence* (working title) (Westport, Conn.: Quorum Books, forthcoming).

20. APQC International Benchmarking Clearinghouse, *Developing a Successful Competitive Intelligence Program: Enabling Action, Realizing Results* (Houston, Tex.: American Productivity & Quality Center, 2000), 8. See also APQC, *Competitive and Business Intelligence*, 8. To the same effect, see Bill Fiora and Paul Houston, "Recruiting for CI Positions," *Competitive Intelligence Magazine* 4, 5 (September–October 2001): 32–36.

21. APQC, *Developing a Successful Competitive Intelligence Program*, 8.

22. See APQC, *Competitive and Business Intelligence*, 10 and APQC, *Developing a Successful Competitive Intelligence Program*, 31, 34.

23. APQC, *Developing a Successful Competitive Intelligence Program*, 31. Experienced CI consultants have previously suggested that this was the preferred option, but did not have any studies on which to base that. See Kenneth Sawka, "The Analyst's Corner: Finding Intelligence Analysts," *Competitive Intelligence Magazine* 2, 1 (January–March 1999): 41–42.

24. Even with technology-oriented CI, where a command of the technology is often considered by outsiders as a critical skill, best-practice firms demonstrate that "While an understanding of technology is important, [a science and technology intelligence] professional needs to develop generalist skills" (APQC, 2001), 39.

25. APQC, *Developing a Successful Competitive Intelligence Program*, 8; APQC, *Competitive and Business Intelligence*, 7, 9–10; APQC International Benchmarking Clearinghouse, *Managing Competitive Intelligence Knowledge in a Global Economy* (Houston, Tex.: American Productivity & Quality Center, 1998), 8–9.

26. APQC, *Managing Competitive Intelligence*, 8; APQC, *Competitive and Business Intelligence*, 10–11; APQC, *Developing a Successful Competitive Intelligence Program*, 8–9. See Neil J. Simon, "Managing the CI Department: CI Teams Must Keep Pace as Companies Grow," *Competitive Intelligence Magazine* 1, 1 (April–June 1998): 47–49. It also involves working with the CI personnel to understand how to work with teams. Neil Simon, "Managing the CI Department," *Competitive Intelligence Magazine* 3, 2 (April–June 2000): 47–50.

27. APQC, *Developing a Successful Competitive Intelligence Program*, 8.

28. Society of Competitive Intelligence Professionals, *CI Team Excellence Award*, 10.

29. Ibid., 12, 14.

30. See, for example, "Shedding Light on Science & Technology," *Competitive Intelligence Magazine* 3, 4 (October–December, 2000): 12–13.

31. APQC International Benchmarking Clearinghouse, *Using Science and Technology Intelligence to Drive Business Results* (Houston, Tex.: American Productivity & Quality Center, 2001), 20.

32. See Sheena Sharp, "Substitutes: Your Next Marketing Headache," *Competitive Intelligence Magazine* 1, 1 (April–June 1998): 44–46.

33. For a discussion of the problems of providing this in economies with minimal public data, see John Price, "Competitive Intelligence in Latin America: New Science Meets Old Practice," *Competitive Intelligence Magazine* 3, 4 (October–December 2000): 16–18.

34. Douglas House, "Getting Inside Your Competitor's Head: A Roadmap for Understanding Goals and Assumptions," *Competitive Intelligence Magazine* 3, 4 (October–December 2000): 22–28. See also Erik Glitman, "Comprehending 'Irrational' Competitor Actions through Futures-Based Analysis," *Competitive Intelligence Magazine* 3, 4 (October–December 2000): 29–32.

35. Herbert E. Meyer, *Real World Intelligence* (Friday Harbor, Wash.: Storm King Press, 1991).

36. See, for example, Laurence A. Carr, "Front-Line CI: Actionable Intelligence for the Business Infantry," *Competitive Intelligence Magazine* 4, 2 (March–April 2001): 11–15.

37. These are the objectives mentioned by 50 percent of the firms surveyed. Survey of SCIP membership conducted by the Pine Ridge Group, Inc. and T.W Powell Company, 1998, as reported in Timothy Powell and Cynthia Allgaire, "Enhancing Sales and Marketing Effectiveness Through Competitive Intelligence." Available at http://www.scip.org/news/cireview_article.asp?id+100.

38. APQC, 2001, 20.

39. Ibid., 20–21.

40. W. Bradford Ashton, "An Overview of Business Intelligence Analysis for Science and Technology," in Gilad and Herring, *Applied Business Strategy 2A*, 246–247.

41. On this topic generally, see McGonagle and Vella, *A New Archetype.*

42. See the Appendix of this chapter for supplemental information on these processes.

43. See Walter D. Barndt, Jr., "New to Competitive Intelligence? 10 Tips for Survival and Success," *Competitive Intelligence Magazine* 2, 3 (July–September 1999): 23, 24. This is in addition to potential indirect competition. See Deborah C. Sawyer, "Defining Your Competition: Turmoil Inside = Disadvantage Outside," *Competitive Intelligence Magazine* 2, 3 (July–September 1999): 47–48 and "Defining Your Competition: Inside Job: Organizational Structure as Competitive Saboteur," *Competitive Intelligence Magazine* 2, 1 (January–March 1999): 45–46.

44. See, for example, APQC International Benchmarking Clearinghouse, *Strategic and Tactical Competitive Intelligence for Sales and Marketing* (Houston, Tex.: American Productivity & Quality Center, 1999), 7, 30–36, 53–55.

45. For more on this, see McGonagle and Vella, *A New Archetype*, 44–49.

46. For an example of this in practice, see Helen N. Rothberg, "Fortifying Strategic Decisions with Shadow Teams: A Glance at Product Development," *Competitive Intelligence Magazine* 2, 2 (April–June 1999): 9–11.

47. This term is properly limited to gaming involving "a simulated military operation." Thomas B. Allen, *War Games* (New York: McGraw-Hill, 1987), 65.

48. For more on this, see McGonagle and Vella, *Internet Age*, 12–13, and McGonagle and Vella, *A New Archetype*, 85–90.

49. James Risen, "GM 'Spy Center' Dissects Competition," *The Los Angeles Times*, reprinted in *The [Allentown] Morning Call*, 6 December 1987, D1, D3.

50. For more on this see McGonagle and Vella, *Internet Age*, 9–11, and McGonagle and Vella, *A New Archetype*, 69–84.

51. For a discussion of how benchmarking is carried on today, see Robert J. Kennedy, "Benchmarking and Its Myths," *Competitive Intelligence Magazine* 3, 2 (April–June 2000): 28–33.

52. For an example of how strategy-oriented CI and benchmarking are combined, see "CI at Avnet: A Bottom-Line Impact," *Competitive Intelligence Magazine* 3, 3 (July–September 2000): 5, 7–8.

53. For more on this, see McGonagle and Vella, *Internet Age*, 8–9, and McGonagle and Vella, *A New Archetype*, 63–68.

5

Which Types of Active Competitive Intelligence Should You Be Using?

THE COMPETITIVE ENVIRONMENT AND THE INTELLIGENCE DIVISIONS

"Figure out what keeps management awake at night."[1]

While every company, regardless of its size, its product and service, or its competitive environment, should be doing some sort of CI, not every company can afford to do all types. In fact, one of the major problems facing CI professionals is that they often do not have a clear understanding of what their internal clients really need in terms of delivered Competitive Intelligence. And their clients may not be able to articulate what kind of Competitive Intelligence they need, as they are not familiar with what effective CI can produce.

Experience shows that a CI unit facing this situation may soon begin to move into a downward, ultimately terminal cycle. If the Competitive Intelligence output does not meet the needs of the ultimate clients, then these clients put less reliance on and faith in the CI program. Over time, experience shows, such programs will wither and then die.

On the other hand, where the CI unit can anticipate and satisfy its customers' real needs, it can then create more valuable Competitive Intelligence products and services, and also create more knowledgeable users. But, if the end users do not precisely know their

Competitive Intelligence needs, or are not familiar enough with the CI process to articulate what it is they really need, it is up to the CI professionals to determine what it is the internal client needs, even if the clients do not know what they need.

To break this closed loop, we have developed a simple system to help CI professionals (or their clients or both) determine which one or more of the four different divisions of CI are most likely to be the types of Competitive Intelligence most needed by and useful to their internal clients.

"Needs are not questions."[2]

The system involves systematically linking what each CI division is best focused to provide with the current CI needs of the business. These CI needs are a function, in turn, of five elements making up the competitive environment faced by the internal clients of the CI professionals. These elements are the

1. environment in which you operate.
2. products and services you produce.
3. companies you face.
4. production and supply chain issues.
5. marketplace dynamics.

In each case, when analyzing your probable CI needs, keep in mind that the CI professional should assume the perspective of the end-user client, with the responsibilities for the products and services that he or she possesses. But you must look at all of these circumstances objectively. By that we mean that, as a CI analyst, it is your obligation to view the marketplace more objectively than do your clients.

In addition, in some cases, your view of the competitive circumstances may have to exclude your own firm from the overall assessment. For example, in the category of the degree of knowledge intensity, you may have a situation where your firm is unique in its high level of knowledge intensity. That means that all of your competitors are significantly less proficient in knowledge management techniques. In such a case, you would characterize your marketplace as one that is not knowledge intensive, even if your own firm were highly knowledge intensive.

Of course, it may well be the case that criteria used below, such as centrality of management, may become a target of the CI process itself, such as when the CI process develops analyses on "organizational infrastructure."[3] That is not a circular problem. All the assessments made to determine the types of CI needed should be reviewed over time.

Competitive Environment

Here you are looking at the overall competitive environment in which your firm (or the part of the firm that you are serving) is now competing. This is, in turn, divided into three separate areas:

1. Level of company regulation
2. Barriers to entry
3. Barriers to exit

Level of Company Regulation

In considering this element, you will be asking, "what is the level of regulation of the company?" as distinguished from regulation of the company's products or services. Such regulation may be aimed at the company because of the industry in which it operates, such as insurance companies, or it may be regulation which is aimed at the company because of how it operates, such as all manufacturing companies that discharge waste products into the air. Or it may be aimed at the company because of how it is structured. For example, a company that is publicly held and that trades on the New York Stock Exchange faces very different regulatory restrictions than a privately held competitor.

In any case, keep in mind only the regulation that impacts, directly or indirectly, the business decisions and operations of your end-user. So, if your parent company owns several businesses, including an insurance company, but your unit makes cookies, you should not take into account the regulatory impact of insurance company financial solvency regulations on your decision.

Companies facing the lowest levels of company regulation are, in general, the most free to act and to respond to market forces. In addition, as they have low levels of regulation, they tend to be able to innovate more quickly, to change their operations and even overall structure more rapidly, and tend to place less information in the public domain. As a result, the CI most likely to have the greatest bottom-line impact on such firms are tactics-oriented, target-oriented, and technology-oriented Competitive Intelligence.

Companies that face a moderate degree of company regulation are, in general, less free to act and to respond rapidly to market forces. They take longer to be able to respond because the regulation directly or indirectly impedes that flexibility. In addition, unlike those facing low levels of company regulation, they tend to have to stretch innovation out over a longer period of time, and find it difficult to change their operations and even overall structure rapidly. Finally, they tend to place more information in the public domain than do the companies facing low levels of company regulation. As a result, the CI most likely to have the greatest bottom-line impact to such a firm are target-oriented and strategy-oriented Competitive Intelligence.

Companies that face a high degree of company regulation are, in general, least free to act and to respond to market forces. In addition, as they face the highest levels of regulation, they tend to be able to innovate relatively slowly, and are unable to change their operations and even overall structure as rapidly as companies facing less company regulation. Finally, they tend to place the greatest amount of information in the public domain. As a result, the CI most likely to have the greatest bottom-line impact to such a firm is strategy-oriented Competitive Intelligence.

Barriers to Entry

Barriers to entry are numerous, varied, and sometimes interrelated. Some are purely regulatory in nature, that is, a company must obtain a license, which entails a review by an agency, often more than mere review, before it can operate as a bank. Others are financial in nature. For example, to make paint, you have to invest in building, buying, or leasing a large manufacturing facility. Sometimes the barriers are strictly political, as where operating permits may be awarded on political grounds. Finally, they may be technologically based. For example, for a firm to compete in the personal digital assistant market, it must have access to a minimum level of technology that it can use and develop.

Companies in a market that has low barriers to entry typically are characterized by higher degrees of flexibility and innovation than are those in other markets. Because of the absence or minimal nature of these barriers, such markets are subject to relatively sudden changes in terms of new participants as well as new products. As a result, the CI likely to have the greatest bottom-line impact tends to be tactics-oriented Competitive Intelligence.

Companies in a market that has moderate barriers to entry typically are characterized by lesser degrees of flexibility and innovation than are those in markets with low entry barriers. Because of these barriers, such markets are not subject to sudden changes in terms of new participants as well as new products. Instead, such changes are more gradual and incremental in nature. As a result, the CI likely to have the greatest bottom-line impact tends to be strategy-oriented, target-oriented, and tactics-oriented Competitive Intelligence.

Companies in a market that have high barriers to entry typically are characterized by significantly lesser degrees of flexibility and innovation than are those in markets with low entry barriers. Because of these high barriers, such markets are not subject to sudden changes in terms of new participants as well as new products. Instead, such changes are much more gradual and often incremental in nature. Companies in such markets do not typically expect nor often engage in aggressive price competition. As a result, the CI likely to have the greatest bottom-line impact tends to be strategy-oriented, target-oriented, and technology-oriented Competitive Intelligence.

Barriers to Exit

Barriers to exit are not as often found as are barriers to entry, but they exist, are similar, and can be as significant. For example, a financial and regulatory barrier to exiting the casualty insurance business might be the requirement that reserves are established to cover all potential future claims which might be made based on past policies and that a licensing body has approved the adequacy of such reserves. Another barrier to exit might be the requirement imposed on an urban ambulance service company that it may not surrender its operating permit, and thus exit the market, on any less than six months notice. A third type of barrier to exit is the existence of a massive capital base, such as a hospital, which cannot easily, quickly, or inexpensively be converted to other uses.

Companies in a market that has low barriers to exit typically are characterized by higher degrees of flexibility and innovation than are those in other markets. Because of the absence or minimal nature of these barriers, such markets are subject to relatively sudden changes, in terms of participants leaving as well as products being taken off the market. As a result, the CI likely to have the greatest bottom-line impact tends to be tactics-oriented Competitive Intelligence.

Companies in a market that has moderate barriers to exit typically are characterized by lesser degrees of flexibility and innovation than are those in markets with low exit barriers. Because of these barriers, such markets are not subject to sudden changes in terms of withdrawing participants as well as withdrawn products. Instead, such changes are more gradual and incremental in nature. As a result, the CI likely to have the greatest bottom-line impact tends to be strategy-oriented, target-oriented, and tactics-oriented Competitive Intelligence.

Companies in a market that has high barriers to exit typically are characterized by significantly lesser degrees of flexibility and innovation than are those in markets with low exit barriers. Because of these high barriers, such markets are not subject to sudden changes in terms of departing participants as well as products taken off the market. Instead, such changes are much more gradual and tend to be incremental in nature. In addition, the high barriers to exit often make those currently in the market more likely to engage in oligopoly-type behaviors. As a result, the CI likely to have the greatest bottom-line impact tends to be strategy-oriented and target-oriented Competitive Intelligence.

Products and Services Produced

Here you are looking at the specific products (or services) that your firm and its competitors provide and that they bring to the marketplace in which you all are now competing. This is, in turn, divided into three separate areas:

- Number of substitutes
- Regulation level of the product or service
- Lead-time to market
- Life cycle of the product or service

Number of Direct Substitutes

What a substitute product or service is varies from industry to industry and from market to market. Too many firms make the mistake of seeking an answer to this question from their single perspective alone. But that is not the only perspective; it is not even the best one.[4]

What a substitute is should be viewed from your perspective; that is, what products or services do you see, in the market today, as operating as a direct substitute for your product or service?

The next perspective to be consulted is that of your competitors; that is, do they see your product or service as a substitute for their products and services? If they do not think so, determine why not. If they do, what other products and services do they appear to consider as substitutes for their products. Are they also direct substitutes for yours as well? They may not be.

Finally, what do those consumers or other end-users, to whom you are seeking to sell your product, see as direct substitutes? Their perspective may surprise you.

For example, the manufacturer of a personal data assistant (PDA) should logically consider the makers of other PDAs as providing substitutes. Looking at the firms making or distributing PDAs, a maker may find that some of these firms also consider that the portable computers are a substitute product. That may or may not be true for the first manufacturer, depending, for example, on the price range. That is, a black and white PDA being sold for $199 may see a color PDA being sold at $349 as a substitute. However, it may not consider a portable computer being sold for $499 as a substitute, even though the color PDA maker may.

Then take the consumer's perceptive. A consumer may see, as a substitute for a $199 black and white PDA, a $129 time organizer, that is a pen and paper system, or a combination of a pager and an inexpensive electronic directory.

Companies whose products and services face very few direct substitutes are typically characterized by the fact that they also face only a few directly competing organizations, that they are often protected from competition by possessing patents or proprietary processes, and that the marketplace may have significant barriers to entry, to exit, or both. Because of these factors, they tend to be involved in more head-to-head competition, with more emphasis on product differentiation than on price, and with some vulnerability to sudden impacts due to technological changes outside of their marketplace. As a result, the CI likely to have the greatest bottom-line impact tends to be target-oriented and technology-oriented Competitive Intelligence.

Companies whose products and services face a moderate number of direct substitutes are typically characterized by the fact that they face several directly competing organizations, that they are poorly protected from competition by patents or proprietary processes, and operate in a marketplace which may have only moderate barriers to entry, to exit, or both. Because of these factors, they tend to be involved in more head-to-head competition with competitors as well as product line competition, with less emphasis on product differentiation and more on price, and with real vulnerability to sudden impacts due to technological changes outside of their marketplace. As a result, the CI likely to have the greatest bottom-line impact tends to be target-oriented and tactics-oriented Competitive Intelligence.

Companies whose products and services face a large number of direct substitutes are typically characterized by the fact that they also face a large number of directly competing organizations, that they are rarely able to rely on any long-term protection from competition by patents or proprietary processes, and operate in a marketplace that may have virtually no barriers to entry, to exit, or both.

Because of these factors, they tend to be involved in head-to-head competition with competitors, product-to-product competition, and product line competition, with very little emphasis on product differentiation and most of the focus on price competition, and with regular impacts due to technological changes outside of their marketplace. As a result, the CI likely to have the greatest bottom-line impact tends to be tactics-oriented Competitive Intelligence.

Regulation Level of Product or Service

The level of regulation of the product or service produced cannot always be separated easily from regulation of the competitor, particularly when we are dealing with services. For example, in the case of legal services, the quality of the services provided is controlled only indirectly, through requirements such as continuing education, as well as through the exercise of disciplinary authority over attorneys whose activities have damaged clients. However, it is useful to try to make such a distinction.

Regulation of a product or service being produced can cover some or all of these areas:

- Price at which it can be offered, such as regulated power utilities
- Terms under which it can be offered, or which it must include, such as individual life insurance policies
- Quality, that is minimum standards, of the product or service, such as in the case of automobiles in the United States where each auto maker must produce a fleet of cars with a certain overall minimum gas mileage
- Restrictions on who can serve as an intermediary, such as rules governing the transportation of human organs for transplantation
- Limitations on to whom or where a product or service can be sold, as in the case of liquor or cigarettes

Companies that are operating in an environment with little or no regulation of the production and sale of their products and services are typically characterized by the fact that they face a market that changes rapidly. New products and services can be introduced and are introduced with relative ease and frequency; existing products and services can be easily and quickly modified. In addition, often there are multiple, flexible channels of distribution, pricing decisions can be quickly transmitted to the marketplace, and competition is on the basis of perceived differences in product and service characteristics and consumer value. As a result, the CI likely to have the greatest bottom-line impact tends to be tactics-oriented and technology-oriented Competitive Intelligence.

Companies that are operating in an environment with moderate levels of regulation of the production and sale of their products and services are typically characterized by the fact that they face a market that changes less quickly. While new products and services can be introduced, their introduction is not as easy so they do not appear as often. Similarly, while existing products and services can be modified, that is not done often or quickly. In addition, often there are fewer, less flexible channels of distribution, so that pricing decisions are transmitted to the marketplace less quickly. Competition is typically conducted on the basis of differences in product and service characteristics as well as on brand-name recognition. As a result, the CI likely to have the greatest bottom-line impact tends to be target-oriented and technology-oriented Competitive Intelligence.

Companies that are operating in an environment with high levels of regulation of the production and sale of their products and services are typically characterized by the fact that they face a market that changes slowly. While new products and services can be introduced, their introduction is not easy so they do not appear with great frequency. Similarly, while existing products and services can be modified, it is not done very often or very quickly. In addition, often there are very few, relatively inflexible channels of distribution. Existing competitors are significantly more important than are potential entrants. Competition is typically conducted on the basis of differences in product and service characteristics as well as on brand-name recognition. As a result, the CI likely to have the greatest bottom-line impact tends to be strategy-oriented and technology-oriented Competitive Intelligence.

Lead-Time to Market

Time to market is, as with so many of these concepts, often a relative concept. In some industries, such as the pharmaceutical industry, the time from the beginning of research and development until a product can be taken to market is often measured in decades. In contrast, in the software industry, it may take only months to convert an idea to a marketable product.

As the Internet Age continues, the time to market for some industries is changing exponentially. For example, take book publishing. Before the advent of personal computers, it took publishers up to one-and-a-half years to bring a manuscript to the public in a bound, hard-copy form. The rise of personal computers meant that publishers could increasingly expect that the text would come from an author to the publisher in a form where it could not only be edited, but where it could also be prepared for printing. That cut the lead-time for the typical bound hard-copy book almost in half. Now, the alternative of e-books, being gradually embraced by mainstream publishers, means that a manuscript provided in electronic form can get to market within weeks, or even days, of its receipt at the publisher.

Companies facing an environment where there is a long lead-time to market typically see the marketplace occupied by relatively few players. These players are concerned with long-range plans and positioning their product or service portfolios to assure a continuing and growing stream of revenues over time. In addition, such markets are often, but not always, dependant on using existing proprietary technology to make the production and/or distribution more efficient and thus squeeze out additional costs.

The reasons for the long lead-time to market may be related to factors such as the product or service that is difficult to produce, to the regulatory environment, which may be rigidly controlling the company and product or service, to low levels of technology, or to operating in a confined environment, one with limits on exit and/ or entry, which permit those in the market to be able to survive with such long lead-times. As a result, the CI likely to have the greatest bottom-line impact tends to be strategy-oriented, target-oriented, and technology-oriented Competitive Intelligence.

Companies facing an environment where there is a moderate lead-time to market typically see the marketplace occupied by a number of players of varying sizes. These players are concerned with positioning their product or service portfolios to assure a continuing and growing stream of revenues over time, but also are alert to respond to shorter-term changes. In addition, such markets are often developing their own technology to make the production and/or distribution more efficient and thus squeeze out additional costs.

The reasons for the moderate lead time to market may be related to factors such as the product or service that is somewhat difficult to produce, to the regulatory environment, with limited controls over the company and product or service, or to operating in a market that has moderate limits on exit and/or entry, which all require that those in the market be able to adapt to survive without long lead-times. As a result, the CI likely to have the greatest bottom-line impact tends to be target-oriented, technology-oriented, and tactics-oriented Competitive Intelligence.

Companies facing an environment where there is a very short lead-time to market typically see the marketplace occupied by a large number of players of widely varying sizes. These players are less concerned with positioning their product or service portfolios to assure a continuing and growing stream of revenues over time than to assure that they identify and then respond to very short-term changes. In addition, such markets are often using their own technology as well as technology from other sectors to continually force the production and/or distribution to be more efficient and thus squeeze out additional costs.

The reasons for the short lead-time to market may be related to factors such as the product or service that is relatively easy to produce, to the regulatory environment, such as one with few controls over the company and product or service, or to operating in a market that has few, if any, real limits on exit and/or entry, which all require that those in the market be able to adapt quickly to survive. As a result, the CI likely to have the greatest bottom-line impact tends to be tactics-oriented Competitive Intelligence.

Product or Service Life Cycle

The life cycle is not the same as the lead-time to market. The former deals with measuring the time between the concept and the realization of the idea in the marketplace. Life cycle deals with the product or service once it is ready to enter that marketplace.

The product or service life cycle can be thought of as the time it takes the product or service to move from being new and revolutionary, through becoming established and evolutionary, to becoming passé and devolutionary. As the product or service moves through these stages, its unit profitably tends to fall, it sales volume tends to rise and then fall, the number and variety of competitors as well as competitive products and services tends to rise, and the number and variety of products which incorporate it in some way first rise and then fall.

Companies that offer a product or service that has a very short life cycle face a market that changes very rapidly, one where prices and costs can take sudden and significant turns. Typically the supporting investment is not relatively significant, but the role of both propriety and nonpropriety technology is. In addition, the products and services usually cannot be protected by legal regimes such as patent and trademark filings. As a result, the CI likely to have the greatest bottom-line impact tends to be tactics-oriented and technology-oriented Competitive Intelligence.

Companies that offer a product or service that has a moderate life cycle face a market that changes quickly, but prices and costs rarely take sudden and significant turns. Typically the supporting investment is somewhat significant, as is the role of both proprietary and nonproprietary technology. In addition, the products and services usually cannot be completely protected by legal regimes such as patent and trademark filings. As a result, the CI likely to have the greatest bottom-line impact tends to be tactics-oriented and technology-oriented Competitive Intelligence.

Companies that offer a product or service that has a long life cycle face a market that rarely changes quickly; that is, prices and costs rarely take sudden and significant turns. Typically the supporting investment is significant, but the role of both proprietary and nonproprietary technology is less so. In addition, the products and services usually receive significant protection from legal regimes such as patent and trademark filings. As a result, the CI likely to have the greatest bottom-line impact tends to be strategy-oriented and technology-oriented Competitive Intelligence.

Companies You Face

Here, you are trying to evaluate the firms with which you directly compete in your market or markets. The determination of who your competitors are should always be under review. In fact, if there are internal changes in process that will impact your firm, you should immediately begin a review of who your competitors will be when the changes have taken effect.[5] If your market is one in which there are currently very few competitors, you may want to evaluate it including the first tier of potential entrants. In any case, you must always make sure that your focus on who and what constitutes a competitor is kept broad.[6]

The way these firms are managed and relate to each other has a direct impact on which types of CI are best for you. This in turn is divided into five separate areas of consideration:

1. Centrality of management
2. Level of cooperation
3. Degree of concentration
4. Level of knowledge intensity
5. Reliance on alliances

Centrality of Management

Here, you are taking into consideration how the firms you face, but not including your own firm, tend to be managed, if there is an overall pattern. While each firm differs from every other firm, experience shows that firms in the same markets often tend to have similar degrees of management centrality.

By centrality of management, we mean the extent to which critical decisions, affecting the product and market, are made at the highest levels of an enterprise, by central managers or, conversely, are made at the level closest to the unit that is actually producing, selling, or otherwise managing the product or service.

By critical decisions, we mean decisions such as these:

- Changing prices of existing products or services
- Developing new products and services
- Launching new products and services and removing existing products and services from the marketplace
- Authorizing the capital investment needed to support these operations
- Entering into long-term contractual relationships with other firms necessary to carry all of these out

By decision making, we mean that the final decision is made at that level, whatever level that is, and is not subject to review at another level before it is implemented. This does not mean that the decisions in a decentralized firm are not reviewed, but rather that they are reviewed only after the fact as a part of the review of the performance of the unit and its executives and employees.

In markets where your competitors tend to be centrally managed, you should expect that response time to market and consumer changes will take longer. In addition, decisions, such as those listed previously, will be made only after taking into account the needs and demands of other, nonrelated operations, as well as the need to satisfy a variety of potentially conflicting constituencies, such as employees, unions, governments, owners, and investors. On the other hand, the centrally managed firm should be making its decisions taking into account performance and success as measured over a relatively long time frame, perhaps even several years. As a result, the CI likely to have the greatest bottom-line impact tends to be strategy-oriented Competitive Intelligence.

In markets where your competitors tend not to be totally centrally managed, but where some decisions are made at lower, more local levels, you should expect that response time to market and consumer changes will be faster. Decisions, such as those listed previously, will take into account the needs and demands of other, nonrelated operations, as well as the need to satisfy a variety of potentially conflicting constituencies, such as employees, unions, governments, owners, and investors, but will also reflect more immediate local pressures, such as those generated by consumers and local interests. The firm that is making its decisions on this mixed model should be making its decisions taking into account performance and success as measured over a moderately long time frame, running from six months up to two years. As a result, the CI likely to have the greatest bottom-line impact tends to be target-oriented as well as strategy-oriented Competitive Intelligence.

In markets where your competitors tend to be least centrally managed, you should expect that response time to market and consumer changes will be quite fast. Decisions, such as those listed previously, may occasionally take into account the needs and demands of other, nonrelated operations, as well as the need to satisfy a variety of potentially conflicting constituencies, such as employees, unions, governments, owners, and investors. However, they will more often reflect local pressures, such as those generated by consumers and local interests. The firm that is making its decisions on this decentralized model should be making its decisions taking into account performance and success as measured over a relatively short time frame, running from three months up to two years. As a result, the CI likely to have the greatest bottom-line impact tends to be tactics-oriented and target-oriented Competitive Intelligence.

Level of Cooperation

By degree of cooperation, we mean the degree to which the firms in this market, in practice, engage in vigorous, rapid moving competition. Those markets in which the firms seem to have the least degree of this may be viewed as having high levels of cooperation, or cartel-type behavior. On the other hand, markets with the lowest levels of cooperation will be ones that would be described as being highly competitive, that is, each firm operates without any evident parallelism in conduct.

In markets where the firms are the most highly competitive, they have the lowest levels of cooperation. Such markets tend to be fast moving, and the actions of one firm cannot often be a useful predictor of the actions of other firms. As a result, the CI likely to have the greatest bottom-line impact tends to be tactics-oriented Competitive Intelligence.

In markets where the firms appear to be more cooperative, the overall degree of competition is somewhat less. In these markets, for example, some firms may engage in joint support of research, or of research and development. Others may actually use competitors in other markets as a source of product or service for this market. Such markets tend to be a little slower moving. Given the linkages and other forms of cooperation, there will be situations when the actions of one firm can be a useful predictor of the actions of some other firms. As a result, the CI likely to have the greatest bottom-line impact tends to be tactics-oriented and target-oriented Competitive Intelligence.

In markets where the firms appear to be cooperating to the greatest degree, they can be said to be operating like a cartel. In those circumstances, the effective levels of competition are even lower. In these markets, for example, most of the firms may engage in joint support of research, or of research and development. Most of them will also be using competitors, in other markets, as a source of product or service for this market. Such markets tend to be much more slow moving. Give high degrees of cooperation, at least tacitly, it will be the usual situation that the actions of one firm can be a useful predictor of the actions of most of the other firms. As a result, the CI likely to have the greatest bottom-line impact tends to be target-oriented and strategy-oriented Competitive Intelligence.

Degree of Concentration

A similar situation involves an evaluation of the degree of concentration. But where the previous section deals with conduct, this one deals instead with structure. And structure influences both present and future competition.[7]

In general, the more concentrated a market is, the less intensive and extensive will direct competition tend to be. The ultimate degree of concentration is the monopoly, where one firm controls 100 percent of a market. There is no competition in that marketplace.

A wide variety of measures of concentration have been developed for a number of reasons. One of the most common reasons to measure the degree of concentration is to enable a government regulator, such as the Antitrust Division of the U.S. Department of Justice, or the European Commission, to determine if a proposed merger or acquisition will materially reduce competition in the future.

For purposes of evaluating the need for CI, we have adopted the following scale, based on those used in antitrust regulation, which measures sales, either in terms of volume or in value:

- A market is highly concentrated if the five largest firms control more than 60 percent of the market.
- A market is moderately concentrated if the five largest firms control at least 25 percent but no more than 60 percent of the market.
- A market is slightly concentrated if the five largest firms control less than 25 percent of the market.

In a highly concentrated market, the largest firms tend to dominate the competitive landscape. In general, they tend to set and defend prices, and also indirectly control the prices of key inputs, simply because of their (relative) size. It is relatively difficult for firms outside of the top five in size to penetrate that tier or to significantly increase market share. Often such radical changes occur only because of major technological shifts. The competition tends to be at two levels: among the very largest, and among the rest, with little real competition between either group. As a result, the CI likely to have the greatest bottom-line impact tends to be target-oriented and strategy-oriented Competitive Intelligence.

In a moderately concentrated market, the largest firms tend to heavily influence the competitive landscape. In general, while they tend to set and defend prices, they are vulnerable to competitive initiatives from smaller, more aggressive firms. Also, the very largest firms have less indirect control over the prices of key inputs. While it is difficult for firms outside of the top five in size to penetrate that tier, it is not impossible. The firms outside of the top five can significantly increase market share even without penetrating the top five. Such changes often occur because of major technological shifts, but the development of proprietary technology as well as the deployment in new ways of existing technology is also highly effective.

The competition tends to be among the very largest as a group, and among all firms in the market as well. As a result, the CI likely to have the greatest bottom-line impact tends to be technology-oriented, target-oriented, as well as tactics-oriented and strategy-oriented Competitive Intelligence.

In a slightly concentrated market, the largest firms tend to have no disproportionate influence on the competitive landscape. They are very vulnerable to competitive initiatives from smaller, more aggressive firms. Also, the very largest firms have very little indirect influence over the prices of key inputs because they do not have significant purchasing leverage. The firms outside of the top five can significantly increase market share and regularly penetrate the tier with the top five firms. Such changes can occur because of major technological shifts, through the development of proprietary technology, due to the deployment in new ways of existing technology as well as due to nontechnology drivers. The competition tends to be among all firms in the market. As a result, the CI likely to have the greatest bottom-line impact tends to be target-oriented and tactics-oriented Competitive Intelligence.

Knowledge Intensity

Knowledge intensity is a relatively new concept. It embodies more than technological sophistication and the effective use of information technology throughout a firm. Increasingly it is an indicator of how important knowledge—information and data that has been captured, processed, and is accessible to employees—is in the marketplace.

That knowledge may be knowledge of production processes, of customer preferences, and of supply chains dynamics. Knowledge intensity also carries with it the inference that the knowledge is easily accessible to all employees who need it, that it is easily and consistently updated, and that end-users can access and manipulate increasing amounts of data to extract the knowledge that they think they need, when they need it.

In a marketplace where companies are very knowledge intensive, the technology base of the companies, as well as the technology that drives the underlying knowledge management processes, tend to be changing relatively rapidly. This allows the firms that are most knowledge intensive to gain, hold, and exploit competitive advantages, so long as they support that process. As a result, the CI likely to have the greatest bottom-line impact tends to be technology-oriented Competitive Intelligence.

In a marketplace where companies are only moderately knowledge intensive, the technology base of the companies, as well as the technology that drives the underlying knowledge management processes, tend to be relatively stable. While this allows the firms that are most knowledge intensive to gain, hold, and exploit competitive advantages, other firms can quickly catch up or even overtake these firms. As a result, the CI likely to have the greatest bottom-line impact tends to be technology-oriented Competitive Intelligence.

In a marketplace where companies are simply not knowledge intensive, the technology base of the companies tends to be relatively stable. This provides no individual firm with any permanent competitive advantages, so all other firms can quickly catch up or even overtake any other firms. As a result, the CI likely to have the greatest bottom-line impact tends to be tactics-oriented Competitive Intelligence.

Reliance on Alliances

The degree to which firms in your market rely on alliances, whether for research, for manufacturing, for distribution, or for new initiatives, actually changes the nature and/or number of competitors.[8] In fact, the control over complementary products, one frequent reason for such alliances, is a well-recognized competitive strategy option.[9]

Take, for example, a small software firm that is developing supply-chain software. As a direct competitor, the way in which they can and will compete changes rapidly in several dimensions in each of the following situations:

- The firm establishes a joint venture with a software firm which offers warehouse management software.
- The firm signs a development contract with one of the four largest food service companies, one which controls over 25 percent of the food service distribution market.
- The firm agrees to partner with Lotus and use only Lotus-based modules in all of its new software products.

A market in which competing firms are relying heavily on alliances is one where the actions of the firm with which you are competing are impacted by the terms of the alliance, the resource and time demands of the alliance. While absolute freedom of action may be curtailed, each firm moves, in a sense, with an impact including that of its allies. As a result, the CI of greatest use tends to be target-oriented Competitive Intelligence.

A market in which competing firms rely moderately heavily on alliances is one where the actions of the firm with which you are competing are only indirectly impacted by the terms of the alliance, and the resource and time demands of the alliance. While absolute freedom of action may be slightly curtailed, each firm moves with its own impact slightly enhanced by that of its allies. Its own interests and a relatively independent strategy still largely drive its overall actions. As a result, the CI likely to have the greatest bottom-line impact tends to be target-oriented and strategy-oriented Competitive Intelligence.

A market in which competing firms never, or at best rarely, rely on alliances is one where the actions of the firm with which you are competing are only occasionally, and usually indirectly, impacted by the terms of the alliance, and the resource and time demands of the alliance. Its own interests and an independent strategy still largely drive its overall actions. As a result, the CI likely to have the greatest bottom-line impact tends to be strategy-oriented Competitive Intelligence.

Production and Supply Chain Issues

Production and supply chains issues are increasingly important. In the past decades, companies have seriously begun to seek and implement new ways to manage the way they produce and distribute the goods and services they provide.[10] This is not to say that production in particular has not been the focus of intensive improvement efforts. Rather, it is that the proper management of the entire supply chain is now an issue. And as companies seek to control and to redefine their own supply chain as well as the way they produce their goods and services, they also change the nature of the firms that you compete with. This is, in turn, divided into four separate areas:

1. Level of technology
2. Number of suppliers
3. Degree of capital intensity
4. Level of innovation

Level of Technology

The level of technology that characterizes your marketplace should be viewed both in terms of product as well as in terms of the entire supply chain. By production technology, we mean everything from the relative trade-off between manual and automated production to the ability of one facility to produce multiple outputs with minimal changeover costs, including lost time. By supply chain technology, we mean everything from the ability to track the status of individual packages being handled by a carrier to the use of the Internet to distribute software by downloading.

In a marketplace that is characterized by high levels of production and supply chain technology, we can expect to see competitors able to control and even reduce production and distribution costs on an ongoing basis, the rapid development and deployment of new products and services, as well as relatively low barrier to exit, but not to entry. As a result, the CI likely to have the greatest bottom-line impact tends to be technology-oriented Competitive Intelligence.

In a marketplace that is characterized by moderate levels of production and supply chain technology, we can expect to see competitors able to control or eliminate increases in production and distribution costs on a short-term basis, the moderately rapid development and deployment of new products and services, as well as relatively low barriers to exit as well as to entry. As a result, the CI likely to have the greatest bottom-line impact tends to be technology-oriented Competitive Intelligence.

In a marketplace that is characterized by low levels of production and supply chain technology, we can expect to see competitors unable to control or eliminate increases in production and distribution cost, the relatively low development and deployment of new products and services, as well as very low barriers to exit as well as to entry. As a result, the CI likely to have the greatest bottom-line impact tends to be tactics-oriented Competitive Intelligence.

Number of Suppliers

The relative number of suppliers to the companies in the marketplace is important since it is a rough approximation of the relative power of these suppliers. For example, if there are only three suppliers of an ingredient in bath soap, which is made by twenty-five different manufacturers, the three suppliers can have a significant impact on the market. For example, if one decides that this market niche is not profitable enough, it could either raise its price or even leave the market. In either case, the companies that currently use that firm as the source face a difficult competitive situation. They may elect to absorb the price or seek alternative sources. But what is the likelihood that either of the two other firms have the capacity or inclination to supply the firm at the old price? Similarly, if the supplier ceases operations, do the firms it supplies have realistic options? They may not.

So, in a marketplace that is characterized by a small number of suppliers of key ingredients, components or inputs, relative to the number of firms in the market, the suppliers have, potentially, great power. In addition, in such markets, the reasons for the number of suppliers are often technological, the technology used by the suppliers is proprietary, or capital; that is, the production of the inputs may be very capital intensive. As a result, the CI likely to have the greatest bottom-line impact tends to be technology-oriented Competitive Intelligence.

In a marketplace that is characterized by a balance between the relative number of suppliers of key ingredients, components or inputs, and the number of firms in the market, the suppliers have, potentially, much less power. In such markets, the reasons for the number of suppliers are often technological; that is, the technology used by the suppliers is proprietary, or capital. The production of the inputs may be very capital intensive. In addition, firms competing in this niche tend to have developed technological abilities allowing them to move freely from one supplier to another. As a result, the CI likely to have the greatest bottom-line impact tends to be technology-oriented Competitive Intelligence.

In a marketplace that is characterized by a relatively large number of suppliers of key ingredients, components or inputs, the suppliers have, potentially, very little power. Firms competing in this niche tend to have developed technological abilities allowing them to move freely from one supplier to another. Regardless of that, they are usually able to play one supplier against another to obtain better terms, including prices. As a result, the CI likely to have the greatest bottom-line impact tends to be target-oriented Competitive Intelligence.

Degree of Capital Intensity

How capital intensive the companies with which you compete are is also a factor driving the kinds of CI you should be focusing on. As with many of the tests, this is also somewhat subjective.

Firms that are very capital intensive tend to have a significant reliance on existing technology, which is imbedded in their investments. In addition, since large capital investments often take time to plan and then implement, these firms will tend to have a long-range view of the market. Their responses to market changes, such as price cuts, will reflect not only current marginal pricing of their output, but the firm's long-term vision of its place in the market, as well as the financial resources available to support the firm's ongoing operations. As a result, the CI likely to have the greatest bottom-line impact tends to be strategy-oriented and technology-oriented Competitive Intelligence.

Firms that are only moderately capital intensive tend to have a less significant reliance on existing technology. That does not mean they do not rely on technology. For example, that technology may be imbedded in strategic partners or suppliers.

Since they are not making large capital investments, these firms will tend to have a short-range view of the market than do firms that are very capital intensive. Their responses to market changes, such as price cuts, will tend to reflect current marginal pricing of their output, as well as the financial resources available to support the firm's ongoing operations. As a result, the CI likely to have the greatest bottom-line impact tends to be strategy-oriented and target-oriented Competitive Intelligence.

Firms that are not capital intensive tend to have no significant reliance on their own existing technology. That does not mean they do not rely on technology. For example, that technology may be imbedded in strategic partners or suppliers.

Since they are not making large capital investments, these firms will tend to have a much shorter-range view of the market than do firms that are moderately capital intensive. Their responses to market changes, such as price cuts, will tend to reflect current marginal pricing of their output, as well as the financial resources available to support the firm's ongoing operations. As a result, the CI likely to have the greatest bottom-line impact tends to be target-oriented Competitive Intelligence.

Level of Innovation

Levels of innovation in an industry impact not only production of products and services; they also impact the development of new products and services, as well as changes in the way in which the supply chain operates.

Firms that have demonstrated low levels of innovation tend to view the immediate future of a market as an extension of the immediate past. In fact, their time horizon tends to be rather short-term in nature. They are also more often reactive rather than proactive, whether the issue is product improvement or workplace modification. As a result, the CI likely to have the greatest bottom-line impact tends to be tactics-oriented Competitive Intelligence.

Firms that have demonstrated moderate levels of innovation tend to view the immediate future of a market as reflecting the immediate past, but expect that many elements of it can and will change. In fact, their time horizon tends to be medium-term in nature. They are also less reactive than they are proactive, whether the issue is launching a new product or changing their own communications infrastructure. As a result, the CI of greatest use tends to be technology-oriented and target-oriented Competitive Intelligence.

Firms that have demonstrated high levels of innovation tend to view the immediate future of a market as only a step towards a longer-term, more radically changed future. In many areas, their time horizon tends to be long-term in nature. They are significantly more proactive than they are reactive, whether the issue is terminating a line of business, even a profitable one, or entering into a new strategic partnership. As a result, the CI likely to have the greatest bottom-line impact tends to be strategy-oriented and technology-oriented Competitive Intelligence.

Marketplace Dynamics

By marketplace dynamics, we mean the way in which the marketplace appears to you and your competitors. The dynamics of each marketplace you face may vary from product or service line, or even just product or service to product or service line. Markets that are chaotic due to underlying dynamics will require a very different CI approach than will markets that are very stable.

The way in which we look at marketplace dynamics is, in turn, divided into three separate indicators:

1. The number of customers
2. The geographic scope of the market
3. The nature of competition

Number of Customers

As with so many of the indicators, the number of customers is a relative concept. Obviously, there are markets where the absolute number of customers is very small, for example less than 100. One example would be the market for civilian jet engines for commercial aircraft. And there are markets where the absolute number of actual and potential customers runs into the hundreds of millions, such as for mutual funds. As we use it, the number of customers is measured relative to the number of firms. As with other terms, those in a marketplace can be fairly comfortable with the terms small, moderate, and large.

In market niches where the firms compete for a relatively small number of customers, these customers individually generally exercise great power over the competitors, and thus should be tracked. Conversely, the change in the relationship between any given competitor and its customer or customers can change the dynamics in the marketplace very quickly. As a result, the CI likely to have the greatest bottom-line impact tends to be target-oriented Competitive Intelligence.

In market niches where the firms compete for a moderate number of customers, these customers individually generally exercise only moderate power over the competitors, and thus should be tracked. But tracking them individually is not necessarily critical. The change in the relationship between any given competitor and its customer or customers will only moderately impact the dynamics in the marketplace quickly. In such niches, the way in which each firm and each customer faces the marketplace and acts in the short-term has a greater impact. As a result, the CI likely to have the greatest bottom-line impact tends to be target-oriented and tactics-oriented Competitive Intelligence.

In market niches where the firms compete for a percentage from a mass of customers, these customers individually exercise no power over the competitors. Rather, in such niches, the way in which each firm faces the marketplace, acts in the short-term, and responds to the actions of the other firms has the greatest impact. As a result, the CI likely to have the greatest bottom-line impact tends to be tactics-oriented Competitive Intelligence.

Geographic Scope of the Market

By geographic scope, we mean the area that your competitors, excluding your own firm, serve. While your firm, for example, may serve customers in a three-county area, your competitors may be serving customers in a thirty-state area. Geographic scope impacts performance issues such as logistics, economies of scale in the production of products, and ability to respond quickly to global versus local changes and thus calls for variations in the strategies available to a firm.[11]

Those markets in which firms compete on a global basis tend to have some larger firms with a global portfolio or products or services. To support such scale, these firms typically must develop or acquire significant internal support for global operations, plan for and respond to long-term trends as well as near-term ones. As a result, the CI likely to have the greatest bottom-line impact tends to be strategy-oriented Competitive Intelligence.

On the other hand, those markets in which firms compete on a regional basis may have some larger firms, but may also see medium-size and small firms in the market. In addition, while the overall strategic goals of the very largest firms will impact the market, the goals and nature of the medium-size firms will impact the present and future directions of the market as well. As a result, the CI likely to have the greatest bottom-line impact tends to be strategy-oriented and target-oriented Competitive Intelligence.

Those markets in which firms compete on a local level tend to have only medium-size and small firms in the market. The ways in which these firms perceive the market and the ways in which they can and do respond to each other's activities has the greatest impact on the nature of competition in that market. As a result, the CI likely to have the greatest bottom-line impact tends to be target-oriented Competitive Intelligence.

Nature of Competition

By nature of competition, we mean the balance between competing on price, which is a commodity-type market, and competing on the basis of features that is a market where products and services tend to be "customized." In the past, customization meant low levels of production. However, as technology grows in importance, markets that were previously considered as commodity-type markets now may be segmented into niches that can be considered as demonstrating mass customization.

In those markets where competition is based exclusively, or almost exclusively, on price, firms face what is also called a commodity situation. That is the product or service provided by any competitor is regarded as a satisfactory substitute for that of another, so the sole or at least dominating determining factor is price. Commodity markets have historically included fungible products such as wheat. Today, they can include services, such as group life insurance, where price is the single most critical element in making a sale. As a result, the CI likely to have the greatest bottom-line impact tends to be tactics-oriented Competitive Intelligence, focusing on issues related to price.

In those markets where competition is based on a combination of price and features, firms face a situation of mixed competition. That is, the product or service provided by any competitor is regarded as a satisfactory substitute for that of another, and the products or services vary in significant ways of importance to the customer. Thus the customers make decisions based on considering both cost and the benefit to them of features found in one product or service but not in another. Today, they can include products, such as a new house, where price and terms are only one or two critical elements in making a sale. In the service sector, home security systems, with a mix of human and electronic elements, meet this definition. It is often the case that the customer is faced with an offering that is actually a mixture of product and service, or where different competitors have adapted or incorporated differing technologies. As a result, the CI likely to have the greatest bottom-line impact tends to be tactics-oriented and technology-oriented Competitive Intelligence.

In those markets where competition is based largely or exclusively on features, firms face a competition based on customization, whether or not the product is actually made in response to a customer order. That is, the products or services vary in significant ways of importance to the customer. Thus the customers make decisions primarily based on the benefit to them of features found in one product or service but not in another. Today, this can include products, such as a portrait painted for an anniversary, as well as services, such as writing a computer program. Most of the true feature-based competition tends to be in the electronic and technology sector. As a result, the CI likely to have the greatest bottom-line impact tends to be technology-oriented Competitive Intelligence.

NEED FOR CI

"Nothing can add more power to your life than concentrating all of your energies on a limited set of targets."[12]

Scoring

To determine what type(s) of CI your firm should be collecting and using, use the prior materials to analyze the market or markets you now ace. One easy approach is to score your responses. That is, you record what your responses illustrate to each of these and then total them up.

If you are in several markets, score each of them separately if you intend to make Competitive Intelligence gathering available to each separate from the other. If you do not intend to do that, then score the market as it appears to you above the individual market level.

Try using this grid to track your overall score. For each area, check the type or types of CI that are best suited to that aspect of the competitive environment, based on the analysis we have just given you.

Preferred CI Orientation

Competitive Environment	Strategy	Target	Tactics	Technology
Environment				
Company Regulation	☐	☐	☐	☐
Entry Barriers	☐	☐	☐	☐
Exit Barriers	☐	☐	☐	
Products and Services				
Substitutes		☐	☐	☐
Regulation	☐	☐	☐	☐
Lead Time	☐	☐	☐	☐
Life Cycle	☐		☐	☐
Companies				
Centrality of Management	☐	☐	☐	
Cooperation	☐	☐	☐	
Concentration	☐	☐	☐	☐
Knowledge Intensity			☐	☐
Alliances	☐	☐		
Production and Supply Chain				
Technology Level			☐	☐
Number of Suppliers			☐	☐
Capital Intensity	☐	☐		☐
Innovation	☐	☐	☐	☐
Marketplace				
Customers		☐	☐	
Geographic Scope	☐	☐		
Type of Competition			☐	☐

Number of Hits

Strategy-oriented CI	_____
Target-oriented CI	_____
Tactics-oriented CI	_____
Technology-oriented CI	_____

Experience shows that if you have indicated one or more types of CI seven times or more, that type of CI is an area in which you should concentrate. If you have more than one with seven points, the one with a higher score is the more important for the competitive environment that you face.

DO REGULAR AND FORWARD-LOOKING REVIEWS

For most firms, this analysis will deal with the environment, products, services, companies, production, supply, and marketplace as they are today. However, it would be a wise firm that would redo this analysis, seeking to evaluate how each of these would look in the near term, that is in one to three years, and in the long-term, that is in two to five years, or even more. Such an analysis should help you point your CI program in the directions where your firm's CI needs will gradually emerge from the present context.

Since the way that you respond to these questions was measured at one point in time, you should make sure to regularly review all these circumstances to see if your overall CI needs have changed. For example, a market niche where the life cycle of a key product has changed should result in an immediate reevaluation of your needs for tactics-oriented Competitive Intelligence versus technology-oriented Competitive Intelligence. In addition, it should trigger a review of your overall CI current needs.

In addition, if your analysis indicates that one or more of these elements are in the process of changing significantly, review your Competitive Intelligence needs assessment too. If you think you know when that change will occur, you can then be prepared to modify your own CI processes and targets to fit those emerging changes.

NOTES

1. Jason Roop, "Low Cost Lowdown." Available at http://www.insidebiz.com/Richmond/cover/cover102898.htm (October 28, 1998).

2. Yves-Michel Marti, "A Typology of Information Needs," in Gilad and Herring, *Applied Business Strategy 2A*, 121, 123.

3. See Fahey, *Competitors*, ch. 14.

4. See Porter, *Competitive Advantage*, ch. 8 for tips on identifying and dealing with substitution issues.

5. Deborah C. Sawyer, "Defining Your Competition: One Step Forward, Two Steps Back," *Competitive Intelligence Magazine* 4, 4 (July–August 2001): 43–44.

6. Deborah C. Sawyer, "Defining Your Competition: The Forest or the Trees?" *Competitive Intelligence Magazine* 4, 3 (May–June 2001): 43–44.

7. See Porter, *Competitive Strategy*, ch. 9.

8. In this we also include other relationships. See Fahey, *Competitors*, ch. 8.

9. See Porter, *Competitive Advantage*, ch. 12.

10. See Porter, *Competitive Strategy*, ch. 6 for a discussion of competitive strategy issues with respect to buyers and suppliers.

11. See Porter, *Competitive Strategy*, ch. 13.

12. Nido Qubein quoted in Davis, *Success*, 40.

6

Where Should You Look for Raw Data for Active Competitive Intelligence?

The data that go into making a CI analysis may be found virtually anywhere. However, CI's more than twenty years experience is that there are only so many places where potentially useful data can be accessed legally and ethically. The collective experience of CI analysts is that there are places where one can usually expect to find useful data and places where it is extremely unlikely to find those data.

In the following sections, we have outlined the most common, typical sources of raw CI data. For each we have very briefly indicated what kinds of data you can expect to find there. And, given these types of expected data, we have then noted which of the four divisions of active CI can be expected to find these data most useful, given its focus, audience, and so forth.

Where can data be found? The question is probably better put thus: Where is it not found? As yet, evidence provided by best-practice firms indicates that "presently it is not used as a tool to create [science and technology intelligence]."[1] That means CI professionals must look for data where they are found. Data move back and forth to an organization as an essential part of its functioning. In fact, viewing the movement of data like the movement of electricity through the body's nervous system produces an interesting way to look at the many pathways these data can flow out from (and back to) any company. Figure 6.1 shows this view. Of course, it is necessarily incomplete.

Figure 6.1
Company Data Flow

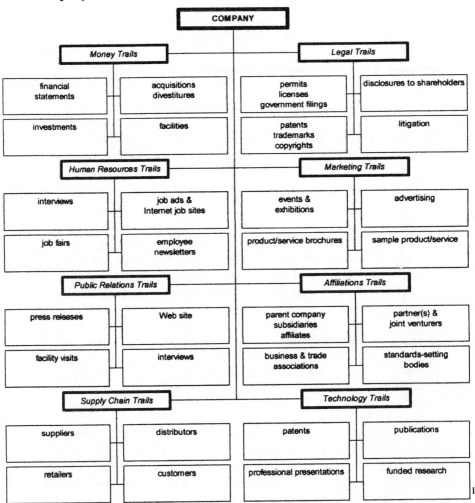

Source: Adapted from *Kent Ridge Digital Labs, Charting Your Course in the Digital Age—An IT Perspective* (Singapore: Kent Ridge Digital Labs, 1999), 65.

TYPICAL SOURCES OF RAW DATA

Data sources for CI research can be divided into two broad, separate groups: secondary and primary.

- By secondary, we mean sources that are primarily prepared for the public to read or to see.
- By primary, we mean sources that have data, but which are not generally prepared for publication.

On the whole, the secondary sources are in print and primary involve interaction with people or nonprint items. But the line between them is not always clear. While a newspaper article may be considered secondary, how would a telephone call to the reporter who did the story be classified? Does it depend on whether he or she relates additional, unpublished but public data collected from the target? What if he or she provides names of potential interviewees at the target?

For each broad type of data source, we will briefly indicate the following:

- *Audience*: To what audience is the document, the publication, or the contact devoted or aimed?
- *Purpose*: Why was this source created, why were these data provided, or why were they originally collected?
- *Sources of underlying data*: Where did the data provided actually come from? For example, did they come directly from a target and if so, from someone at the target who would be expected to have those data?
- *Level of Detail and Scope*: How much depth or breadth can you typically expect to find in data at this source? Would it be considered as superficial to individuals in your position, or as having a great deal of depth? Would it be considered as very narrow and focused, such as on production details, or would it be written for a general audience?
- *Age*: How old are the data provided here likely to be? Are they very current (that is less than one week old), current (that is less than one month old), dated (that is up to twelve months old), or old (which is over twelve months old)?
- *Accuracy and Completeness*: How likely is it that data obtained from or through this type of source are accurate as well as complete?

And then we will indicate the type or types of CI for which this is usually a good source of raw data.

Researchers tend to spend too much time looking to published sources and using the library before they begin to tap field sources.[2]

Secondary Sources of Raw Data for CI

Trade Journals

Audience: Employees and executives of firms in the industry; suppliers and customers to a lesser degree.

Purpose: Keep readers up to date with news in the industry and factors impacting that industry niche. Often includes interviews on future developments, trends, and strategies.

Sources of underlying data: Companies in the industry, trade associations, government agencies, wire services.

Level of detail and scope: Usually highly focused on industry, assuming its readers understand who is who and what the major issues, technologies, and so on are. Less detailed on matters only peripheral to the industry.

Age: Materials are usually fairly current. As a general rule, daily publications have materials one to two days old, weekly publications, one to two weeks old; monthly publications, one to two months old; and annuals are usually six months old before they are published.

Accuracy and completeness: Tend to be fairly accurate and complete. Only problems tend to be in publications that have a high turnover in editorial personnel, which produces a degree of loss of institutional memory.

CI most likely to find it useful:

Strategy-oriented CI

Target-oriented CI

Technology-oriented CI

Tactics-oriented CI

Trade Associations and Chambers of Commerce

Audience: Publications tend to aim at senior-level management and other key decision makers in a particular industry or local businesses.

Purpose: To communicate changes affecting the overall industry or local economic conditions and to marshal support from members for legislation, research and development, and so forth.

Sources of underlying data: Members, particularly their public relations offices.

Level of detail and scope: On matters impacting the industry, deals with issues at a more common or strategic level. When dealing with individual members, can provide a detailed profile of people and processes.

Age: As a general rule, monthly publications have materials about one to two months old, and quarterlies about three to five months old.

Accuracy and completeness: Fairly accurate, but rarely put in data not obtained from individual or business members.

CI most likely to find it useful:
Strategy-oriented CI
Target-oriented CI

Government Reports

Audience: Government policy makers, industry regulators, companies in a particular industry.

Purpose: Collect, analyze, and publish data, often highly aggregated, to inform government officials or to report on the impact of government policies. Can also provide independent look at policies and trends.

Sources of underlying data: Usually original data collection efforts, such as surveys and interviews. Sometimes also use data collected and provided by trade associations and specialized research centers.

Level of detail and scope: Vary widely. Data are usually aggregated but can be disaggregated in some cases. Will not contain proprietary data, except by accident.

Age: Tends to be dated; that is, up to twelve months old; or old, that is over twelve months old, in most cases. When dealing with issues with high-level political or economic impacts, data may occasionally be less dated.

Accuracy and completeness: Data collected directly from companies surveyed tend to be very accurate but often, due to definitional issues, may not be directly comparable with other published data. Due to ability of governments to compel cooperation, even when compulsion is not an issue, there tends to be a high level of cooperation.

CI most likely to find it useful:
Strategy-oriented CI
Target-oriented CI
Technology-oriented CI
Tactics-oriented CI

Government Records and Files

Audience: Agencies and offices regulating the business or industry in question. Due to open records laws and regulations, much of this is also open to the general public.

Purpose: To allow agencies to conduct their business.

Sources of underlying data: Most often, these records contain materials provided by individual persons and companies to the agency or office.

Level of detail and scope: Tend to be highly detailed, as they are designed to provide data requested by the agency for the conduct of its business, to ensure compliance with rules and permits, and so forth.

Age: Vary widely. The contents can go back for decades in some cases. On the other hand, the frequency with which an agency updates its files depends on filing and reporting requirements, which can be from weekly to annual.

Accuracy and completeness: Materials, sometimes filed under oath, tend to be accurate. However, the scope of the materials can be very narrow, depending on the agency's filing and compliance requirements.[3]

CI most likely to find it useful:

Strategy-oriented CI

Target-oriented CI

Security Analyst Reports

Audience: Investors in the securities of publicly traded enterprises. This ranges from individual to institutional investors.

Purpose: To demonstrate capability of research departments of the securities dealers, with the aim of improving its image, and thus its sales business.

Sources of underlying data: Usually data come directly from the firm being profiled. On occasion, key suppliers and distributors are interviewed. Industry-level data may be developed from company-by-company sources or from trade associations, as well as taken from government reports.

Level of detail and scope: Most reports tend to be focused in terms of time, covering events over the past weeks or quarters. Some are annual. Detail varies widely, with most of the detail coming from company sources. It is heavily financial in orientation.

Age: Fairly current. Many reports will note the date of the last report.

Accuracy and completeness: In the past, there have been questions raised about objectivity of reports from researchers working for firms having a major interest in the stock of the company profiled. SEC efforts since 2000 are aimed at making these reports more objective and credible.

CI most likely to find it useful:

Strategy-oriented CI

Target-oriented CI

Tactics-oriented CI

Academic Case Studies

Audience: Graduate-level students in business, management, and related courses.

Purpose: To provide detail of specific business actions, set in a competitive context, so that students can prepare their own analyses of these cases.

Sources of underlying data: The targeted companies, including unpublished materials, studies by the professor writing the case, trade associations, and government agencies.

Level of detail and scope: Tend to focus either on history and long strategy or on tactics in an unusual market and economic context.

Age: Usually two or more years old.

Accuracy and completeness: Very accurate, but often have a very narrow focus or only a summary of the overall context.

CI most likely to find it useful:

Strategy-oriented CI

Research Centers

Audience: Companies in the industry, government agencies involved in the industry, companies whose business is dependent on that industry.

Purpose: To develop new information for sale or to influence legislation and regulation, as well as to support academic research needs.

Sources of underlying data: Companies in the industry and government agencies, as well as independent research conducted by the centers and students.

Level of detail and scope: Tend to be very industry-centric. Often heavily focused on strategy and policy. But can provide industry-level data not available elsewhere.

Age: Rarely current. They are usually dated or even very old.

Accuracy and completeness: Except for advocacy pieces, they tend to be both accurate and complete. That is because accuracy and completeness is a part of the reputation the centers seek to develop.

CI most likely to find it useful:

Strategy-oriented CI

Business Information Services

Audience: Companies extending credit to individuals or businesses; businesses seeking market-level data.

Purpose: Allow customers to utilize the data in managing their businesses.

Sources of underlying data: For credit, creditors, and the target himself or herself, as well as public records. For others, government surveys, as well as proprietary surveys.

Level of detail and scope: Credit-based sources tend to have a great deal of financial data from third parties. The degree of information on the individual business in noncredit categories tends to be significantly less. Surveys vary widely in scope and depth.

Age: Credit-based information tends to be current, with the exception of information provided by the target. That may be old, or nonexistent, depending on the cooperation of the target. Survey-based resources tend to be dated to old.

Accuracy and completeness: The accuracy of data provided by creditors and from public records tend to be very high. Data provided directly from the target are most often not crosschecked, and so must be considered as unconfirmed. Data from surveys, in the aggregate, tend to be accurate, but care must be taken to make sure that the survey encompasses all potential targets.

CI most likely to find it useful:

Strategy-oriented CI

Target-oriented CI

Technology-oriented CI

Tactics-oriented CI

Advertisements

Audience: Primarily existing and potential customers and consumers. However, advertisements in industry publications may also be aimed at developing or enhancing company image.

Purpose: To sell product and services, either by featuring the product (or service) or by convincing potential customers and consumer that the advertiser is the right place to buy the product or service.

Sources of underlying data: The company that places the advertisement is usually the sole source of data and photographs in the advertisement.

Level of detail and scope: Typically these are very low in detail and general in scope. However, sometimes photographs in advertising provide data that the advertiser did not intend to provide.

Age: They tend to range from being current to being dated.

Accuracy and completeness: Are not subject to legal action unless they are clearly fraudulent. Trade regulation authorities tend to allow significant "puffing" so that their reliability can be questionable.

CI most likely to find it useful:

Target-oriented CI

Technology-oriented CI

Tactics-oriented CI

Want Ads

Audience: Potential employees of the target.

Purpose: To obtain employees or executives to fill existing or anticipated needs.

Sources of underlying data: The advertiser alone is responsible for the details of the position provided in a want ad.

Level of detail and scope: While many want ads tend to be general, some can provide a great deal of detail about the position to be filled, allowing inferences to be drawn about marketing tactics and strategy, as well as technology to be used.

Age: They range from being very current to being somewhat current. Most companies do not keep republishing a want ad, or keep it continually posted on-line for very long after the position is filled.

Accuracy and completeness: As the ad is selling the position, they tend to be incomplete. The details provided tend to be accurate, for reasons associated with equal employment opportunity and related laws.

CI most likely to find it useful:[4]

Target-oriented CI

Technology-oriented CI

Tactics-oriented CI

Local Newspapers and Magazines

Audience: Individuals, and to a lesser extent businesses, living or working in the circulation area.

Purpose: Provide news and articles with a local focus, as well as providing a local angle on national stories. Also provides national wire services, columns, and so forth.

Sources of underlying data: Most local stories are developed by staff or local writers who rely heavily on what they are told, except in investigative pieces.

Level of detail and scope: Most business articles are moderately detailed, but are not written for those in the particular industry. Sometimes local businesses provide data to a local paper or magazine that they would not give to a trade publication.

Age: Stories in the business section can range from the very current to those that are somewhat dated, while nonbusiness stories tend to range from those that are very current to some that are only current.

Accuracy and completeness: These sources tend to be able to check most of the facts on which they rely, but sometimes they can be manipulated to generate disinformation.

CI most likely to find it useful:

Strategy-oriented CI

Target-oriented CI

Tactics-oriented CI

Competitor Reports

Audience: Companies in competition with, or dependent on, the target.

Purpose: Provide data for industry or investment research.

Sources of underlying data: Trade publications, government reports, target company filings, occasionally interviews.

Level of detail and scope: Varies widely. Some, on public companies, do little more than repackage filings with the U.S. Securities and Exchange Commission. Others are parts of larger studies on the industry as a whole.

Age: Usually dated. The longer it is, the more likely it is to be dated.

Accuracy and completeness: Companies providing these strive to keep them accurate. However, they tend to be superficial when it comes to technical material. In addition, there are some industry-specific situations where such data should be closely questioned.[5]

CI most likely to find it useful:

Strategy-oriented CI

Target-oriented CI

Tactics-oriented CI

Competitor News Releases

Audience: A broad range of company constituencies, including its shareholders, creditors, suppliers, employees, and customers.

Purpose: Keep constituencies informed, keep the company name before the public and its customers, and build a positive image.

Sources of underlying data: Data in releases almost always come directly from the company, or from filings or reports it has made public.

Level of detail and scope: Varies widely depending on the aim of the release. A release announcing a new officer will have less detail than one announcing the closing of a plant.

Age: They usually range from the very current to merely current.

Accuracy and completeness: While the material in the releases tends to be accurate, they are usually written by professionals to accomplish one or more particular ends. Often they disclose less than they conceal.

CI most likely to find it useful:

Strategy-oriented CI

Target-oriented CI

Technology-oriented CI

Tactics-oriented CI

Competitor Home Page

Audience: A broad range of company constituencies, including its shareholders, creditors, suppliers, employees, and customers.

Purpose: Keep constituencies informed, keep the company name before the public and its customers, offer products, take orders, and build a positive image.

Sources of underlying data: Data almost always come directly from the company or from filings or reports it has made public. Many companies link the site to other sources rather than reprint or report what is said there.

Level of detail and scope: Varies widely depending on the aim of each page of the site. Also, some pages are written by technical personnel, seeking to communicate with other technical personnel, while hiring opportunity pages may offer a look at the vision of the business. Visuals, such as photographs, charts, or streaming media can contain significant detail.

Age: Ranges from very current to dated. This depends on how aggressive the Webmaster is in removing dated materials.

Accuracy and completeness: While the material in the text tends to be accurate, it should be read in light of what that page is seeking to communicate and to whom. Often these Web sites disclose less than they conceal. The analysis of the contents of Web sites, including what you should not expect to find there, is an emerging area of research.[6]

CI most likely to find it useful:

Strategy-oriented CI

Target-oriented CI

Technology-oriented CI

Tactics-oriented CI

Directories and Reference Aids

Audience: Businesses, academics, reference centers, such as libraries.

Purpose: Collect and provide tabulated, or crossindexed data on a large number of companies or businesses that have something in common.

Sources of underlying data: Almost always based on a combination of government sources, trade association data, and surveys voluntarily completed by the targets themselves.

Level of detail and scope: Usually has significant detail, but within a very narrow spectrum. Sometimes it is the only source of names to associate with a target.

Age: Most range from dated to old.

Accuracy and completeness: Tend to be accurate, but since they rely on voluntary surveys, completeness varies widely.

CI most likely to find it useful:

Target-oriented CI

Technology-oriented CI

Technical Publications

Audience: Practitioners of the technology in question, both business and academic.

Purpose: Source of information on current technology, especially trends.

Sources of underlying data: Companies involved with the technology in question.

Level of detail and scope: While companies may cooperate, often that is at the cost of not allowing their names to be associated with particular elements of research and development.

Age: Current to dated. Technical publications that contain data over one year old tend to have a very small market.

Accuracy and completeness: Tend to be very accurate on technical matters, but show mixed results when dealing with company- or even industry-level issues.

CI most likely to find it useful:

Technology-oriented CI

Tactics-oriented CI

Catalogs

Audience: Customers and clients.

Purpose: Sell products and services. Enable customers and clients to understand target's offerings.

Sources of underlying data: With the exception of generic catalogs, the target provides all data. However, if the catalog includes products and services not developed by the target, then descriptions and technical information almost always originate with the source of the product or service.

Level of detail and scope: Provides sufficient detail to allow potential customers and clients to differentiate among competing products and services. May also (but not always) provide pricing or cost data.

Age: These are usually current to dated. However, a comparison of a current version with an older one can often provide interesting data on trends.

Accuracy and completeness: Unless they are on-line, catalogs are incomplete due to lead-time issues. If the products or services originate elsewhere, the data are only as accurate and complete as the ultimate provider.

CI most likely to find it useful:

Target-oriented CI

Tactics-oriented CI

General News Publications

Audience: Readers, usually subscribers, across the national and economic spectrum.

Purpose: Provide current news, and, in the case of magazines, provide a context for that news.

Sources of underlying data: Usually have their own reporters and contributors. They, in turn, use a wide variety of sources, including but not limited to the target.

Level of detail and scope: Level of detail tends to be less than in trade publications, but they are more likely to talk to experts and commentators to provide a sense of context and trends.

Age: Materials are usually fairly current. As a general rule, daily publications have materials one to two days old, weekly publications one to two weeks, and monthly publications one to two months.

Accuracy and completeness: While they tend to be fairly accurate, they are often less precise with critical details than are trade publications.

CI most likely to find it useful:

Strategy-oriented CI

Target-oriented CI

Tactics-oriented CI

Books

Audience: Composed of general interest readers, along with those interested in a particular company, industry, or even executive.

Purpose: Some are historical studies, some are personal memoirs, and some are expansions of feature stories or series in general interest publications.

Sources of underlying data: Vary widely. May include data not previously published or even disclosed elsewhere.

Level of detail and scope: Varies widely.

Age: Usually old (over twelve months in age), due to publication lead times.

Accuracy and completeness: Depends on the author and purpose of the work.

CI most likely to find it useful:

Strategy-oriented CI

Target-oriented CI

Technology-oriented CI

Internet Aggregators and Portals

Audience: General interest Internet users or industry-specific users, depending on the portal or aggregator.

Purpose: Sell products or services associated with the site as well as collect money from advertising on the site directed to users. For those that are fee-based, the primary source of revenue is from subscriptions.

Sources of underlying data: Most data are actually sited elsewhere on the Internet or are collected, sometimes developed, by the site owner. The typical portal is a mixture of each, with the boundaries often unclear.

Level of detail and scope: Varies widely form site to site.

Age: Varies widely. While most Internet-based data sources sell currency, in fact that data to which they have access or provide are rarely any more current than hard-copy equivalents.

Accuracy and completeness: Varies widely. Site owners cannot (and do not) vouch for the accuracy of sties to which they direct (or even drive) visitors.

CI most likely to find it useful:

Target-oriented CI

Technology-oriented CI

Tactics-oriented CI

Primary Sources of Raw Data for CI

The availability, accessibility, accuracy, and level of detail of primary sources of raw data for CI will vary widely from industry to industry, from country to country, and from time to time.[7] At times it will be almost impossible to obtain; at others, it will be freely available.

Your Own Employees

Sources of underlying data: Personal contact with competitors, customers, suppliers, as well as previous employment with them.

Level of detail and scope: Varies widely, but rarely very detailed. Gaining cooperation from employees, particularly from the sales force,[8] may take significant efforts.[9]

Age: Data developed during previous employment tend to be dated, even if stated in the present tense. Other data tend to be as current as the contacts from which they are developed.

Accuracy and completeness: Accuracy tends to be high but completeness varies significantly.

CI most likely to find it useful:

Strategy-oriented CI

Target-oriented CI

Technology-oriented CI

Tactics-oriented CI

Industry Experts

Audience: You, your competitors, your investors, and those dependent on you and your competitors, such as suppliers and distributors.

Sources of underlying data: Vary widely, but generally include direct contact with the industry segment in question.

Level of detail and scope: Level of detail tends to be very significant. Scope can vary from wide to highly focused.

Age: Industry experts attempt to keep their data as current as possible.

Accuracy and completeness: Tends to be very accurate and very complete.

CI most likely to find it useful:

Strategy-oriented CI

Target-oriented CI

Technology-oriented CI

Tactics-oriented CI

Sales Representatives, Nonemployee

Sources of underlying data: Customers and competitors.

Level of detail and scope: Can be very detailed, particularly in terms of product or service characteristics and pricing, but rarely detailed with respect to strategic and technology issues.

Age: Varies. When sales representatives collect data, they are often dated when they get them. There is additional lead-time until you get the data from them.

Accuracy and completeness: Can be very accurate, if sales representative is willing to share the data. Completeness is likely only with respect to marketing and product or service concerns.

CI most likely to find it useful:

Target-oriented CI

Tactics-oriented CI

Customers

Sources of underlying data: Direct experience with you and your product or service and direct contact with your competitors.

Level of detail and scope: Can be very detailed, particularly in terms of product or service characteristics and pricing, but rarely detailed with respect to strategic and technology issues.

Age: Current as of the time collected and experienced by the customer. But you must make allowance for the time between collection and experience and the time it is actually collected by you.

Accuracy and completeness: Can be very accurate, if customer is willing to share the data and the data are current. Completeness is likely only with respect to marketing and product or service concerns.

CI most likely to find it useful:

Target-oriented CI

Tactics-oriented CI

Security Analysts

Audience: Investors in the target company and its competitors.

Purpose: To develop customers of the investment firm itself.

Sources of underlying data: Target companies, including interviews, as well as industry experts, trade associations, and government data.

Level of detail and scope: Moderately detailed, and fairly broad in scope, including strategy. Has significantly less detail and scope in technology areas.

Age: Most analysts produce reports at least quarterly, and sometimes more frequently. Data underlying reports tend to be very current.

Accuracy and completeness: Data tend to be accurate and complete, particularly financial data.

CI most likely to find it useful:

Strategy-oriented CI

Target-oriented CI

Tactics-oriented CI

Direct Contact with Competitors

Sources of underlying data: Competitor's own records and personnel.

Level of detail and scope: Can be very detailed and of very wide scope, depending on who is contacted, if this is a person-to-person contact.

Age: Can be extremely current.

Accuracy and completeness: While direct contact should provide the most accurate data, care should be taken to make sure that the contact in fact has regular access to such data. In technical areas, it is not usually effective.

CI most likely to find it useful:

Strategy-oriented CI

Target-oriented CI

Tactics-oriented CI

Suppliers

Sources of underlying data: Themselves as well as competing firms that they serve.

Level of detail and scope: Level of detail can be very good, but the scope is most often highly restricted.

Age: Can be reasonably frequent, if supplier is in regular contact with competitors.

Accuracy and completeness: If supplier will share competitor-sourced information, can be highly accurate and, within its limited scope, very complete.

CI most likely to find it useful:

Strategy-oriented CI

Target-oriented CI

Technology-oriented CI

Tactics-oriented CI

Product or Service Purchases

Sources of underlying data: Reverse engineering of the product or service, as well as sales, warranty, and service materials.

Level of detail and scope: Fairly detailed with respect to product or service details and performance. Narrow in scope, effectively providing support only for research and development as well as marketing-associated processes.

Age: May be dated with respect to other products or services mentioned in materials, as they reflect the situation as of the date prepared, which may be a long time before the product or service is purchased.

Accuracy and completeness: Accurate and complete, but only as of the date prepared.

CI most likely to find it useful:

Technology-oriented CI

Tactics-oriented CI

Focus Groups

Purpose: Used to determine consumer attitudes towards competing products or services.

Sources of underlying data: Members of the group interviewed.

Level of detail and scope: Varies widely, depending on what other data are being sought and what are captured by those moderating the groups. Most of the data deal with interests of members and with characteristics of competing products or services.

Age: Tends to be fairly current.

Accuracy and completeness: Depends on the recollection of the members of the group.

CI most likely to find it useful:

Tactics-oriented CI

Questionnaires and Surveys

Purpose: Broad-scale collection of data, usually from a sample representing a larger group or population.

Sources of underlying data: Analysis of responses to questions posed.

Level of detail and scope: Depends on depth of questions and design of instrument.

Age: Allowing for the processing time, can be fairly current.

Accuracy and completeness: Varies widely. They can be useful for capturing information on competitors and their actions, if the primary focus is on competition based on particular products or services.

CI most likely to find it useful:

Target-oriented CI

Trade Shows

Purpose: Provide opportunity for companies in the same market niche(s) to meet potential customers, distributors, suppliers, and so forth.

Sources of underlying data: Direct contact with attendees, as well as materials provided to attendees.

Level of detail and scope: Can be somewhat detailed, particularly with respect to technical and product or service characteristics. Also, direct contact may elicit significant gems of data on intentions in the marketplace in the near term.[10]

Age: Very current.

Accuracy and completeness: Can be very accurate and often quite complete.

CI most likely to find it useful:

Target-oriented CI

Technology-oriented CI

Tactics-oriented CI

Business Conferences

Purpose: Multicompany meetings to deal with current and future developments facing a particular industry or market niche.

Sources of underlying data: Speakers at the conference, attendees, and exhibitors, or vendors, if any.

Level of detail and scope: Can be quite detailed, and scope is usually broad. These are rarely useful for data on marketing issues.

Age: Reasonably current. However, the speakers usually prepare their presentations when invited, so that these may be somewhat dated.

Accuracy and completeness: Can be very accurate and complete.

CI most likely to find it useful:

Strategy-oriented CI

Target-oriented CI

Technology-oriented CI

Technical and Professional Meetings

Purpose: Bring together technical or professional employees within the context of their common discipline and technology.

Sources of underlying data: Presentations made at the meeting by speakers, direct contact with attendees, and exhibitors (vendors).

Level of detail and scope: Can be quite detailed, and scope is usually not very broad. However, they are rarely useful for data on marketing or strategy issues.

Age: Reasonably current. However, the speakers usually prepare their presentations when invited, so that these may be somewhat dated.

Accuracy and completeness: Can be very accurate and complete if very focused.

CI most likely to find it useful:

Technology-oriented CI

Facility Tours

Purpose: Public relations effort by facility owner to familiarize the public with its business.

Sources of underlying data: Actual viewing of working facility. Rarely is contact with employees at work permitted.

Level of detail and scope: Very general in terms of information. Close examination is usually not permitted. The result of that technical information, while potentially accessible through direct observation, can only be acquired if the person taking the tour is a trained observer.

Age: Current.

Accuracy and completeness: Most, but not all, tours are highly controlled. However, employees can become so inured to the presence of a tour that they may inadvertently discuss business matters in presence of the tour.

CI most likely to find it useful:

Target-oriented CI

Technology-oriented CI

Tactics-oriented CI

Retailers and Distributors

Sources of underlying data: Customers, competitors, and sales representatives.

Level of detail and scope: Can be very detailed, particularly in terms of product or service characteristics and pricing, but rarely detailed with respect to technology issues.

Age: Varies. Data collected by retailers and distributors are often dated when they get them. There is additional lead-time until you get the data from them.

Accuracy and completeness: Can be very accurate, if retailer or distributor is willing to share the data. Completeness is likely only with respect to marketing and product or service concerns or general changes in strategy, as expressed to these sources.

CI most likely to find it useful:

Strategy-oriented CI

Target-oriented CI

Tactics-oriented CI

Banks

Purpose: Collect data from customers as a part of their financial services relationship.

Sources of underlying data: Direct contact with company.

Level of detail and scope: Very deep, in financial terms, reasonably broad scope, except for technical matters. Rarely deals with intentions or strategy in any detail.

Age: Moderately current, depending on frequency with which client contacts bank with financial data.

Accuracy and completeness: Very accurate. Financial data tend to be complete.

CI most likely to find it useful:

Strategy-oriented CI

Target-oriented CI

Advertising Agencies

Purpose: Collect data from clients and develop marketing campaigns as a part of service relationship.

Sources of underlying data: Direct contact with company and media.

Level of detail and scope: Very deep in the marketing arena and reasonably broad in scope, except for technical matters. Often may have access to client intentions or strategy.

Age: Very current. May often be prospective as well.

Accuracy and completeness: Very accurate and complete, at least with respect to products and services represented.

CI most likely to find it useful:

Strategy-oriented CI

Target-oriented CI

Tactics-oriented CI

Television, Radio Programs, and Interviews

Purpose: Provide business information and news to readers and viewers.

Sources of underlying data: Interviews with key officers of target companies, sometimes accompanied by analysis from industry experts and/or securities analysts.

Level of detail and scope: Often very high level and, if carefully reviewed, can provide insights into the way in which executive(s) view the competitive environment and how they plan to deal with it.[11]

Age: May not always be very current. Print and even taped interviews may be done one or more weeks before release.

Accuracy and completeness: Very accurate, but not necessarily complete. That often depends on how informed and aggressive the interviewer is.

CI most likely to find it useful:

Strategy-oriented CI

Target-oriented CI

Technology-oriented CI

Tactics-oriented CI

Speeches

Purpose: Vary widely. May be promotional, defensive, or even personal appearances.

Sources of underlying data: Speaker and those assisting in preparing remarks, as well as preparing for questions and answers.

Level of detail and scope: Often very high level and can provide insights into the way in which executives view the competitive environment and how they plan to deal with it.

Age: May not always be very current. Text may be prepared weeks before presentation.

Accuracy and completeness: Very accurate, but not necessarily complete. Depends on the speaker's perceptions of the audience.

CI most likely to find it useful:

Strategy-oriented CI

Target-oriented CI

Technology-oriented CI

Tactics-oriented CI

Internet Chat Groups

Purpose: Communication among individuals with common interests. These may be as investors, retirees, potential investors, consumers with complaints, and so forth.

Sources of underlying data: Personal experiences of those on the list or sending messages to the site.

Level of detail and scope: Usually not very deep. Scope generally limited to subjects of the list itself. May contain technical detail if the list is comprised of technical personnel. Those that are complaint or feedback sites may include data on how companies actually handle complaints as well.[12]

Age: Very current, but sometimes old data, even misinformation, can resurface.

Accuracy and completeness: Very hard to gauge. Many members conceal identities under Internet handles. Some members of investment groups have reportedly used the lists to manipulate stock prices up or down to their benefit. On the other hand, an insider may provide insights on current events, such as lay-offs.

CI most likely to find it useful:

Target-oriented CI

Tactics-oriented CI

Both secondary and primary data sources and their orientation can be summarized as follows:

	Orientation of CI			
Typical Sources of Raw Data	**Strategy**	**Target**	**Tactics**	**Technology**
Secondary sources				
Trade journals	×	×	×	
Trade associations and chambers of commerce	×	×		
Government reports	×	×	×	×
Government records & files	×	×		
Security analyst reports	×	×		×
Academic case studies	×			
Research centers	×	×	×	
Business information services		×	×	
Advertisements		×	×	×
Want ads		×	×	×
Local newspapers & magazines	×	×	×	
Competitor reports	×	×	×	
Competitor news releases	×	×	×	×
Competitor home page	×	×	×	×
Directories and reference aids		×		×
Technical publications			×	×
Catalogs		×	×	
General news publications	×	×	×	
Books	×	×		×
Internet aggregators and portals		×	×	×
Primary sources				
Your own employees	×	×	×	×
Industry experts	×	×	×	×
Sales representatives (nonemployee)		×	×	
Customers		×	×	

Security analysts	×	×	×	
Competitors (direct contact)	×	×	×	
Suppliers	×	×	×	×
Product/service purchases			×	×
Focus groups			×	
Questionnaires/surveys		×		
Trade shows		×	×	×
Business conferences	×	×		×
Technical/professional meetings				×
Facility tours		×	×	×
Retailers and distributors	×	×	×	
Banks	×	×		
Advertising agencies	×	×	×	
TV & radio programs & interviews	×	×	×	×
Speeches	×	×	×	×
Internet chat groups		×	×	

APPENDIX: LOOKING AT SOURCES OF RAW DATA

The most often used potential sources of raw data can be viewed in a number of different ways. One way is to look at them and then try to assign them to one of four basic categories:

1. *Government.* Government sources generally provide CI analysts with high-level or indirect assistance. That is, the data that they can release may have to be aggregated, or the government unit may only provide data that are already collected and sold by a commercial provider, such as a commercial directory. However, many government units do receive some data through channels other than data, such as census, collection, licensing, regulation, and litigation files. These data tend to be more company specific than industry level.

2. *Specialized interests.* This group is composed of sources that collect data to advance their own interests. That interest may be professional or may be what the group's members see as a public or industry interest.

3. *Private sector.* The private sector includes persons and organizations whose business involves holding or collecting the data you seek. For some, providing the data is their business. Others come across data you may need as a part of their own business.

4. *Media.* The media collects, generates, and digests data for a specific audience. To fully understand both the data you may find and how to analyze them, you must understand from whom the media collects them, how, and why. The media, in the broadest sense, can be one of the most fruitful resources. In particular, always remember that many publica-

tions exist to serve a particular industry or market. Thus they are, or should be, positioned to help you locate important data and develop leads for additional data.

This grouping forces you to think about the characteristics each group has in common.[13] Knowing what characteristics the data sources have in common becomes very useful when you must categorize, analyze, and evaluate the data they have provided.

NOTES

1. APQC, 2001, 54.

2. Porter, *Competitive Strategy*, 371.

3. For example environmental filings are both broad and deep. See Steve Rice, "Public Environmental Records: A Treasure Chest of Competitive Information," *Competitive Intelligence Magazine* 3, 3 (July–September 2000): 13–19.

4. For a brief example of how to use them, see Peggy R. Stover, "Shoestring Intelligence: The Want Ads," *Competitive Intelligence Magazine* 1, 2 (July–September 1998): 43–44.

5. Thomas Yake, "Why Retailers Fail: Discovering the Telltale Signs," *Competitive Intelligence Magazine* 4, 3 (May–June 2001): 15–19.

6. See Conor Vibert, *Web-Based Analysis for Competitive Intelligence* (Westport, Conn.: Quorum Books, 2000).

7. In this section, we are, of course, assuming that either your firm or a contractor is collecting the primary data in a legal and ethical manner. The involvement of government in this process, as is the model in some countries outside of the United States, has potential problems. Compare Bill Lisse, "Should U.S. Intelligence Agencies Provide CI?" *Competitive Intelligence Magazine* 2, 2 (April–June 1999): 25–26 with Jonathan Calof and Bill Skinner, "Government's Role in Competitive Intelligence: What's Happening in Canada?" *Competitive Intelligence Magazine* 2, 2 (April–June 1999): 20–23.

8. Ellen Naylor, "Capturing Competitive Intelligence From Your Sales Force," *Competitive Intelligence Magazine* 3, 1 (January–March 2000): 24–28; Cody Thomas, "Surviving Deregulation: Using Field Reps for CI in the Electric Utility Industry," *Competitive Intelligence Magazine* 3, 1 (January–March 2000): 30–31.

9. Enrico Codogno, "Getting CI from Internal Sources," *Competitive Intelligence Magazine* 2, 1 (January–March 1999): 21–23.

10. See, for example, Anne Barron, "Three Easy Steps for Gathering Intelligence at Trade Shows," *Competitive Intelligence Magazine* 3, 3 (July–September 2000): 19–21.

11. For an example of how two such pieces telegraphed a major strategic change, see Peggy R. Stover, "Shoestring Intelligence: When the Press Interviews Your Competitors," *Competitive Intelligence Magazine* 2, 1 (January–March 1999): 37.

12. See Tim Powell, "Tech Knowledge: Spotting Lemons on the Web," *Competitive Intelligence Magazine* 4, 2 (March–April 2001): 45.

13. For more on this approach, see John J. McGonagle and Carolyn M. Vella, *Outsmarting the Competition: Practical Approaches to Finding and Using Competitive Information* (Naperville, Ill.: Sourcebooks, 1990), ch. 6.

7

How and When Should You
Deliver Active Intelligence Results?

HOW IS CI MADE AVAILABLE NOW?

"The CI process contains user-friendly and organizationally wide accepted forms of communication to disseminate information."[1]

The fourth step of the CI cycle requires that the results of the research and analysis be actionable, able to be acted upon. And that in turn requires that the results be delivered to the end-user in a timely manner and in a form that the end-user can utilize.

Over the past fifteen years, the form in which CI is delivered to its end-users has changed. In the mid-1980s, the majority of CI communications were made in one of three forms: the occasional written report, the periodic and regularly scheduled report (written or oral), as well as making files of research materials available as needed. If you consider the internal database as another form of passive access, like the file system, then we see that a significant majority of the CI was not truly communicated but rather collected. This distribution pattern reflected the fact that the bulk of the end-users of CI were receiving it for strategic purposes.

Forms in Which CI Was Made Available—1988

Occasional Written Reports	68 percent
File Materials Available on Request	60 percent
Periodic Reports	55 percent
Occasional Presentations	43 percent
Newsletters	29 percent
In-house Electronic Database	28 percent
Periodic Presentations[2]	22 percent

Within fifteen years, the manner in which CI was communicated had gradually but perceptibly changed. One reason for the change was the rise of Internet-based technologies, such as e-mail and Intranets. The other was due to changes in the types of CI being communicated and in the audiences to which it was communicated.

Forms in Which CI Was Made Available—2001

Occasional Written Reports	65 percent
Periodic Reports	60 percent
Occasional Presentations	40 percent
Intranets	35 percent
Newsletters	25 percent
Periodic Presentations	25 percent
File Materials Available on Request[3]	10 percent

Among the results is that the provision of CI in the form of files and internal databases has fallen sharply in favor. However, a part of what had formerly been provided in this way is now posted on firm Intranets.[4] The philosophy is the same: Collect the data and develop CI and then let the users access them when and as needed.

HOW SHOULD CI BE MADE AVAILABLE?

What is being done is not necessarily what should be done. There are two issues involved in determining the best ways to communicate particular types of CI: the form of communication and the frequency of communication, or manner of access to the CI.

Looking at the way in which CI is being communicated, as well as evaluating how the best-practice firms distribute CI, we can see that there are only a limited variety of intelligence outputs that are typically being provided. In addition, there are only a limited variety of patterns for distribution or access.

"Wisdom is perishable. Unlike information or knowledge, it cannot be stored in a computer or recorded in a book."[5]

Typical CI Outputs

Each of the forms in which intelligence is delivered to end-users has unique characteristics, strengths, and limitations. While every CI analyst may handle them in a different manner, some of these characteristics can be used to help define where they are best used to communicate what types of CI, and where they are least likely to be beneficial.

This is not to say that a particular kind of CI can only be delivered in these ways. The goal is to see that the CI reaches the end-user in time for it to be useful and in a form that the end-user can deal with. Given a choice between taking additional time to communicate critical CI in the right form or sending it in the wrong way, keep in mind that form is never more important than substance.[6]

Typical intelligence outputs are the following:

Newsletters
Source data and raw inputs
Flash alerts
Face-to-face briefings and presentations
Written reports
Forecasts and modeling[7]
Gaming and shadowing exercises[8]
Internal training on CI

Newsletters

Purpose: Provide short, current reports of particular changes in competitive environment.

Manner of communication: Hard copy as well as e-mail and Intranet distribution.[9] Typically done on a fairly frequent basis, such as weekly or biweekly.

End-user participation: Minimal. Most end-users will quickly scan shortly after receipt.

Currency: Relatively current. Tends to be no older than one to two weeks.

Ability to be updated: Any changes must be captured and noted in succeeding issues. But noting how well past estimates of competitor behavior track with actual behavior can help in promoting CI.

Balance of data versus analysis: While they contain some analysis, both in text and in terms of what is reported, they tend to be heavily weighted toward relatively raw data.

Source Data and Raw Inputs

Purpose: Allow end-user to see the original inputs, documents, interview notes, and so on.

Manner of communication: By e-mail, as well as in hard copy form. Also can be made accessible in files on an Intranet.

End-user participation: End-user provides virtually all of analysis. In case of data and inputs that are filed or on an Intranet, requires that the end-user act to access these in the first instance.

Currency: Can range from quite old to very current, depending on the frequency with which it is collected and archived.

Ability to be updated: Can be updated as often as needed, but end-user must usually return to original distribution source for the update.

Balance of data versus analysis: While they may contain some analysis, in terms of what is collected, these tend to be almost exclusively raw data.

Flash Alerts

Purpose: Communicate new, important events as soon as they are known.

Manner of communication: E-mail and voice mail are the most common. Typically done on a sporadic basis.

End-user participation: None. But may prompt end users to ask additional questions.

Currency: Extremely current. May be only hours old.

Ability to be updated: None. Updates are usually accomplished through other means, such as newsletters.

Balance of data versus analysis: While they are the results of some analysis, in terms of what is distributed, these tend to be almost exclusively reports of raw data.

Face-to-Face Briefings and Presentations

Purpose: Present end-users with findings as well as access to those who did the analysis.

Manner of communication: Typically PowerPoint®-style; that is, the use of overheads with summary points, accompanied by oral presentations.[10] Often followed by question and/or discussion period. Another option is to create a formal dialogue process.[11]

End-user participation: Depends on the specific end-user. The format allows significant participation.

Currency: Tends to be somewhat dated, given the fact that the presentation is prepared and duplicated in advance of what is often a scheduled meeting.

Ability to be updated: Presenters can do this in their oral presentation, but the materials may not reflect some updates.

Balance of data versus analysis: Tend to be more heavily oriented toward analysis, with only those data needed to provide background and to make the case persuasive usually provided.

Written Reports

Purpose: Provide a detailed, highly documented report of both analysis as well as data. May also offer a comparison of the firm's own strategy and position vis-à-vis key competitors.

Manner of communication: Written document. May also be made available on an Intranet.

End-user participation: Whether an end-user reads it often depends on issues such as available time. Sometimes only conclusions and recommendations are read.

Currency: Given the long lead-time, can be dated, weeks, even months old, when delivered.

Ability to be updated: Updates can be provided easily, either by written supplements, or replacements of the entire document.

Balance of data versus analysis: Contains significant data, but are typically heavily weighted toward analysis and advocacy.

Forecasts and Modeling

Purpose: Provide management with ability to predict changes in markets, in competitor behavior[12] and even in macro-level cultural and political trends.[13] It may also provide management with the predictions themselves.[14]

Manner of communication: Forecasts are typically communicated in the form of a report or presentation as well as integrated into another product, such as a strategic plan, a strategic intelligence report, or market projection. Models are created and results generated that are also communicated to management. Either one may produce an analysis with alternative futures.[15]

End-user participation: Varies. Management may be involved in establishing the assumptions underlying the process and occasionally in developing the conclusions as well.

Currency: While used to predict the future, due to their complexity the underlying data and work are often dated.

Ability to be updated: Either can be updated, but it takes a considerable effort.

Balance of data versus analysis: While often relying on vast amounts of data, the end products are heavily, almost exclusively, analysis and conclusions.[16]

Gaming and Shadowing Exercises

Purpose: Provide interactive way for managers and executives to work out the impact of strategic and tactical decisions. Both involve some individuals playing out the role of one or more competitors.

Manner of communication: Usually face-to-face over an extended period of time. However, there are Internet-based and Intranet-based opportunities for participation without all players being present.

End-user participation: Usually requires those making the decisions to "play" themselves or their opposite numbers. They are rarely effective without the personal participation of key decision makers.

Currency: While used to predict the future, due to their complexity the underlying data and work is often dated.

Ability to be updated: Underlying process can be updated, but it takes a considerable effort.

Balance of data versus analysis: While based on vast amounts of data, the process requires the articulation and then application of analysis to generate conclusions.

Internal Training on CI

Purpose: Stated purpose is to train end-users to be better clients by creating an understanding of how CI really works, as well as its ethical and legal limitations. Unstated purpose is to help the CI process and the CI unit to institutionalize CI within the firm.

Manner of communication: Usually face-to-face, although there are multimedia course materials increasingly available.

End-user participation: Typically most participation is passive, although good trainers and materials will affirmatively generate participation to enhance learning.

Currency: Fairly current, as the legal, ethical, collection, and analytical principles do not change rapidly.

Ability to be updated: Fairly easily updated.

Balance of data versus analysis: Not applicable.

Frequency of Distribution and Access to CI

Having established the most common ways that intelligence outputs, it only remains to define the small number of options. There are really two major divisions: active and passive. For each there are a limited number of variations.

Active

"In intelligence situations it is usually best to deliver the findings and recommendations using an interactive process, especially for high stakes situations."[17]

As Requested

By this we mean that the intelligence product is provided to the end-user if and when the end-user asks for it. When it is provided, it is not again provided until the end-user asks for it again. This can mean that the end-user requests, for example, a report on a specific competitor's research and development capabilities. It can also mean that an end-user has requested that it receive a flash alert if certain narrowly defined circumstances, such as prices, change.

Occasional

By this we mean that the intelligence product is provided to the end-users from time to time, but not on a regular schedule. Typically, the decision to provide it, if it is an emergent matter, is made by the CI professional rather than by the end-user. On the other hand, the end-user may initiate an intelligence effort, which the CI professional then keeps current, as developments require.

Regular

By this we mean that the intelligence product is provided to the end-users on a predetermined schedule. That schedule may be weekly, even daily, or it may be annual. This usually occurs when the end-user and CI professional have identified and agreed on a series of intelligence tasks and targets, such as in the Key Intelligence Topics or Key Intelligence Questions (KIT/KIQ) process.

Passive

"Simply transferring information automatically does not increase its value for action."[18]

The use of passive means, at least in the context of technology-oriented CI, may be declining in popularity. A 2001 report of best practices in this area noted that "there has been the presumption that once [CI] deliverables were established, the [technology-oriented] intelligence group had minor interactions with intelligence users until they delivered the final product. The findings from this study provide counter evidence to this widely espoused view.[19]

On Intranets

By this we mean that the CI professionals post, usually on a regular basis, both finished intelligence as well as data and third-party reports on an internal Internet, usually called an Intranet. End-users are then free to access these data and intelligence to use themselves. Usually, the site also provides for some way to connect to an analyst for further assistance. In many cases, access to the site is limited through the use of passwords and other security protections. This approach has been increasing in popularity, particularly with respect to technology-oriented CI, where its use is now "commonplace."[20]

The selection of the materials and topics placed on the Intranet may be made in any number of ways. Most common are these:

- CI professionals work from KITs and KIQs to select materials that meet these profiles.[21]
- End-users may identify data and intelligence which they want made available, but which they do not wish distributed on a regular basis.
- CI professionals may post abstracts or entire reports from assignments completed for internal clients for the use of other employees.

In Files and Databases

By this we mean that the CI professionals collect and either input (databases) or collate (files) on a regular basis, both finished intelligence as well as data and, to a lesser degree, third-party reports. End-users are then free to access the files or databases to use themselves.

The selection of the materials and topics placed in the files or databases may be made in any number of ways. Most common are these:

- CI professionals work from KITs and KIQs to select materials that meet these profiles.
- End-users may identify data and intelligence that they want to access, but that they do not wish to be distributed on a regular basis.

How Should You Distribute Each Type of CI?

Taking now the characteristics of each type of active CI from Chapter 4 and matching them with the characteristics of the channels of distributions and frequency or access provides us with an overview of which channels, used at what frequency, are best-suited for delivering each particular type of active CI.

"Analysis refers to extracting larger meaning from data and information to support evaluation, decision making, and operational improvement. Analysis entails using data to determine trends, projections, and cause and effect that might not otherwise be evident."[22]

Strategy-Oriented

In general, end-users of strategy-oriented CI need deliverables that stress analysis over data, that are provided to them on a fairly predictable basis, that may provide ways for the end-users to probe further and develop their own understanding of the analysis and recommendation.

Target-Oriented

In general, end-users of target-oriented CI need deliverables that provide a wide rage of data and analysis and that capture both base line analysis as well as current new pieces of data. Experience indicates that passive programs rarely provide actionable CI, so the delivery must heavily rely on the more active approaches.

Technology-Oriented

In general, end-users of technology-oriented CI need deliverables that allow them to have direct access to the underlying data and other raw materials. While active delivery systems are in widespread use, the end-users of technology-oriented CI are, in many cases, content to have passive delivery systems as long as the data and other materials are constantly refreshed. Recent studies also indicate that best-practice firms in technology-oriented CI sponsor training to a broad set of employees, broader than training at other firms, and use assignments as training vehicles more than do other companies.[23]

Tactics-Oriented

In general, end-users of tactics-oriented CI need deliverables that stress immediacy and currency over those that provide long-term and highly refined analyses. They rarely avail themselves of passive channels.

The interplay of these factors in is summarized in the following list:

	Orientation of CI			
	Strategic	Target	Technology	Tactics
Newsletters				
Occasional		×	×	×
Regular		×	×	×
On Intranets		×	×	×

Source Data/Raw Input				
As requested	×	×	×	×
Occasional event		×	×	×
Regular event			×	×
On Intranets		×	×	×
On file/database			×	×
Flash Alerts				
As requested		×	×	×
Occasional event	×	×	×	×
Regular event	×	×	×	×
On Intranets		×		×
Face-to-face Briefings and Presentations				
As requested		×	×	×
Occasional event	×	×	×	×
Regular event	×		×	×
On Intranets		×	×	×
Written Reports				
As requested	×	×	×	×
Occasional event	×	×	×	×
Regular event	×	×		×
On Intranets		×	×	×
On file/database				×
Forecasts and Modeling				
As requested	×	×	×	×
Occasional event	×	×	×	×
Regular event	×			
On Intranets				×
On file/database	×	×	×	×
Gaming & Shadowing Exercises				
As requested	×	×	×	
Occasional event	×	×	×	
Regular event	×			
Internal Training on CI				
As requested				×
Occasional event	×	×	×	×
Regular event		×		×
On Intranets		×		×

NOTES

1. Society of Competitive Intelligence Professionals, *CI Team Excellence Awards*, 11.

2. The Conference Board, "Competitive Intelligence: Research Report No. 913" (New York: Conference Board, 1988).

3. Unpublished Helicon Group estimates.

4. For a study of the issues involved in creating and managing an Intranet, see Linda Rosen, "Capturing and Sharing Competitive Intelligence: Microsoft's Intranet," *Competitive Intelligence Magazine* 1, 2 (July–September 1998): 9–12; and Allan T. Laalo, "Intranets and Competitive Intelligence: Creating Access to Knowledge," *Competitive Intelligence Review* 9, 4 (Fourth Quarter 2000): 63–72.

5. Sid Taylor quoted in Davis, 332.

6. There may also be a trade-off between data access on the one hand and analysis and decision making on the other, depending on the location of the CI unit. See William M. McGrath, Jr., "Improving Competitor Intelligence's Value to Management," in John E. Prescott, ed., *Advances in Competitive Intelligence* (Vienna, Va.: Society of Competitive Intelligence Professionals, 1989), 177–181.

7. This also includes practices such as scenario development where the final results are delivered to management. See Alexander Fink and Oliver Schlake, "Scenario Management—An Approach for Strategic Foresight," *Competitive Intelligence Review* 11, 1 (2000): 37–45; A. Lee Gilbert, "Using Multiple Scenario Analysis to Map the Competitive Landscape: A Practice-Based Perspective," *Competitive Intelligence Review* 11, 2 (2000): 12–19; and Franz Tessun, "Scenario Analysis and Early Warning Systems at Daimler-Benz Aerospace," in Prescott and Miller, *Proven Strategies*, 259–273. In cases where managers help develop the scenario, it would be classified with gaming. See, for example, David J. Reibstein and Mark J. Chussil, "Putting the Lesson Before the Test: Using Simulation to Analyze and Develop Competitive Strategies," *Competitive Intelligence Review* 10, 1 (First Quarter 1999): 34–48.

8. This term includes what some call "war games." For the reasons noted in the Glossary, we are trying to minimize the use of such terms.

9. One expert suggests that newsletters never be sent to anyone who has not asked for them and that a newsletter should not be replaced with a link to the Intranet. See Dale Fehringer, "Hot Off the Wires! Improve the Effectiveness of Your CI Newsletter," *Competitive Intelligence Magazine* 4, 3 (May–June 2001): 11, 14.

10. For a valid criticism of the way some of these are done, see Kenneth Sawka, "The Analyst's Corner: Keep Your Message Short and Sweet," *Competitive Intelligence Magazine* 3, 1 (January–March 2000): 54–55.

11. Bob J. Holder, "Scouting: A Process for Discovering, Creating and Acting on Knowledge," *Competitive Intelligence Magazine* 4, 2 (March–April 2001): 17, 20–21.

12. See Porter, *Competitive Advantage*, 446 et seq.

13. Guntram F.A. Werther, "Profiling 'Change Processes' as a Strategic Analysis Tool," *Competitive Intelligence Magazine* 3, 1 (January–March 2000): 19–22.

14. See, for example, Louis-Jacques Darveau, "Forecasting an Acquisition: 5 Steps to Help You See it Coming," *Competitive Intelligence Magazine* 4, 1 (January–February 2001): 13–17.

15. Guntram F.A. Werther, "Beyond the Blocking Tree: Improving Performance in Future-Oriented Analysis," *Competitive Intelligence Magazine* 3, 4 (October–December 2000): 40–44; Sarah Breacher, "Tools for Predicting Alternative Futures," *Competitive Intelligence Magazine* 2, 3 (July–September 1999): 19–22.

16. For a discussion of how and when to develop competitive scenarios, see Fahey, *Competitors*, ch. 16 and Kenneth Sawka, "The Analyst's Corner: Scenario Analysis: Alternative Worlds," *Competitive Intelligence Magazine* 4, 5 (September–October 2001): 41–42. For an example of such efforts applied to the future of CI, see Steven M. Shaker and Mark P. Gembicki, "Competitive Intelligence: A Futurist's Perspective," *Competitive Intelligence Magazine* 2, 1 (January–March 1999): 24–27.

17. W. Bradford Ashton, "An Overview of Business Intelligence Analysis for Science and Technology," in Gilad and Herring, *Applied Business Strategy 2A*, 265.

18. Kent Ridge Digital Labs, *Charting Your Course*, 120.

19. APQC, 2001, 47.

20. APQC, 2001, 39.

21. Key Intelligence Questions are developed from KITs when the KITs are very broad. On this process generally, see Jan P. Herring, "Key Intelligence Topics: A Process to Identify and Define Intelligence Needs," in Prescott and Miller, *Proven Strategies*, 240–258; and David B. Francis and Jan P. Herring, "Key Intelligence Topics: A Window on the Corporate Competitive Psyche," *Competitive Intelligence Review* 10, 4 (1999): 10–19.

22. Baldrige National Quality Program, *2001 Criteria*, 3.

23. APQC, 2001, 32.

8

Untangling the Problems
of Metrics in CI

Almost since its inception, CI practitioners have struggled with the interrelated problems of demonstrating that CI has a positive impact on a particular business and quantifying, or measuring, that impact. Demonstrating such a connection and an impact is not only important to achieving program success and growth; experience shows that it may be critical to protecting the very existence of a CI program.[1]

There are four major reasons for such failures:

1. Efforts to measure the impact of CI on business may involve the overextension of quantitative methods to what is more properly a qualitative process. Of course, it is important to determine that CI is having a positive impact on a business. But it not always as critical to determine the extent of that impact. This is the issue of qualitative versus quantitative measurements.

2. The impact of CI is most often indirect rather than direct. That is, CI is an effective, if not critical, contribution to improved decision making. And it is the effective decision, which may combine many inputs, that actually has the impact on the bottom line.

3. Efforts to measure the impact of CI on business ignore one critical reality that CI professionals face: There is no way to compel an end-user to utilize CI. In fact, there is often no way to know if the CI has been utilized at all. As one observer put it: "Another key point of differentiation for competitive intelligence analysis [from other forms of analysis] is that it is fiercely decision-driven. . . . The "tradecraft" of competitive

intelligence demands that no analysis is generated unless it contributes to or prompts a specific management action. This requires that the senior executive become a full participant in the analysis process, a situation that typically is absent from most American corporations today."[2] Put another way, we have to decide if we should be measuring process, or product, or both.

4. Most efforts to measure the impact of CI assume that all CI is strategy-oriented. So they have applied measures that have some relevance to strategy-oriented efforts. However, as we have shown in Chapter 5, in fact much, if not most of the CI provided today is other than strategy-oriented. The result is that we are trying to measure several types of CI using tools which are, at best, somewhat useful for only one type.

In spite of these problems, there are ways to show the CI has an impact on the bottom line of a business and to show the extent of that impact. To understand these methods, each of these problems must first be dealt with.

"CI directly affects decisions at the senior level."[3]

QUANTITATIVE EFFORTS IN A QUALITATIVE WORLD

The first issue to be dealt with is whether a process like CI can ever be properly measured; that is, evaluated on a quantitative basis, when the process itself is necessarily quantitative. While this sounds like a very theoretical debate, in fact it is a consideration that some observers contend underlies the failure of many efforts to measure business processes and success.[4]

To summarize this argument, CI and other similar processes are essentially qualitative in nature, that is, they operate in contexts where the end product is the result of "sift[ing] through mountains of data in search of nuggets of actionable information. . . . The conclusions drawn from [this] . . . are usually not based on 'hard facts'; instead they result from a number of independent observations that are woven together with subjective judgment and intuition."[5]

This approach, in turn, enables CI professionals to provide results that quantitative methods cannot: "Using intuition, insight, and non-verifiable knowledge . . . researchers can shorten the time required for a project, use all relevant information made available from whatever source, and examine any question—even those which cannot be explored in a rigorous [quantitative] manner."[6]

To preserve and advance the qualitative benefits of CI, it is argued that the best way to measure the success of CI is to use a qualitative audit. In that audit, two types of questions are posed, one dealing with the CI professionals and the other dealing with the end-user organization of the other. The key questions are:[7]

- Are CI analysts allowed to gain expertise in specific areas through training?
- Are CI analysts allowed to use appropriate qualitative tools?
- Have the CI analysts mastered the traditional tools of CI?
- Have the CI analysts mastered other appropriate qualitative methodologies?
- Can the CI analysts integrate the full range of qualitative methods into their analysis?
- Do end-users recognize the limitations inherent in quantitative analysis?
- Do the end-users acknowledge the CI analyst's choice of methods?
- Do end-users acknowledge the trade-offs inherent in the choice of research techniques?
- Do the end-users rely on quantitative research to protect themselves?
- Is the firm willing to invest in qualitative-oriented analysts?

However, at the same time, it is argued that "scientific/quantitative methods have dominated business research and analysis," so that "yardsticks of evaluation based on . . . qualitative methods continue to dominate."[8]

In other words, the argument goes, businesses increasingly take the position that, if they cannot measure it, it does not exist, or at least does not have any impact on the business, even if they are dealing with qualitatively oriented processes that cannot easily be measured with quantitative means. And this does not even allow for additional concerns among many who try to apply value-based metrics to support processes. Those concerns are that many such efforts fail simply because they are not well designed[9] or because they are so difficult to use that results are increasingly "fudged."[10]

However, the ways that CI is practiced encompass methods and results that encompass both the qualitative and the quantitative.

- An example of the first might be CI provided in a target-oriented context predicting that a competitor would not raise prices. What can be measured here? The CI analyst was correct. What the end-user did (or did not do) with the CI may be unclear.
- An example of the second might be a projection that a competitor would lower prices in two months. Their success might be able to be measured by the additional new sales made in the two-month window to accounts that would be lost to lower prices.

Therefore, CI professionals should consider the use of either or both appropriate.[11]

DIRECT MEASUREMENTS VERSUS INDIRECT
(SUBSTITUTE) MEASUREMENTS

"The team can demonstrate that intelligence has been acted on; that CI contributed to decisions or actions that led to beneficial outcomes."[12]

Direct Measurements

Direct measurements, sometimes called first-order, are those where we have the classic cause–effect relationship. That is, you add an additional line to an existing plant that could produce no more than 1,000 units per day, on an annual basis. Now that plant produces 1,500 units per day, on an annual basis. So, the net contribution of the line to the plant's overall output is 500 units per day.

In the case of CI, opportunities for direct measurements may be quite few. The principle reason is that CI does not operate directly on any corporate process. An additional dollar spent on CI cannot be tied to additional revenues to the end-user. This is not because that does not happen; rather it is because it is a very complex process to track such events.

For confirmation of that, we have only to look at the raging debate in the Information Technology (IT) community over the use of direct financial measures, such as return on investment (ROI), to determine the effectiveness of IT investments:

[One benchmarking firm] argues that a strict short-term return on investment approach to measuring Web technology investment in service of e-business goals is doomed. . . . ROI is of limited strategic value when companies straitjacket the formula to literally mean profit divided by investment. . . . By its nature, the collection of technology driving e-business can create second-, third-and fourth-order benefits such as online brand building, increased in-store sales and referral business—value that strict ROI will miss every time.[13]

Indirect Measurements

Indirect measurements are often referred to as second-order, third-order, and so on. That refers to the distance, in terms of steps, that they are from the eventual end event. So, for example, distributing a coupon redeemable in connection with online sales might be seen to have generated $100,000 in direct sales; that is, sales made with the coupon. But it also may have generated sales in retail stores from people who saw the advertising and remembered the store or the brand. This is not a first-order effect, but it is just as real as one. The difficulty with indirect measurements is that they are inherently less precise and able to be validated than are direct measures. But the lack of precision is not the same as a lack of existence.

Other types of indirect measure are the indicator and the vector approaches. The former describes an effort to measure something that is not yet complete, a situation where direct measures are often unable to be applied. The latter is an effort to demonstrate the existence, direction, and relative size of a trend.[14]

However indirect, measures also allow those looking at a topic to consider not only how to measure its impact, but, conversely, to try and consider the cost of its absence over both the near term and the distant future. For example, one observer compared the elimination of critical information over time to the impact on a body of reducing its intake to only nutraceuticals and vitamins, eliminating solid food:

> A large financial institution had . . . run an in-house library staffed by professionals. This center fielded some 40,000 requests a year. . . . The answers . . . were used to support pitches for new business, develop new products, and make purchasing decisions. The cost of all this activity . . . was in the seven-figure range.

> The number crunchers . . . closed it down. Initially, there was no immediate impact, but . . . the bank began to suffer. Staff preparing bids . . . were less well-informed than the competition and so the bank won fewer bids. . . . New product development lost its edge. . . . [Technology] purchase decisions were not always the best. By the time the damage could be fully assessed, the cost of re-starting a fully staffed information center had soared into the eight-figure range.[15]

Surveys

One way in which indirect measurements are often handled is by surveying the end-users. This can be split into two options: One is to use surveys to supplement or enrich the data available from direct measurements; the other is to use it in the absence of such measures.

- As an example of the first option, take the reported efforts of a major freight company to calculate the ROI of a new Web site. The efforts had two parts. First, the company determined that moving its customer contacts to the Web allowed it to offer an expanded range of services far more cheaply than if its customers had to rely on telephone contact with customer service representatives, as had been done in the past. But, to this it added a factor representing the increase in its "customer capture rate," the rate that customers doing business with it are likely to come back again. This rate increase was correlated to a rise in sales. So a survey was used to supplement the more traditional model.[16]

- As an example of the second option, look at the experiment of a major pharmaceutical company to measure customer satisfaction with a CI department. The end-users were asked to complete a value questionnaire after a CI activity was performed. The anonymous questionnaire had eleven questions, asking for the end-user to rate the value of the specific CI on a scale from 1 (very low) to 5 (very high). The results were then tabulated, allowing the staff to compare how the end-users rated the CI staff's responsiveness and accuracy against how the end-users regarded the service as allowing them to make better decisions or to lower expenses.[17]

The utility of surveys of CI effectiveness seems to vary according to the relationship between those providing the CI and those using it. E-mail and mailed surveys do not seem to work nearly as well as face-to-face surveys when the end-users of the CI are internal. On the other hand, the non-face-to-face surveys seem to work when the end-users are strictly external.[18]

Inclusion in Other Corporate Initiatives

Another way that firms have tried to develop indirect measures for processes and products such as those provided by CI is to link CI activities to other initiatives, often Total Quality Management (TQM), that are already operating with well-established and accepted systems of metrics.[19] Frankly, this seems more to be a political decision than a selection of an effective option.

MEASURING PROCESS AND END PRODUCT IMPACT

The final distinction that should be kept in mind is the measurement of process versus the measurement of End Product Impact. For example, you might decide that you want to measure the accuracy of the predictions and forecasts provided by your CI unit. That would be measuring the End Product Impact, the CI provided by the unit. However, measures that focus exclusively on End Product Impact can actually distort the underlying process.

Taking this example, if you expect a CI unit to be 100 percent accurate all of the time, you are actually setting the stage for an ineffective unit. When you expect perfection, you are actually asking for the unit to provide you with CI and draw conclusions of such breadth and depth, subject to such qualifications, as to be virtually useless to you. Staff will cease to be aggressive for fear of being wrong; their results will cover all potential options.[20]

On the other hand, if you make it clear that perfection is not and cannot be expected from your CI unit, you may encourage it to take the small risks necessary to ensure consistent, quality, usable CI. Not only should you accept the fact that the output from this unit cannot always be perfect, but you should expect failures from time to time.

Measuring process, on the other hand, looks at the *how* more than the *what* of CI. Taking our example of accuracy, a process measure might involve a determination of how, and how well, CI analysts confirm their findings and conclusions. However, a process measure can ignore one or more key End Product Impact issues. In this case, looking only at this process measure would ignore the issue of whether or not the predictions and forecasts were of use to the end-user.

The choice of process versus End Product Impact measurements sometimes reflects a failure to decide who is doing the measuring as well as what is being measured. As one study found,

Currently there is a significant gap between management's expectations and CI professionals' beliefs. Management wants CI to produce a strategic, tangible impact on the company's business operating and financial performance. CI professionals, on the other hand, focus their efforts on the intelligence operations, products, and process.[21]

Thus, any system of showing the impact of CI must reflect not only the perspectives of the CI professionals, which are largely on process, but also the perspectives of end-users, which are largely on impacts or End Product Impacts.[22]

NOTES

1. See, for example, James A. Langabeer, "Exploring the CI Value Equation," *Competitive Intelligence Review* 10, 3 (Third Quarter 1999): 27–32: "departments avoiding layoffs have been shown to be either: (1) valuable resources, or (2) essential to the business' primary mission."

2. Kenneth Sawka, "Competitive Intelligence Analysis: Filling the Corporate Analytic Void," *Competitive Intelligence Review* 8, 1 (Spring 1997): 87–89.

3. Society of Competitive Intelligence Professionals, *CI Team Excellence Awards*, 13.

4. For a highly developed and very approachable defense of this, see Alf H. Walle III, *Qualitative Research in Intelligence and Marketing: The New Strategic Convergence* (Westport, Conn.: Quorum Books, 2001).

5. Walle, *Qualitative Research*, 14.

6. Ibid., 60.

7. Adapted from Walle, *Qualitative Research*, 200–209.

8. Ibid., 53.

9. See, for example, Bill Birchard and Alix Nyberg, "On Further Reflection," *CFO* 17, 3 (March 2001): 56–64.

10. See, for example, David Lewis and Mike Koller, "ROI: Little More Than Lip Service," *InternetWeek*, 1 October 2001, 1, 49.

11. See Craig S. Fleisher and David L. Blenkhorn, "Effective Approaches to Assessing Competitive Intelligence Performance," in Craig S. Fleisher and David L. Blenkhorn, eds., *Managing Frontiers in Competitive Intelligence* (Westport, Conn.: Quorum Books, 2001), 111, 113.

12. Society of Competitive Intelligence Professionals, *CI Team Excellence Awards*, 15.

13. John Berry, "IT Dividends: Short-term ROI Approach Won't Pay," *InternetWeek*, 10 September 2001, 50.

14. Julie L. Davis and Suzanne S. Harrison, *Edison in the Boardroom* (New York: John Wiley & Sons, 2001), 137.

15. Deborah C. Sawyer, "Defining Your Competition: Are You Blunting Your Own Strategic Weapons?" *Competitive Intelligence Magazine* 3, 1 (January–March 2000): 44–45.

16. "Mad to Measure," *eCFO* 17, 12 (Special Fall 2001 issue): 29, 30–31.

17. James Russell, "Measuring the Value of Competitive Intelligence (CI) Activities: A Pilot Study," in Society of Competitive Intelligence Professionals, *Conference Proceedings—2000 Annual International Conference and Exhibit* (Alexandria, Va.: SCIP, 2000).

18. APQC, 2001, 65.

19. See APQC, *Competitive and Business Intelligence*, 11.

20. See, for example, Richard H. Giza, "The Problem of the Intelligence Consumer," in Roy Godson, ed., *Intelligence Requirements for the 1980's: Analysis and Estimates* (Washington, D.C.: National Strategy Information Center, 1986), 202.

21. Jan P. Herring, *Measuring the Effectiveness of Competitive Intelligence—Assessing & Communicating CI's Value to Your Organization* (Alexandria, Va.: SCIP, 1996), 53.

22. In any case, it has been effectively argued that the very act of having management engaging in such assessment activities may actually help encourage senior management to "review the intelligence reports [themselves] and [thus] make more use of the insights provided." Nick Wreden, "Business Intelligence—Turning on Success," *Beyond Computing*, September 1997: 19, 24.

9

Choosing the Right Measurements for the Active CI You Are Using

To work our way through this, and determine what measurements are best for which type of active CI, we have first identified what appear to be the most common types of financial metrics and other measurements now in use by CI professionals. We have then combined them into broader categories to allow you to understand each and to determine where and when they should be used, and not used. These broad categories are as follows:[1]

- Assignments and Projects
- Budget[2]
- Efficiency[3]
- End-users
- Feedback[4]
- Financial
- Internal Relationships[5]
- New Products and Services
- Performance
- Reports and Presentations
- Sales Effectiveness
- Surveys[6]
- Time[7]

Since some of these may partially overlap with others, we have elected to put concepts in one place rather than to duplicate them.

Finally, for each we have provided a brief explanation of what the measurement does, classified it, and commented on its utility. Then, we look at each type of CI and the related issues of data sources and delivery of the final product to match up those measurements that are most appropriate in your unique situation.

MASTER LIST OF CI MEASURES

Assignments and Projects

Meeting Objectives

This involves a determination of what the end-user's objectives were in initiating the assignment. That is not the same as receiving the report. It is really a question whether the end-user received CI that supported a decision he or she was facing.

Classification:

- Qualitative Metric
- Direct Metric
- Process Metric

Observations: This requires direct contact with the end-users as to the goals of the CI assignments that they initiated. Of course, if the end-user asked the wrong questions, then the likelihood that the assignment will provide any assistance is negligible.

Number Completed

In this situation, the CI unit would track the number of assignments and projects completed. It is probably useful to divide this into a number of different types, such as flash alerts, in-depth briefings, and so on for without separating out the complex from the simple, the pressure on the CI unit will be to generate more low-value reports.

Classification:

- Quantitative Metric
- Indirect Metric
- Process Metric

Observations: Some potential limitations should be noted. First, by contracting out, a CI unit can quickly increase the number of assignments completed. Second, there is not necessarily a direct link between the number of assignments and the impact of CI on a firm's decision making.

Number Completed on Time

In this case, the metric should separate on-time from not on-time, and also separate out reports by complexity or other differentiation at the same time. It helps to show that the CI unit is continuing to deal with work on the end-user's schedule, or that it is improving over time.
Classification:

- Quantitative Metric
- Indirect Metric
- Process Metric

Observations: This does not effectively deal with assignments or reports initiated by the CI unit. These events are, almost by definition, always on time. Also, end-users who establish unrealistic due dates will skew results unless the evaluation also separates out timeliness by the end-user. In that case, it might help identify end-users who are not calling for CI on a timely enough basis.

Number Requested

In this situation, the CI unit would have to record every request for any CI or raw data. Over time, it should show growth, except in units with a strategy-orientation. There, the number of assignments should probably stay constant over time.

To be useful, it should at least be divided into groups reflecting assignments, from the end-users the CI unit is authorized to serve, and other requests. Also, if the CI unit were allowed to decline, refer, or transfer requests, it would be valuable to note this as well. Indicating where these requests went and from whom they came might indicate areas where training on CI needs and research for end-users could be useful.
Classification:

- Quantitative Metric
- Direct Metric
- End Product Impact Metric

Observations: This is a very crude metric, as it provides numbers, but rarely a sense of the value and impact of the CI unit. It is more properly adapted to an information center-style operation.

Number Requested—Increase by End-Users

This metric, when sorted by end-users, will serve to show the penetration of CI among end-users. Where requests have fallen, additional inquiry should be made to see if additional training of these end-users is appropriate. Where requests rise, it may be appropriate to see if that function should have its own CI function.
Classification:

- Quantitative Metric
- Indirect Metric
- Process Metric

Observations: This is useful in only a limited number of situations. A growth in number of requests does not necessarily prove that CI is having an increased impact on the bottom line. For example, if the CI unit does not charge back for its services, this could be evidence of the phenomenon known as "abuse of a free resource."[8]

Number of Follow-Up Assignments

This metric should be designed to indicate increasing interest by end-users, and thus, indirectly, increased impact on the firm. The absence of follow-up assignments, however, may not necessarily mean problems. It could indicate that the CI unit is actually anticipating what the end-user needs and will need.
Classification:

- Quantitative Metric
- Indirect Metric
- Process Metric

Observations: Follow-up assignments should be clearly distinguished from efforts that are the result of an incomplete first project or a need to clarify the findings of a report.

Number of Projects Assisted

This metric involves an assessment of the number of times the CI unit is involved in other projects or on internal teams. The belief is that an expansion of such activity marks an affirmative, broadening recognition of the value of CI to the firm.
Classification:

- Quantitative Metric

- Indirect Metric
- Process Metric

Observations: In a firm that is highly structured and does not use teams, networking, or similar cross-functional process, this metric has no real utility. Also, if a firm has many small, decentralized CI units, the likelihood of such contacts is also much lower.

Number of Suggestions Submitted

This assumes that the CI unit is permitted to undertake its own assignments and to provide appropriate end-users with its conclusions and recommendations.
Classification:

- Quantitative Metric
- Indirect Metric
- Process Metric

Observations: Since these suggestions are generated by the CI unit, and not driven by the requests or even requirements of end-users, there can be a tendency for the CI unit to turn into a "push" clipping service. Also, this carries no way to evaluate the importance or suggestions, nor any evaluations of how many of them were actually used.

Budget

Comparative Costs Savings

Compared with Cost of Outsider

This metric is probably best used in efforts to show the worth of a CI unit in its very earliest stages.[9] To accomplish this, a CI manager could work with an outside vendor to "cost out" the majority of the work of the CI unit. Even doing that for a few projects can produce persuasive evidence. This, of course, assumes that the firm would have been wiling to contract these out.
Classification:

- Quantitative Metric
- Indirect Metric
- Process Metric

Observations: It would be very expensive to cost out all of a CI unit's work against an outside contractor. While a CI unit may be able to prevail on a regular CI contractor to provide gross estimates of doing a limited number of projects for no fee, it is unfair to do so on a broader basis.[10] Also there are functions carried on by a CI unit, such as serving as an internal advocate, which an outside contractor would generally not deal with. And finally, this assumes that all of the CI work is (1) of value and (2) would still be of value if conducted at the higher costs.

Compared with Cost of Untrained Person

In contrast with the prior metric, in this case, there is no easy source to which the CI unit can go for such an estimate. Otherwise it is relatively similar.
Classification:

- Quantitative Metric
- Indirect Metric
- Process Metric

Observations: This metric carries with it the implicit assumption that the work product of the untrained person would be as valuable as that of the trained person. That error makes this of even less value.

Meeting Project and Function Budget Constraints

The first would apply only when the CI unit has a way to allocate budget to an assignment or to bill another function for its work. The second, testing against the overall function budget, presumes that the CI unit can control the costs of outside contractors whose work is actually supervised by end-users. In such cases, experience indicates that there can be a significant loss of cost control.
Classification:

- Quantitative Metric
- Indirect Metric
- Process Metric

Observations: Use of this metric alone can have the unintended consequence that the CI unit shies away from large, complex, and potentially costly assignments and tasks that might have a very great potential to benefit the firm.

Efficiency

Accuracy of Analysis

This metric requires that the CI analyst and end-user both review previous estimates, projections, and analyses to determine how accurate the analysis was. This should be focused on determining accuracy at the time it was made rather than its ultimate accuracy. This is because intervening, unpredictable events may render an otherwise valid analysis inaccurate in retrospect. Its most effective use is to assure that the CI unit is using the most appropriate analytical tools correctly, as applied to the best available data.

Classification:

- Quantitative Metric
- Direct Metric
- End Product Impact Metric

Observations: This should be limited to those key elements of CI analyses that may lead to a firm's action or inaction. But its utility may be limited in strategy-oriented CI units, since this would entail reviewing predictions and analyses made years before. Care must be taken to see that this requirement does not cause analysts to make such vague, qualified conclusions that, in retrospect, cannot ever be found to be wrong and that provide no actionable intelligence.

Data Quality

This is similar to Accuracy of Analysis except that the test deals with the efficiency of the data collection and evaluation. To that extent, it removes the problem of tracking analyses over long periods of time and through unpredictable circumstances. However, having good data is only an interim step to developing good CI. It is not the end, except in situations where tactics-oriented or technology-oriented CI end-users are expecting data in most cases.

Classification:

- Qualitative Metric
- Indirect Metric
- Process Metric

Observations: This offers a good test of the data gathering and data evaluation efforts of the CI unit. But an excessive stress on the quality of the data may accidentally place emphasis on this part of the CI cycle, rather than on the more critical phase, the analysis.

First Time Results (No Reworking)

This requires the CI unit and end-users to record instances when the end-user pushes back an assignment or report to have it reworked. The goal is to see the progress of the CI unit toward meeting the end-user's expectations the first time. Over time, this should decline, as long as the CI professionals have anticipated the likely changes in end-user expectations.[11]
Classification:

- Quantitative Metric
- Indirect Metric
- Process Metric

Observations: This metric is a valid measure only when the end-user already understands CI and is able to express and communicate his or her needs to the CI professional. A case where there is a high reworking ratio may as well reflect problems with the end-user as with the CI professional.

Meeting Project Time Line

This requires that the CI unit record the due date for each assignment, including dates for interim deliverables. Then it would have to record when these events actually occurred. The goal is to assure that the CI unit is responding to end-users in a consistently timely manner. Timeliness of CI is one of the keys to its value.[12]
Classification:

- Quantitative Metric
- Indirect Metric
- Process Metric

Observations: Fairness should require that any failures to meet schedules should carry explanations for that. For example, the sale of a target's distribution subsidiary during an assignment on its supply chain may, understandably, cause the entire project to have to be rescheduled. In addition, the time lines should be those to which the CI unit has agreed. Calibrating its failure to meet time lines that end-users were warned were not possible is not a measurement of inefficiency.

Time for Research versus Time for Response

For this metric to be an effective measurement tool, there would have to be agreement on what is the appropriate balance of the research time in comparison with the response, or turn-around time. The problem here is that the research effort includes within it virtually all of the CI cycle. For this measure to have any significance, it should probably be applied to situations where the CI unit is providing an ongoing series of reports, quickly updated and delivered to the end-users.

Classification:

- Qualitative Metric
- Quantitative Metric
- Direct Metric
- Indirect Metric
- Process Metric
- End Product Impact Metric

Observations: In using this measure, extreme care must be taken not to shorten what the end-user might view as the postresearch phase, that is the time during which the final analysis is made and the results prepared for presentation to the end-user. While timeliness is important the value that CI brings to the decision-making process lies in its ability to deliver analysis, even at the expense of data collection efforts.[13] Excessive reliance on this measure could have the unintended effect that end-users would receive more data and less analysis, thus causing a decline in the value of the CI process itself.[14]

End-Users

Creating Compelling Reasons to Use CI

This approach is actually a way of measuring how effectively the CI process is being marketed within the firm.[15] It involves identifying and then assessing the way in which end-users regard the use of CI. It is probably best conducted using either surveys or other forms of feedback (see Feedback section). The underlying premise is that if the end-users see more and more reasons to use CI in their operations and decision making, then CI is adding additional value to the firm and its activities.

Classification:

- Quantitative Metric

- Indirect Metric
- End Product Impact Metric

Observations: What this may not capture, unless very carefully designed, are the perceptions of those who do not use the internal CI unit at all. That they do not call upon an existing unit is not the same as saying that they do not use CI. They may collect the CI themselves or contact out for it, which might make them strong advocates of CI, but not strongly supportive of the way in which the CI unit provides CI to them.

Effectiveness of Implementation of Findings

This metric assumes that all CI deliverables carry within them recommendations for actions by the firm, or at least such strong statement of the CI findings that certain actions are almost inevitable. Thus it would not be very useful for types of CI that had relatively higher levels of data. And it assumes that the end-users not only accept the validity of the findings but that they then implement them.

Classification:

- Qualitative Metric
- Direct Metric
- End Product Impact Metric

Observations: This requires a significant degree of contact with the end-users. In addition, it has the potential for distorted findings when the end-user, relying on other forces, elects not to take the CI recommendations. For example, it may seem obvious to a CI analyst that the best step for the firm is to invest in new technology. However, unknown to the analyst, the firm may have already committed significant capital to the acquisition of another firm, leaving it unable to implement the findings.

Meeting Needs

This is a highly subjective measure, but one which is at the very core of the CI process. Does the CI meet the end-user's needs? As mentioned earlier, surveys and interviews are the only sources of such ratings.

Classification:

- Qualitative Metric

- Direct Metric
- End Product Impact Metric

Observations: For this to be an effective measure, the firm must feel certain that not only is the CI analyst able and the CI unit properly staffed and trained, but also that the end-user is trained to be able to help the CI professionals determine the intelligence needs to be satisfied.

Number of Referrals

This can be accomplished simply by recording and later adding up such referrals. The value of this metric is somewhat limited, since an end-user might consider a CI unit very valuable and still decline to overload it with requests from others. Conversely, he or she might not find its output to be particularly valuable, and might use referrals as a way to move the CI unit to another home in the firm, or to avoid using it at all.

Classification:

- Quantitative Metric
- Indirect Metric
- Process Metric

Observations: In firms where the CI unit is not available to serve other than its primary end-user, this measure would be of no real benefit.

Number Served

As with the previous measure, the number of end-users served does not always have a direct correlation with the overall value of the CI unit and process to the firm. This is most appropriate when the CI unit is serving a large number of individuals who have to ask to receive its output, typically flash alerts, newsletters, and other forms of mass communication.

Classification:

- Quantitative Metric
- Indirect Metric
- Process Metric

Observations: As with other indirect quantitative measures, there is always the danger that heavy reliance on such measures will have the effect of driving the CI unit to value quantity of output and customers over quality of CI produced.

Feedback

Written

This usually involves the use of formal instruments, best kept short, sent to all end-users after each assignment. They should be completed only by the end-user. They seem most effective when they ask not only for response to specific questions, such as, "Was the assignment returned on time?" but also ask that the end-user assign a grade or weight (the 1 to 5 scale is very useful here). Asking for comments in addition to the answers can occasionally produce valuable insights, but most often generates anecdotal remarks.
Classification:

- Qualitative Metric
- Indirect Metric
- End Product Impact Metric

Observations: For this to be effective, all end-users must be involved. Those who do not wish to be involved can often be the source of the most important insights. While direct feedback after a report, given to the individual or team working on it, can be valuable in building skills and a strong relationship with the end-user, that often results in evaluations which are always slightly higher than satisfactory. One option would be to divide the results into two parts—one shared with the CI unit, and one kept for annual statistical purposes, and used without attribution.

Oral

This is typically used to collect anecdotal remarks, often as a part of a regular face-to-face feedback process. Without using a scoring system, which can cause oral feedback to become rather stilted, it is best used to capture after-the-fact estimates of impact. These can be expressed in a wide variety of ways, but it is best to try to get them with an attached value. Thus, for example, in addition to having a report called "powerful," it would be useful to get the end-user to say that it saved the firm from spending $2.5 million to develop technology it could license.
Classification:

- Qualitative Metric

- Indirect Metric
- End Product Impact Metric

Observations: As with written feedback, it is critical to get it directly from the end-user, and not an intermediary, as well as to get it from all end-users.

Financial

Cost Avoidance

As CI in any form operates in a decision-support manner, one way of valuing it has historically been to determine what costs, including losses, the firm has avoided due to the CI.[16] Accomplishing this requires the complete cooperation, and frankness, of the end-user of the CI. The end-user must, after executing the decision(s) supported by CI, make an evaluation of what money he or she did not, or will not, spend as a result of the CI. To be effective, this must be done with every assignment, even when the purpose of the assignment was not in this direction. This measure can be particularly difficult for end-users to make in situations where the CI is providing regular alerts and updates on rapidly changed market situations.

Classification:

- Quantitative Metric
- Direct Metric
- End Product Impact Metric

Observations: Use of this metric requires a significant degree of honesty on the part of the end-user. It is most difficult to apply when the CI confirmed an end-user's preexisting analysis of a situation. Then the measurement of the value of the CI is further reduced to a calculation of what changes in the odds of success or failure was accomplished by the use of the CI. Then this change is applied to the costs avoided by the decision. While it appears scientific, it is actually highly subjective.

Cost Savings

The issues involved here are similar to those just noted in the previous section with one significant change.[17] In the case of cost avoidance, the estimate of the costs avoided tends to be more subjective than an estimate of cost savings. Usually in the case of cost savings, there is more precision in identifying either the total amount of costs saved, or in identifying the steps, processes, and so forth which can now be dispensed with. In the latter case, it is fairly simple to then determine the cost savings. Otherwise, the comments on cost avoidance apply here as well.

Classification:

- Quantitative Metric
- Direct Metric
- End Product Impact Metric

Observations: See the comments under Cost Avoidance.

Goals Met

In this measurement, the metric is financial goals met. In most firms, such metrics are some function of cash flow, or of changes in other measures, such as return on investment, or profitability. The underlying presumption is that everything done in the firm must somehow impact, for example, cash flow, and that which does not do so is extraneous. However, this misses the vital intellectual link— there is a difference between having a positive impact and being able to isolate the exact extent of that positive impact.

Classification:

- Quantitative Metric
- Indirect Metric
- End Product Impact Metric

Observations: As for the first, cash flow, there is no real way that a rational first-order connection can be made between cash flow and CI, just as there is none that can be made between cash flow and, for example, the law department. Any impacts on cash flow tend to be data captured with respect to a particular assignment, rather than from CI overall. As for the others, these are covered in the following sections.

Linking CI to Specific Investments

The basis of this measure is that CI's bottom impact can be demonstrated by assigning to it at least partial credit for specific positive steps, that is investments that would not have been made, but for CI, or that are being changed, again due to the impact of CI.[18]

Classification:

- Quantitative Metric
- Indirect Metric
- End Product Impact Metric

Observations: For this to be a valid measure, from an intellectual basis, the firm would first have to have assessed the expected return on the planned investment without the use of CI. It would then have to either (1) recalculate the expected return factoring in the analysis provided by CI or (2) determine the final rate of return, over time, and assign some or all of the excess returns to CI. In the first case, while it produces numbers, it is a series of subjective estimates, followed by more subjective estimates. In the latter case, actual data cannot be calculated for several years after the fact.

Linking CI to Investment Enhancement

This metric varies only slightly from the previous one. In this case, management seeks to assign to CI any improvements in the return on specific investments. For example, if a CI report indicates that a competitor will soon face distribution problems, the excess return generated by a factory turning out additional products might be considered such an enhancement.

Classification:

- Quantitative Metric
- Indirect Metric
- End Product Impact Metric

Observations: This metric is subject to the same limitations and considerations as the prior one. In addition, CI that is not produced to support investment decisions or investment-related decisions, such as tactics-oriented CI, would find this extremely difficult to apply.

Linking CI to Specific Savings from Unneeded Investments

This concept is similar to the prior two, except that the end-user(s) may estimate savings based on the cancellation of or reduction in already planned or budgeted investments.[19] If that is the case, then the metric has a hard figure savings which it then must allocate among competing inputs.

Classification:

- Quantitative Metric
- Indirect Metric
- End Product Impact Metric

Observations: This metric is subject to the same limitations and considerations as Linking CI to Specific Investments and Investment Enhancement.

Revenue Enhancement

Revenue enhancement first requires that the CI in question be supporting processes that, in turn, generate or improve the revenue stream.[20] Thus, this measure would not be easily applied to CI that is strategy-oriented, while it may be very useful with technology-oriented CI.[21] In the latter case, the CI unit may be able to point to new technologies brought into the firm that have direct bottom line impacts.

Classification:

- Qualitative Metric
- Direct Metric
- End Product Impact Metric

Observations: This metric is subject to the same limitations as the previous three sections.

Value Creation

By value creation, those advocating use of this metric are referring to the numerous value analyses being used by many different firms.[22] While all of these have in common an effort to measure what works better in a firm by contributing to its value, many are falling into disrupt or disuse.

Classification:

- Quantitative Metric
- Direct Metric
- End Product Impact Metric

Observations: These systems of value assessment are falling into disuse for a number of reasons:

- They are regarded as too difficult to implement, either in terms of complexity or costs.
- As used, they place too heavy a reliance on subjective, rather than objective, assessments.
- They often produce anomalous results, such as having five units responsible for 278 percent of the total profit of the firm while no one is responsible for any shortfalls.
- The connections to values such as improved value to the consumer are real, but they are are no closer than second-order connections or third order-connections, and thus not easily subjected to repeatable quantitative assessments.

Internal Relationships

Building Strong with End-Users

This measure requires an interview or survey with end-users as well as with CI professionals to assess not only the current relationship between the CI professional and the end-user, but also its change, if any, over time.[23] The underlying premise is that end-users will develop stronger relationships with CI professionals as the quality and impact of the CI provided improves over time. Also, this measure is probably better done no more than quarterly.

Classification:

- Qualitative Metric
- Indirect Metric
- Process Metric

Observations: In addition to being subjective, this measure has the disadvantage that the scoring by one end-user may not be comparable to that of another. That, in turn, means that the scores provided by a new end-user of CI cannot be compared in any meaningful way with those of the end-user he or she replaced.

Formulating Relevant Strategy and Tactics

This is similar to building strong with end-users, but it takes the inquiry one step further, in that it focuses on the use of the CI.[24] To that extent, the degree of input by the CI professional is significantly more limited.

Classification:

- Quantitative Metric

- Direct Metric
- End Product Impact Metric

Observations: This measure is not appropriate in situations where the end-user is seeking CI for a purpose other than the creation of a strategy or mapping out tactics. That makes it a poor measure for most technology-oriented CI units, as one of the primary goals could be the acquisition of new technology, which is technically only the implementation of an already existing strategy. Also, for those situations where the contact between the CI professional and the end-user is quite frequent, it is probably counterproductive to ask the end-user to assess the contribution of each assignment or report.

Quality of CI with End-Users

Unlike the first measure in this section, this measure seeks to quantify the nature of the current relationship between the end-user and the CI professional. This may permit additional depth to the questions asked of the end-user. Otherwise, it is quite similar to the first measure in this section.
Classification:

- Qualitative Metric
- Indirect Metric
- Process Metric

Observations: Unlike the first measure, this does not seek to compare changes in the relationship over time.

Quality of Participation on Cross-Functional Teams

This involves surveys or questionnaires given to both the CI professionals as well as the term or teams on which they work. At best, it deals with only a small part of the CI professional's efforts. The underlying assumption is that the reception of the CI professional on such teams will increase as the value of his or her contributions increase.
Classification:

- Qualitative Metric
- Indirect Metric
- Process Metric

Observations: This measures only a part of the job of the CI professional. It would not be applicable to those situations or corporate cultures where such team effort is not utilized.

New Products and Services

Number Developed Due to Use of CI

This measure is quite effective for use in situations where the CI professional is supporting marketing and research or development efforts. It requires that those persons developing the new products or services are willing to assign credit to the CI professional for new products and services. In most cases, it can be done once a year. The troublesome question of assigning partial credit must be dealt with as well.
Classification:

- Quantitative Metric
- Indirect Metric
- End Product Impact Metric

Observations: This measure makes no distinction as to the value of various new products or services. This should not be used in such situations as strategy-oriented and target-oriented CI where the needs of the end-users deal remotely, if at all, with the development of new products and services.

Cost Savings and Avoidance in Development from Use of CI

As with the former measure, this entails the cooperation of those actually developing the new products and services.[25] Unlike that one, it is best if the assessment of the value of the CI in saving actual or potential expenditures were done at the close of individual assignments. Those using this metric should remember that cost savings and cost avoidance figures might not be comparable. One may be based on budget allocated but not spent while the other may involve a very subjective determination of what might have been spent under a particular set of assumptions.
Classification:

- Quantitative Metric
- Direct Metric
- End Product Impact Metric

Observations: As with the previous measures, this is not appropriate for CI professionals supporting nonproduct or service development initiatives.

Performance

Profitable Growth for the Unit

This measure focuses on another measure, the performance of the unit or firm supported by the CI process.[26] It assumes that if CI is available, then the unit or firm is using it and if the unit or firm is using it, it will be showing profitable growth. To that degree, it is an accurate look at CI as imbedded in a unit or firm.

Classification:

- Quantitative Metric
- Indirect Metric
- End Product Impact Metric

Observations: There is no generally acceptable, objective way to allocate what part of the profitable growth is due to the CI process versus other processes. In addition, this measure has a tendency to have many inputs claiming some portion of the credit for growth, but none claiming any for declines or loss of profitability.

Impact on Strategic Direction of the Unit

This measure seeks to capture the impact of CI on the decision making and resulting direction of the firm or unit. As with similar other measures, it requires the end-users to regularly participate in surveys or interviews to allow ongoing and comparable assessments of the impacts of CI. It may also help to determine if that impact has changed over time.

Classification:

- Qualitative Metric
- Indirect Metric
- End Product Impact Metric

Observations: This metric has associated with it the same limitations as other similar measures, including its reliance on subjective assessments and the lack of comparability between different end-users. In addition, it is very little use for measuring CI processes such as technology-based CI and target-based CI where the end-users are not always directly involved in setting strategic direction.

Market Share Gains for the Unit

This measure focuses on another measure, the performance of the unit or firm supported by the CI process. It assumes that if CI is available, then the unit or firm is using it and if the unit or firm is using it, it will be showing an increase in market share. To that degree, it is an accurate look at CI as imbedded in a unit or firm.

Classification:

- Quantitative Metric
- Indirect Metric
- End Product Impact Metric

Observations: There is no generally acceptable, objective way to allocate what part of the increase in market share is due to the CI process versus other processes, including the departure of a competitor from the market space. In addition, this measure has a tendency to have many inputs claiming some portion of the credit for increases, but none claiming any for declines or loss of profitability.

Reports and Presentations

Number

In this situation, the CI unit would track the number of reports and presentations made. One question of course, is what is a report or presentation? If it is a formal contact with the end-user communicating finished CI, then a two-minute conversation before a meeting on a new product's prices carries the same weight as a four-hour briefing on overall strategy. So it is probably useful to divide this into a number of different types, such as flash alerts, in-depth briefings, and so on, for without separating out the complex from the simple, the pressure on the CI unit will be to generate more low-value reports.

Classification:

- Quantitative Metric
- Indirect Metric
- Process Metric

Observations: Some potential limitations should be noted. First, by contracting out, a CI unit can quickly increase the number of assignments completed. Second, there is not necessarily a direct link between the number of assignments and the impact of CI on a firm's decision making. In addition, this measure is not very appropriate for CI processes such as technology-oriented CI and some instances of tactics-oriented CI where formal reports and presentations are not frequently used.

Number of Follow-Ups

This metric should be designed to indicate increasing interest by end-users, and thus, indirectly, increased impact on the firm. The absence of follow-up reports and presentations, however, may not necessarily mean problems. It could indicate that the CI unit is actually anticipating what the end-user needs and will need.
Classification:

- Quantitative Metric
- Indirect Metric
- Process Metric

Observations: Follow-up reports and presentations should be clearly distinguished from efforts that are the result of an incomplete first project or a need to clarify the findings of a prior presentation or report.

Production of Actionable CI

While this measure encompasses within it one of the deliverables of CI, its success is highly dependent on the ongoing cooperation of the end-users.[27] In addition, it has the slight advantage that the end-user is asked whether the CI is usable rather than whether and to what extent it was actually used. This overcomes, in theory, the problem that CI professionals cannot force end-users to use the finished product.
Classification:

- Qualitative Metric
- Direct Metric
- Process Metric

Observations: As with other similar measures, this relies on higher subjective assessments, and can produce results from different end-users that cannot be compared. This measure can have the unintended consequence of concealing a misconnect between the CI professionals and end-users. That is, the end-users can get actionable CI, but if they are not using it, then there may be a failure of the needs phase of the CI cycle.

Sales Effectiveness

Customer Satisfaction

Customer satisfaction should be linked to another measure, presumably already established and refined by the unit or firm supported by the CI process. It assumes that if CI is available, then the unit or firm is using it and if the unit or firm is using it, it will be showing improvements in customer satisfaction. To that degree, it is an accurate look at CI as imbedded in a unit or firm.

Classification:

- Quantitative Metric
- Indirect Metric
- End Product Impact Metric

Observations: There is no generally acceptable, objective way to allocate what part of the increase in customer satisfaction is due to the CI process versus other processes. In addition, this measure has a tendency to have many inputs claiming some portion of the credit for improvements, but none claiming any for declines. As with the balance of this section, this measure is effectively limited to tactics-oriented CI, with significantly fewer applications to technology-oriented and target-oriented CI.

Linking to Specific Customer Wins

In contrast with the previous measure, this one can often be done easily and frequently. The best situation is where the firm or unit makes formal bids and those making the proposals can point to the support of CI as an element contributing to the award of a new contract. However, there are no valid, objective ways in which the contribution of the CI to the award can be assessed. In addition, there is no way to determine if the CI made a poor bid better, but still not a winner.

Classification:

- Quantitative Metric
- Indirect Metric
- End Product Impact Metric

Observations: This measure is effectively limited to tactics-oriented CI, supporting sales and marketing operations, with significantly fewer applications to technology-oriented and target-oriented CI. It is also of little application in firms or markets where formal bids are not used or where the number of customers makes the gain or loss of individual customers impossible to determine.

Number of Customers Retained

While this seems to be a more focused version of the previous measure, this one can be significantly different. That is because it is difficult to determine, in the first instance, that any firm action has resulted in retained specific customers. There may be situations where one or two can be identified as having been retained, usually by actions such as anticipating competitor changes in price, terms, product support, and the like. However, this is very close to merely using anecdotal reports to measure a CI unit's success.

Classification:

* Quantitative Metric
* Indirect Metric
* End Product Impact Metric

Observations: This measure is effectively limited to tactics-oriented CI, supporting sales and marketing operations, with significantly fewer applications to technology-oriented and target-oriented CI. It is also of little application in firms or markets where the number of customers makes the gain or loss of individual customers impossible to determine.

Number of Leads Generated

The underlying assumption here is that a CI unit, supporting the sales and marketing effort, can assist sales and marketing to succeed by identifying new customers, or new ways to access existing potential customers. From there, the assumption goes that success in converting the leads is a function of the skill of the sales and marketing functions, so that the CI unit should neither be rewarded nor penalized by what sales and marketing do with its efforts. A measure as limited as this should not be used alone, as that would, in the long run, result in the CI unit having as its sole mission lead generation.

Classification:

* Quantitative Metric

- Indirect Metric
- End Product Impact Metric

Observations: This measure should be refined to measure only qualified leads that are worth following up on. In addition, this measure is effectively limited to tactics-oriented CI, supporting sales and marketing operations, with significantly fewer applications to technology-oriented and target-oriented CI. And even in those cases, its greatest utility would be in other than mass markets.

Repeat Business

While this seems to be a more focused version of a previous measure, number of customers retained, this one can be significantly different. That is because it is difficult to determine, in the first instance, that any firm action has resulted in having customers return, absent specific surveys of these customers on that subject. There may be situations where one or two can be identified as having returned, usually by actions such as anticipating competitor changes in price, terms, product support, and the like.

Classification:

- Quantitative Metric
- Direct Metric
- End Product Impact Metric

Observations: This measure is effectively limited to tactics-oriented CI, supporting sales and marketing operations, with significantly fewer applications to technology-oriented and target-oriented CI. It is also of little application in firms or markets where the number of customers makes the gain or loss of individual customers impossible to determine so that the only data are on an aggregate increase in customer repeat business.

Improvement in Win–Loss Ratio

The best situation for use of this is where the firm or unit makes formal bids and those making the proposals can point to the support of CI as an element contributing to the relative increase in new contracts. However, there is still no valid, objective way in which the contribution of the CI to the win can be assessed. While there is no way to determine if the CI made a poor bid better, but still not a winning one, by measuring the improvement in this ratio over time, such contributions would be captured, at least to a limited degree.

Classification:

- Quantitative Metric
- Direct Metric
- End Product Impact Metric

Observations: This measure is effectively limited to tactics-oriented CI, supporting sales and marketing operations, with significantly fewer applications to technology-oriented and target-oriented CI. It is also of little application in firms or markets where formal bids are not used or where the number of customers makes the gain or loss of individual customers impossible to determine.

Surveys

Written

This usually involves the use of formal instruments, best kept short, sent to all end-users on a regular basis, or after each assignment. They should be completed only by the end-user. They typically ask that the end-user assign a grade or weight (the 1 to 5 scale is very useful here). Asking for comments in addition to the answers can occasionally produce valuable insights, or subjects about which to ask in the future, but most often generates anecdotal remarks.
Classification:

- Quantitative Metric
- Indirect Metric
- End Product Impact Metric

Observations: For this to be effective, all end-users must be involved. Those who do not wish to be involved can often be the source of the most important insights. While direct feedback after a report, given to the individual or team working on it, can be valuable in building skills and a strong relationship with the end-user, that often results in evaluations which are always slightly higher than satisfactory. One option would be to keep the results for annual statistical purposes, and use without attribution, but to provide the CI unit with a summary of the grades on a regular basis, such as quarterly.

Oral

This is typically better used to collect anecdotal remarks, often as a part of a regular face-to-face feedback process, rather than used with a scoring system, Use of a scoring system can cause oral feedback to become rather stilted. So oral surveys are better used to capture after-the-fact estimates of impact. These can be expressed in a wide variety of ways, but it is best to try to get them with an attached value and probability. Thus, for example, it would be useful to get the end-user to say that a certain CI report reduced the probabilities for failure from 80 percent to 20 percent. Since the project involved risking $10 million, the CI thus saved the firm $6 million in risk reduction.

Classification:

- Quantitative Metric
- Indirect Metric
- End Product Impact Metric

Observations: As with written surveys, it is critical to get it directly from the end-user, and not an intermediary, as well as to get it from all end-users.

Time

Gained by CI Input

This entails an evaluation, after the fact, of the contribution CI made to the timeliness of a project. The assumption is that a project that comes on-line faster will thus generate greater revenues and profits. This is highly subjective, as it involves estimating not only the total time a project might have taken, absent the CI, but the total time it will take with the CI. Then the end-user must allocate that timesaving among competing supporting services. It is the operation of subjective judgments on unverifiable estimates.

Classification:

- Quantitative Metric
- Indirect Metric
- End Product Impact Metric

Observations: This is typically useful only for CI processes, such as tactics-oriented and target-oriented, which operate in support of marketing, research, and related processes. That is because it is difficult to assign a value to time savings that are not market oriented.

Projects Delivered on Time

See the sections "Assignments" and "Number Completed on Time."

Saved by CI Input

This is quite similar to the previous section, Time Gained by CI Input. In the case of time saved, however, the estimate of the time saved may be slightly less subjective than an estimate of time gained.[28] Usually in the case of time saved, there is slightly more precision in identifying either the total amount of time saved, or in identifying the steps, processes, and so on which can now be dispensed with. In the latter case, it can be fairly simple to then determine the time saved. Otherwise, the comments on time gained apply here as well.

Classification:

- Quantitative Metric
- Direct Metric
- End Product Impact Metric

Observations: Use of this metric requires a significant degree of honesty on the part of the end-user. It is most difficult to apply when the CI confirmed an end-user's preexisting analysis of a situation. While it appears scientific, it can actually be quite subjective.

SPECIFIC MEASUREMENT TOOLS FOR SPECIFIC SITUATIONS

As we have shown, there is no single perfect metric for CI. In fact, every potential metric has its shortcomings and even flaws. That does not mean that they should not be used. It is up to you to understand these metrics and to select the best for your particular situation from among them. To aid in considering your choices, we have summarized the situations in which these metrics tend to work best. And from there, it is up to you to select a small number to adapt to your unique context.

When deciding which among these metrics are those that are the most appropriate for your firm and your situation, keep in mind the following guidelines:[29]

1. *Less is better than more.* Aim at creating and capturing a small number of key measures on a limited group of activities.
2. *Linkage is vital.* The measure you select should be tied to the significant underlying strategies, tactics and operations of your firm. In other words, if they change, so too should your CI program and the way in which you measure its impact.
3. *Look in all directions.* Find ways to measure what you have done, what you are doing, and what you will be doing in the future.

4. *Connect with all critical parties.* Ideally, the measures you select should provide information to everyone deeply involved with the CI process. That includes not only the CI unit and its end-users, but also those providing raw data to the process as well as those authorizing a budget for it.

5. *Use some verifiable measures.* While anecdotal support, such as interviews, may provide critical information on the effectiveness of a CI program, it is always better to have some quantitative measures supporting these key qualitative findings.

6. *Change is inevitable.* Just as what the CI unit does will change, and the perspective of its end-users will change, so also should you be ready to change the measures you are using.[30]

Tables 9.1 through 9.4 summarize those that are most often useful by the type of CI process, the major source of raw data, and modes of delivery. We suggest you use these as follows.

On Table 9.1, identify those potential metrics that usually fit your individual CI situation. If you, for example, use a combination of tactics-oriented CI and target-oriented CI, you would check the metrics that are usually relevant in Table 9.4.

From Table 9.2, determine if your CI is based most heavily of primary data or secondary data. If the raw data you use are obtained approximately equally from both types of sources, then just skip this one. Here, you are seeking indications that a particular measure is not usually relevant to processes that rely heavily on those data sources. On Table 9.4, you would delete these from your list.

On Table 9.4, first establish which are the most common ways in which you distribute the CI in your organization or firm. For each of the remaining measures, count the number of times you see the mark "usually relevant." Put that number in the last column.

Then rank the remaining measures in order of the number of hits in the last column. And from that list, using the six rules previously noted you can identify those measures most likely to be relevant to the CI processes in your firm or unit.

This analysis should be repeated at least every two years, if not more often. If your CI unit radically changes its direction, sources of CI data, and/or manner of delivery, you should review this analysis.

NOTES

1. Developed from The Futures Group, *Ostriches & Eagles*, 29; APQC, *Competitive and Business Intelligence*, 64 et seq.; Neil J. Simon, "Managing the CI Department: Determining Measures of Success," *Competitive Intelligence Magazine* 1, 2 (July–September 1998): 45–47; APQC, *Managing Competitive Intelligence*, 70 et seq.; APQC, *Strategic and Tactical Competitive Intelligence*, 64 et seq.; Kenneth Sawka, "The Analyst's Corner: Are We

Table 9.1
CI Orientation

	Strategic	Tactics	Target	Technology
Assignments and Projects				
Meeting objectives	●	●	●	●
Number completed	●	●	●	●
Number completed on time	◘	●	●	●
Number requested	◘	●	●	●
Number requested - increase by end-users	●	●	●	●
Number of follow-up assignments	●	●	●	●
Number of projects assisted	◘	●	●	●
Number of suggestions submitted	◘	●	●	●
Budget				
Comparative costs savings				
compared with cost of outsider	●	●	●	●
compared with cost of untrained person	●	●	●	●
Meeting project and function budget constraints	●	●	●	●
Efficiency				
Accuracy of analysis	●	●	●	◘
Data quality	●	●	●	●
First time results (no reworking)	●	●	●	●

Table 9.1 (*continued*)

Meeting project time line	●	●	●	●
Time for research versus time for response	◘	●	●	●
Endusers				
Creating compelling reasons to use CI	●	●	●	●
Effectiveness of implementation of findings	●	◘	●	◘
Meeting needs	●	●	●	●
Number of referrals	◘	●	●	●
Number served	◘	●	●	◘
Feedback	–			
Written	●	●	●	●
Oral	●	●	●	●
Financial				
Cost avoidance	◘	●	●	●
Cost savings	◘	●	●	●
Goals met	●	●	●	●
Linking CI to specific investments	●	◘	●	●
Linking CI to investment enhancement	●	◘	●	●
Linking CI to specific savings from unneeded investments	●	◘	●	●
Revenue enhancement	●	●	●	●
Value creation	●	◘	◘	●
Internal Relationships				
Building strong with end-users	●	●	●	●

Table 9.1 (*continued*)

Formulating relevant strategy and tactics	●	●	●	◻
Quality of relationship with end-users	●	●	●	●
Quality of participation on cross-functional teams	●	●	●	●
New Products and Services				
Number developed due to use of CI	◻	●	◻	●
Cost savings/avoidance in development from use of CI	◻	●	◻	●
Performance				
Growth, profitable for the unit or firm	●	●	●	●
Impact on strategic direction of unit or firm	●	●	◻	◻
Market share gains for unit or firm	●	●	●	●
Report and Presentations				
Number	●	◻	●	◻
Number of follow-ups	●	●	●	●
Production of actionable CI	●	●	●	●
Sales effectiveness				
Customer satisfaction	◻	●	◻	◻
Linking to specific customer wins	◻	●	◻	◻
Number of customers retained	◻	●	◻	◻
Number of leads generated	◻	●	◻	◻
Repeat business	◻	●	◻	◻
Improvement in win-loss ration	◻	●	◻	◻

Table 9.1 (*continued*)

Surveys				
Written	●	●	●	●
Oral	●	●	●	●
Time				
Gained by CI input	◘	●	●	◘
Projects delivered on time	◘	●	●	●
Saved by CI input	◘	●	●	◘

Key: Usually relevant   - ●

       Rarely relevant   - ◘

Table 9.2
Dominant Data Source

	Secondary	Primary
Assignments and Projects		
Meeting objectives	●	●
Number completed	●	●
Number completed on time	●	●
Number requested	●	●
Number requested - increase by end-users	●	●
Number of follow-up assignments	●	●
Number of projects assisted	●	●
Number of suggestions submitted	●	●
Budget		
Comparative costs savings		
compared with cost of outsider	●	●
compared with cost of untrained person	●	●
Meeting project or function budget constraints	●	●
Efficiency		
Accuracy of analysis	●	●
Data quality	●	□
First time results (no reworking)	●	●
Meeting project time line	●	●
Time for research versus time for response	●	□
End-Users		

Table 9.2 (*continued*)

Creating compelling reasons to use CI	●	●
Effectiveness of implementation of findings	●	●
Meeting needs	●	●
Number of referrals	●	●
Number served	●	●
Feedback		
Written	●	●
Oral	●	●
Financial		
Cost avoidance	●	●
Cost savings	●	●
Goals met	●	●
Linking CI to specific investments	●	●
Linking CI to investment enhancement	●	●
Linking CI to specific savings from unneeded investments	●	●
Revenue enhancement	●	●
Value creation	●	●
Internal Relationships		
Building strong with end-users	●	●
Formulating relevant strategy and tactics	●	●
Quality of relationship with end-users	●	●
Quality of participation on cross-functional teams	▫	●

Table 9.2 (*continued*)

New Products and Services		
Number developed due to use of CI	●	●
Cost savings/avoidance in development from use of CI	●	●
Performance		
Profitable growth for the unit or firm	●	●
Impact on strategic direction of unit or firm	●	●
Market share gains for unit or firm	●	●
Reports and Presentations		
Number	●	●
Number of follow-ups	●	●
Production of actionable CI	●	●
Sales effectiveness		
Customer satisfaction	●	●
Linking to specific customer wins	●	●
Number of customers retained	●	●
Number of leads generated	●	●
Repeat business	●	●
Improvement in win - loss ratio	●	●
Surveys		
Written	●	●
Oral	●	●
Time		

Table 9.2 (*continued*)

Gained by CI input	●	●
Projects delivered on time	●	●
Saved by CI input	●	●

Key: Usually relevant   ●

Rarely relevant   ◘

Table 9.3
CI Delivery

	Nws	Dat	Alt	Pre	Rpt	Mdl	Gam	Trn
Assignments and Projects								
Meeting objectives	●	●	●	●	●	●	●	●
Number completed	●	●	●	●	●	●	□	●
Number completed on time	●	●	●	●	●	●	□	●
Number requested	□	●	□	●	●	●	□	●
Number requested, increase by end-users	□	●	□	●	●	●	●	●
Number of follow-up assignments	●	●	●	●	●	●	●	●
Number of projects assisted	□	●	□	●	●	●	●	□
Number of suggestions submitted	□	□	□	●	●	□	□	□
Budget								
Comparative costs savings								
compared with cost of outsider	●	●	●	●	●	□	□	●
compared with cost of untrained person	●	●	●	●	●	□	□	□
Meeting project or function budget constraints	●	●	●	●	●	□	□	□
Efficiency								
Accuracy of analysis	●	□	●	●	●	●	□	□
Data quality	●	●	●	●	●	●	●	□
First time results (no reworking)	□	□	□	●	●	□	□	□

Table 9.3 (*continued*)

Meeting project time line	□	●	□	●	●	●	●	□
Time for research versus time for response	□	●	□	●	●	□	□	□
End-Users								
Creating compelling reasons to use CI	●	●	●	●	●	●	●	●
Effectiveness of implementation of findings	□	□	□	●	●	●	●	□
Meeting needs	●	●	●	●	●	●	●	●
Number of referrals	●	●	●	●	●	●	●	□
Number served	●	●	●	●	●	●	●	●
Feedback								
Written	●	●	●	●	●	●	●	●
Oral	●	□	●	●	●	●	●	●
Financial								
Cost avoidance	●	●	●	●	●	●	●	□
Cost savings	●	●	●	●	●	●	●	□
Goals met	●	●	●	●	●	●	●	□
Linking CI to specific investments	●	●	□	●	●	●	●	□
Linking CI to investment enhancement	●	●	□	●	●	●	●	□
Linking CI to specific savings from unneeded investments	●	●	□	●	●	●	●	□
Revenue enhancement	●	●	●	●	●	●	●	□
Value creation	●	●	●	●	●	●	●	□
Internal Relationships								
Building strong with end-users	●	●	●	●	●	●	●	●

Table 9.3 (*continued*)

Formulating relevant strategy and tactics	●	◻	●	●	●	●	●	◻
Quality relationships with end-users	●	●	●	●	●	●	●	●
Quality of participation on cross-functional teams	◻	◻	◻	●	◻	◻	●	◻
New Products and Services								
Number developed due to use of CI	●	●	●	●	●	●	●	◻
Cost savings or avoidance in development from use of CI	●	●	●	●	●	●	●	◻
Performance								
Profitable growth for the unit or firm	●	●	●	●	●	●	●	◻
Impact on strategic direction of unit or firm	●	◻	◻	●	●	●	●	◻
Market share gains for unit or firm	●	●	●	●	●	●	●	◻
Reports and Presentations								
Number	◻	◻	●	◻	●	◻	◻	◻
Number of follow-ups	◻	◻	●	◻	●	◻	◻	◻
Production of actionable CI	◻	◻	◻	◻	●	◻	◻	◻
Sales effectiveness								
Customer satisfaction	●	●	◻	●	●	◻	◻	◻
Linking to specific customer wins	●	●	●	●	●	◻	◻	◻
Number of customers retained	●	●	●	●	●	◻	◻	◻
Number of leads generated	◻	●	●	●	●	◻	◻	◻
Repeat business	●	●	●	●	●	◻	◻	◻
Improvement in win-loss ration	●	●	●	●	●	●	●	◻

Table 9.3 (*continued*)

Surveys								
Written	●	●	●	●	●	●	●	●
Oral	●	●	□	●	●	●	●	●
Time								
Gained by CI input	●	●	●	●	●	●	●	□
Projects delivered on time	□	□	□	●	●	●	□	□
Saved by CI input	●	●	●	●	●	●	●	□

Key: Nws = Newsletters

Dat = Source data and raw inputs

Alt = Flash alerts

Pre = Face-to-face briefings and presentations

Rpt = Written reports

Mdl = Forecastsand modeling

Gam = Gaming and shadowing exercises

Trn = Internal training on CI

Key: Usually relevant   ●

Rarely relevant   □

Table 9.4
Summary Table

	Orientation	Data Source	Delivery
Assignments and Projects			
Meeting objectives			
Number completed			
Number completed on time			
Number requested			
Number requested - increase by end-users			
Number of follow-up assignments			
Number of projects assisted			
Number of suggestions submitted			
Budget			
Comparative costs savings			
compared with cost of outsider			
compared with cost of untrained person			
Meeting project or function budget constraints			
Efficiency			
Accuracy of analysis			
Data quality			
First time results (no reworking)			
Meeting project time line			
Time for research versus time for response			
End-Users			

Table 9.4 (*continued*)

Creating compelling reason to use CI			
Effectiveness of implementation of findings			
Meeting needs			
Number of referrals			
Number served			
Feedback			
Written			
Oral			
Financial			
Cost avoidance			
Cost savings			
Goals met			
Linking CI to specific investments			
Linking CI to investment enhancement			
Linking CI to specific savings from unneeded investments			
Revenue enhancement			
Value creation			
Internal Relationships			
Building strong with end-users			
Formulating relevant strategy or tactics			
Quality of relationships with end-users			
Quality of participation on cross-functional teams			

Table 9.4 (*continued*)

New Products and Services			
Number developed due to use of CI			
Cost savings and avoidance in development from use of CI			
Performance			
Profitable growth for the unit or firm			
Impact on strategic direction of unit or firm			
Market share gains for unit or firm			
Reports and Presentations			
Number			
Number of follow-ups			
Production of actionable CI			
Sales effectiveness			
Customer satisfaction			
Linking to specific customer wins			
Number of customers retained			
Number of leads generated			
Repeat business			
Improvement in win-loss ratio			
Surveys			
Written			
Oral			
Time			

Table 9.4 (*continued*)

Gained by CI input			
Projects delivered on time			
Saved by CI input			

Valuable?" *Competitive Intelligence Magazine* 3, 2 (April–June 2000): 53–54; APQC, *Developing a Successful Competitive Intelligence Program*, 97 et seq.

2. On cost, see Fleisher and Blenkhorn, eds., *Managing Frontiers*, 113.

3. Ibid., 114.

4. See Klavans, "So, What Is the Value of Technical Intelligence?"; Leigh Davison, "Measuring CI Effectiveness: Insights from the Advertising Industry," in Society of Competitive Intelligence Professionals, *Conference Proceedings—2001 Annual International Conference and Exhibit* (Alexandria, Va.: SCIP, 2000); and James Russell, "Measuring the Value of Competitive Intelligence (CI) Activities: A Pilot Study," in Society of Competitive Intelligence Professionals, *Conference Proceedings—2000 Annual International Conference and Exhibit* (Alexandria, Va.: SCIP, 2000).

5. See Fleisher and Blenkhorn, *Managing Frontiers*, 114.

6. See Russell, "Measuring the Value of Competitive Intelligence Activities," and Davison, "Measuring CI Effectiveness."

7. See Fleisher and Blenkhorn, *Managing Frontiers*, 113.

8. See McGonagle and Vella, *Outsmarting the Competition*, 349–350.

9. See Herring, *Measuring the Effectiveness*, and Solomon, "The Intelligence Asset-Building Process."

10. Cf. John J. McGonagle and Carolyn M. Vella, *How to Use a Consultant in Your Company: A Manager's and Executive's Guide* (New York: John Wiley & Sons, 2001), 104–105.

11. John J. McGonagle, Jr., "Patterns of Development In CI Units," *Competitive Intelligence Review* 3, 1 (Spring 1992): 11–12.

12. "The usefulness of [an intelligence] paper is closely connected with its timeliness." Washington Platt, *Strategic Intelligence Production* (New York: Frederick A. Praeger, 1957), 35.

13. Cf. Robert A. Margulies and Andre G. Gib, "Making Competitive Intelligence Relevant to the User: A Case Example," *The Competitive Intelligencer* 3, 1 (Spring 1988): 9.

14. See Telofski, *Dangerous Competition*, 8.

15. Cf. Hovis, "CI at Avnet."

16. See Herring, *Measuring the Effectiveness*.

17. Ibid.

18. For a careful look at trying to use ROI techniques for CI, see S. David Kilmetz and R. Sean Bridge, "Gauging the Returns on Investments in Competitive Intelligence: A Three-Step Analysis for Executive Decision Makers," *Competitive Intelligence Review* 10, 1 (First Quarter 1999): 4–11.

19. See Sawka, "The Analyst's Corner: Drills and Holes," 36–37; "The Analyst's Corner: Finding Intelligence Analysts," 41–42; and "The Analyst's Corner: Keep Your Message Short and Sweet," 54–55.

20. See Herring, *Measuring the Effectiveness*.

21. See Merrill S. Brenner, "Technology Intelligence and Technology Scouting," *Competitive Intelligence Review* 7, 3 (Fall 1996): 20–27.

22. See Herring, *Measuring the Effectiveness*.

23. Cf. Fleisher and Blenkhorn, *Managing Frontiers*, 118.

24. Cf. Hovis, "CI at Avnet."

25. See Sawka, "Drills and Holes," "Finding Intelligence Analysts," "Keep Your Message Short and Sweet"; Solomon, The Intelligence Asset-Building Process"; and Herring, *Measuring the Effectiveness.*

26. See Herring, *Measuring the Effectiveness.*

27. Cf. Hovis, "CI at Avnet."

28. Cf. Graef, *Executive Briefing.*

29. Adapted from Fleisher and Blenkhorn, *Managing Frontiers*, 120.

30. See John J. McGonagle, Jr., "Patterns of Development," 11–12.

PART III

DEFENSIVE COMPETITIVE INTELLIGENCE

As we noted in Part I, defensive CI is another variation of CI. However, because of the way in which it functions, it must be approached slightly differently from active CI, but using the same approach set forth in Part II.

10

Defensive CI

THE ESSENCE OF A DEFENSIVE CI PROGRAM

"It is unawareness far more than a wantonly careless attitude per se that leads to the needless compromise of much important business data."[1]

Deciding what you need to protect from you competitors actually has two separate elements:

1. Determining if your firm is in a competitive environment which demands a defensive program.
2. Determining what kinds of intelligence efforts your competitors are or should be mounting against you.

From there, you can focus on what sources of data on your firm you should be reviewing in connection with a defensive program.

Why Become Involved with a Defensive CI Program?

You need to become involved with defensive CI activities because your competition is already obtaining competitive intelligence, or CI, on your firm, or soon will be. Many companies still operate under the mistaken impression that CI is something a few giant multinationals do, and that it doesn't affect them. They are wrong.

CI is operating today at an almost staggering breadth and depth. Look for example at the promotion conducted by the Society of Competitive Intelligence Professionals (SCIP), the global society representing practitioners of this profession.

SCIP has been heavily promoting CI to members and nonmembers over the past decade.

These promotional efforts suggest how your competitors are profiling you. In addition to numerous workshops and special sessions at its annual meetings, SCIP sponsors public sessions throughout the year and around the world. Special sessions sponsored by SCIP in the recent past have included the following:

- Intelligence in the sales and bidding processes
- CI in the Canadian communications market (technical competitive intelligence)
- Gathering CI through your sales force
- CI and e-business
- CI and counterintelligence for small and medium enterprises and individual entrepreneurs
- CI in the financial services industry
- International corporate intelligence and protection of intellectual property
- Business journalism and CI

The lesson is that no enterprise of any size or kind is safe in assuming that its competitors are not conducting competitive intelligence against them. Protective activities are vital.

The Philosophy Underlying Cloaking Programs

The philosophy underlying cloaking appears simple because CI itself is deceptively simple. Recall that CI consists of collecting publicly available data, analyzing them, drawing conclusions, and transmitting those conclusions to management in a form that can be acted upon.

Basic ground rules, not complexity, should be the foundation of your cloaking effort. A good starting ground rule is that, instead of trying to censor everything, just make people aware of the fact that competitors are listening to everything they say.

The key to a cloaking program is to make sure that every employee understands that information that seems fairly harmless is really considered sensitive by your company.

Why "Harmless" Information May Be Sensitive

Consider two important facts: One is that the most valuable competitive information often now comes from direct contact—often telephone calls from one person to another. You can, of course, learn a great deal from press releases and securities filings. But to get really good CI, you need to talk to people.

And the closer the intelligence source is to the target, the more valuable what they have to say is, no matter how insignificant it seems to them. Everyone from the receptionist to the CEO needs to be made aware that anything they say to an outside party could be useful to a competitor's CI operation.

The other important fact is that around 80 percent of the information needed for a typical CI study is in the public domain. Your other data may be protected by law or by contracts and nondisclosure agreements. The point of a cloaking program is to provide some protection for the public 80 percent, without trying to hide every last bit of it. The bottom line is that by treating all information as sensitive, you won't stop the flow of information into the public domain, but you will stop revealing things you don't have to reveal.

KEY ISSUES INVOLVED IN SETTING UP AND RUNNING A DEFENSIVE CI PROGRAM

Panic and Paranoia

You have to avoid the panic and paranoia that may arise when your firm sees what kind of information on it is already out there. Your firm may be tempted to try to lock down everything. Your firm can't do it. It is impossible and even dangerous to try to protect all your firm's information from the outside world.

Remember that cloaking is to conceal, not to make invisible. If you're invisible to your competitors, you're invisible to your customers. If you're invisible to your customers, you're out of business.

Keeping it simple is the key. Protect limited amounts of data, for a limited period of time, at a limited cost, so there's only a limited impact, if any, on sales and marketing, on customer relations or on shareholder relations. For example:

- Has your Web site administrator considered controlling what pages a competitor sees on your Web site?[2]
- Have you considered educating employees on how to properly answer outside phone calls?[3]

If everyone takes reasonable efforts to protect the company's sensitive information, cloaking will cost little or nothing.

Now look at some of the key steps that will help you get a cloaking program off the ground:

- Selling the program to management
- How cloaking relates to intellectual property protections
- Cloaking and corporate security
- Cloaking and your CI unit

Selling a Cloaking Program to Management

Sell your cloaking program by making these four key points to management:

1. Cloaking works and is proven to work.
2. It will often save money.
3. The competition can find out a lot about us right now with little effort.
4. Other companies are already doing it.

Cloaking Works and Is Proven to Work

In a well-known case, Bristol-Myers tried to launch a new pain reliever, Datril®. It ran two trial launches, which led it to the conclusion that a reduced-priced strategy was the only way to penetrate the market. It set a launch date. Two weeks before the launch date, a competitor, McNeil, lowered the price of Tylenol®, a head-to-head competitor, dramatically; McNeil even gave rebates on existing inventories. The Datril® launch failed. It later became known that CI had played an important part in McNeil's discovery of the pending Datril® launch.[4] Had Bristol-Myers been able to prevent its competitor from finding out about the launch, the story might have been very different.

Saving Money

Savings on printing and mailing by eliminating inappropriate recipients and trimming content can be substantial. For example, if your internal newsletter prints detailed technical articles, consider printing abstracts instead. By reviewing current distribution and tightly controlling distribution to keep it internal, you may cut printing and distribution costs significantly.

The Competition Can Find Out a Lot about Us
Right Now with Little Effort

"What's going on in the inside shows on the outside."[5]

Take a few minutes to show management what can be learned about your company right now, taken from data in the public domain. Be prepared for management to be petrified.

Other Companies Are Already Doing It

If you have a competitor you are following and there appear to be some blind spots in your analysis of it, the odds are this firm is already cloaking. The lesson to management is that we are operating (partially) blind, but at least one of them, the competition, is not. No one survives in business like that.

Cloaking Programs and Intellectual Property Programs

Before setting up a cloaking program, you should evaluate where a cloaking program fits in relation to existing intellectual property programs. By intellectual property programs, we mean those that deal with patents, trademarks, and copyrights.

These classes of intellectual property all benefit from legal protection. In essence, by using these programs, your company claims exclusive rights to material that is publicly known. Copyright does not hide a document from your competitors; it just keeps them from using the document. A similar principle also applies to patents and trademarks.

Cloaking does not supplant these areas, it supplements them:

- A trademark filing may be very protective. However, filing trademarks for new processes or products may disclose to your competitors that something new is happening. As part of cloaking, take care to avoid premature filings.

- Cloaking should work with your company's patent process before the disclosure of the patent. Why? You can lose the right to a patent if information about the process becomes public prematurely.

Cloaking is a good way to maximize their effectiveness.

Cloaking Programs and Corporate Security

Corporate security is the responsibility of any department focused on physical protection of the company and its property. It normally protects your firm against acts that have an element of criminality while, in contrast, cloaking generally protects against legal activities. However, it can be hard to tell the difference between what was based on legal activity and what was based on illegal activity, so locating the exact source of an information leak may require both corporate security and a CI specialist.

Usually the inadvertent leak—for example, accidental omission of a nondisclosure clause combined with legitimate distribution to someone with a conflict of interest—is more harmful and harder to detect. If a party on the other end of such a leak is reasonably sophisticated in CI, the problem is compounded.

Too many people assume it can never happen, so they never look to see if it could. You should be looking at what's out there on your company and your products every couple of months. Always ask yourself: Where does the information flow?

Where Does Cloaking Fit within a CI Unit?

If you have an active CI unit, it can be a great source of people with the skills needed to establish a cloaking program. It can help sensitize all of your personnel as to what they should be doing to keep the competitors off balance. For example, ask the CI unit to identify key pieces of information that were particularly useful in cracking cases—seemingly innocuous information like casual remarks by executives, or trade show flyers. Then look at how your company presents comparable information.

Your CI personnel may be able to tell you which key competitors already have formal and vigorous CI units. More specifically, they may be able to tell you who is watching you now, who is probably watching you, and who may start watching you tomorrow. You should be able to learn from your own unit's activities against your competitors. Consider the data analysis techniques they are using; you can assume that your competitors are probably using the same ones against you.

Look at those analytical tools and ask: Is there one key piece of information that if withheld would ruin this analysis? That is the information you will focus on in your cloaking program.

NOTES

1. "Editorial," *Forum* magazine, 16 May 1990, 3.
2. "Beware Rival's Web Subterfuge," *Competitive Intelligence Magazine* 3, 1 (January–March 2000): 8.
3. See Peggy R. Stover, "Shoestring Intelligence: Preventative Medicine Against CI Attacks," *Competitive Intelligence Magazine* 2, 2 (April–June 1999): 37.
4. For additional details, see John Nolan, *Confidential: Uncover Your Competitors' Top Business Secrets Legally and Quickly—and Protect Your Own* (New York: HarperBusiness, 1999), 194–195.
5. Earl Nightingale, quoted in Davis, 27.

11

Is Your Firm in a Competitive Environment That Demands a Defensive CI Program?

Returning to the structure we presented in Part II, there are particular competitive environments that quite literally demand the creation of a defensive intelligence program. In this case, you should view the marketplace with your firm in it, not excluding it as we did in Chapter 4.

COMPETITIVE ENVIRONMENT

Here you are looking at the overall competitive environment in which your firm, or the part of the firm which you are serving, is now competing. This, in turn, is divided into three separate areas:

1. Level of company regulation
2. Barriers to entry
3. Barriers to exit

Only the area of barriers to entry has the ability to trigger the immediate need for a defensive CI program.

Barriers to Entry

Companies in a market that has low barriers to entry typically are characterized by higher degrees of flexibility and innovation than are those in other markets. Because of the absence or minimal nature of these barriers, such markets are subject to relatively sudden changes in terms of new participants as well as new products. This is an indicator of the need for a defensive CI program.

PRODUCTS AND SERVICES YOU PRODUCE

Here you are looking at the specific products or services that your firm provides and brings to the marketplace where it is now competing. This, in turn, is divided into four separate areas:

1. Number of substitutes
2. Level of regulation of the product or service
3. Lead time to market
4. Life cycle of the product or service

Only the areas of lead-time to market and life cycle have the ability to trigger the immediate need for a defensive CI program.

Lead-Time to Market

Companies facing an environment where there is a very short lead-time to market typically see the marketplace occupied by a large number of players of widely varying sizes. These players are less concerned with positioning their product or service portfolios to assure a continuing and growing stream of revenues over time, than to assure that they identify and then respond to very short-term changes.

The reasons for the short lead-time to market may be related to factors such as the product or service, which is relatively easy to produce, to the regulatory environment, which may have few controls over the company and product or service, or to operating in a market which has few, or even no, limits on exit and/or entry, which all require that those in the market be able to adapt quickly to survive. This is an indicator of the need for a defensive CI program.

Product or Service Life Cycle

Companies that offer a product or service that has a very short life cycle face a market that changes very rapidly, one where prices and costs can take sudden and significant turns. Typically the supporting investment is not relatively significant, but the role of both propriety and nonpropriety technology is. In addition, the products and services usually cannot be protected by legal regimes such as patent and trademark filings. This is an indicator of the need for a defensive CI program.

COMPANIES YOU FACE

Here, you are trying to evaluate the firms with which you directly compete in your market or markets. If your market is one in which there are currently very few competitors, you may want to evaluate it including the first tier of potential entrants.

The way these firms are managed and related to each other has a direct impact on which types of CI are best for you. This is, in turn, divided into five separate areas:

1. Centrality of management
2. Level of cooperation
3. Degree of concentration
4. Level of knowledge intensity
5. Reliance on alliances

All the areas, with the exception of centrality of management and reliance on alliances, have the ability to trigger the immediate need for a defensive CI program.

Level of Cooperation

In markets where the firms are the most highly competitive, they have the lowest levels of cooperation. Such markets tend to be fast moving, and the actions of one firm cannot be a useful predictor of the actions of other firms. This is an indicator of the need for a defensive CI program.

Degree of Concentration

In general, the more concentrated a market is, the less intensive and extensive will direct competition tend to be. The ultimate degree of concentration is the monopoly, where one firm controls 100 percent of a market. There is no competition in that marketplace.

In a highly concentrated market, the largest firms tend to dominate the competitive landscape. In general, they tend to set and defend prices, and also indirectly control the prices of key inputs, simply because of their (relative) size. This is an indicator of the need for a defensive CI program.

Knowledge Intensity

In a marketplace where companies are very knowledge intensive, the technology base of the companies, as well as the technology that drives the underlying knowledge management processes, tend to be changing relatively rapidly. This allows the firms that are most knowledge intensive to gain, hold, and exploit competitive advantages, so long as they support that process. This is an indicator of the need for a defensive CI program.

Production and Supply Chain Issues

As companies seek to control and to redefine their own supply chain as well as the way they produce their goods and services, they also change the nature of the firms that you compete with.[1] This is divided into four separate areas:

1. Level of technology
2. Number of suppliers
3. Degree of capital intensity
4. Level of innovation.

Two of these areas, the level of technology and level of innovation, have the ability to trigger the immediate creation of a defensive CI program.

Level of Technology

The level of technology that characterizes your marketplace should be viewed both in terms of product as well as in terms of the entire supply chain.

By production technology, we mean everything from the relative trade-off between manual and automated production to the ability of one facility to produce multiple outputs with minimal changeover costs, including lost time. By supply chain technology, we mean everything from the ability to track the status of individual packages being handled by a carrier to the use of the Internet to distribute software by downloading.

In a marketplace that is characterized by high levels of production and supply chain technology, we can expect to see competitors that are able to control and even reduce production and distribution costs on an ongoing basis, as well as the rapid development and deployment of new products and services and relatively low barrier to exit, but not to entry. This is an indicator of the need for a defensive CI program.

In a marketplace that is characterized by moderate levels of production and supply chain technology, we can expect to see competitors able to control or eliminate increases in production and distribution costs on a short-term basis, the moderately rapid development and deployment of new products and services, as well as relatively low barriers to exit as well as to entry. This is an indicator of the need for a defensive CI program.

Level of Innovation

Levels of innovation in an industry impact not only production of products and services; they also impact the development of new products and services, as well as changes in the way in which the supply chain operates.

Firms that have demonstrated moderate levels of innovation tend to view the immediate future of a market as reflecting the immediate past, but expect that many elements of it can and will change. In fact, their time horizon tends to be medium-term in nature. They are also less reactive than they are proactive, whether the issue is launching a new product or changing their own communications infrastructure. This is an indicator of the need for a defensive CI program.

Firms that have demonstrated high levels of innovation tend to view the immediate future of a market as only a step towards a longer-term, more radically changed future. In many areas, their time horizon tends to be long-term in nature. They are significantly more proactive than they are reactive, whether the issue is terminating a line of business, even a profitable one, or entering into a new strategic partnership. This is an indicator of the need for a defensive CI program.

MARKETPLACE DYNAMICS

The way in which we look at marketplace dynamics is divided into three separate indicators:

1. The number of customers
2. The geographic scope of the market
3. The nature of competition

Only the number of customers has the ability to trigger the immediate creation of a defensive CI program.

Number of Customers

In market niches where the firms compete for a relatively small number of customers, these customers individually generally exercise great power over the competitors, and thus should be tracked. And, conversely, the change in the relationship between any given competitor and its customer, or customers, can change the dynamics in the marketplace very quickly. This is an indicator of the need for a defensive CI program.

SCORING

To determine if you should be initiating a defensive CI program immediately, use the prior materials to analyze the market or markets you face. As in Chapter 4, one easy approach is to "score" your responses. That is, you record your responses to each of these and then total them up.

If you are in several markets, score each of them separately as well as jointly to see if you need to begin a defensive CI program.

Try using this grid to track your overall score.

Is Defensive CI Needed?

Competitive Environment

Environment	
Entry Barriers	×
Products and Services	
Life Cycle	×
Companies	
Cooperation	×
Concentration	×
Knowledge Intensity	×
Production and Supply Chain	
Technology Level	×
Innovation	×
Marketplace	
Customers	×
Type of Competition	×

Experience shows that if you have indicated the need for defensive CI four times or more, then you should begin establishing such a program now.

DO REGULAR AND FORWARD-LOOKING REVIEWS

This analysis of the need for defensive CI deals with the environment you face and your products and services, production, supply, and marketplace as they are now. If you do not score high enough to warrant the immediate establishment of a defensive CI program that does not mean one is not useful. It only means that you do not necessarily need one right now.

As with active CI, try evaluating how each of these factors would look in the near term, that is one to three years, and in the long-term, that is two to five years or more. Such an analysis should warn you when the need for a defensive CI will emerge.

If you do not set up a defensive CI program, it would be wise to redo this analysis at regular internals, at least annually, regularly reviewing all these circumstances to see if you now need a defensive CI program. For example, a market niche where the number of competitors suddenly declines, making it a highly concentrated niche should generate an immediate reevaluation of your needs for defensive CI.

NOTE

1. In fact, the supply chain itself can also be an appropriate CI target. See Kevyn Kennedy, "Minding the Supply Chain: Gray-Market Goods, Production 'Leakage,' and Global CI," *Competitive Intelligence Magazine* 3, 3 (July–September 2000): 20–22; Deborah C. Sawyer, "Defining Your Competition: Balance of Power: When Suppliers Are Your Main Threat," *Competitive Intelligence Magazine* 3, 3 (July–September 2000): 51–52; Kevyn Kennedy, "Doing Business Globally? Focus CI on Suppliers," *Competitive Intelligence Magazine* 3, 1 (January–March 2000): 11–13.

12

What Kinds of Intelligence Efforts Should Your Competitors Be Mounting Against You?

Here too, we return to the basic analytical structure outlined in Part II. However, instead of looking at the overall marketplace and all of the competitors in the market, often excluding your own firm, we must look at it from the perspective of your competitors, with the focus being on you and your operations. That means you may find that your competitors' needs are somewhat different from ones you have identified for your own program.

As you recall, the system involves systematically linking what each CI division is expected to provide with the needs of the business. These needs are a function, in turn, of five elements making up the competitive environment faced by the internal clients of the CI professionals. These are the following:

1. Environment in which you operate
2. Products and services you produce
3. Companies you face
4. Production and supply chain issues
5. Marketplace dynamics

In each case, when analyzing your competitor's probable targeting of your operations, keep in mind that you are also still assuming the perspective of your end-user client, with the responsibilities and products and services that he or she possesses. You must look at all of these circumstances objectively.

In this context, your view of the circumstances must have to exclude other firms from the overall assessment. For example in the category of the lead-time to market which will be discussed later, you may have a situation where your firm is unique in that it has a very short lead-time to market, and all your competitors are significantly less quick in getting new products and services to market. In such a case, you would characterize your competitor's view that the marketplace is one that is both one with a short lead-time to market; that is, your firm, and a medium lead-time to market, that is, your *other* competitors. Remember, your competitors will be tracking you and your competitors, so while your operations may call for tactics-oriented CI, their operations may warrant the additional use of target-oriented CI. And once having established a unit with a particular focus, you should expect that focus on you, as a part of the overall market focus.

COMPETITIVE ENVIRONMENT

Here you are looking at the overall competitive environment in which your firm, or the part of the firm which you are serving, is now competing. This, in turn, is divided into three separate areas:

1. Level of company regulation
2. Barriers to entry
3. Barriers to exit

Level of Company Regulation

Companies facing the lowest levels of regulation are, in general, most free to act and to respond to market forces. In addition, as they have low levels of regulation, they tend to be able to innovate more quickly, to change their operations and even overall structure more rapidly, and tend to place less information in the public domain. As a result, the CI most likely to have the greatest bottom-line impact on your competitors are tactics-oriented, target-oriented, and technology-oriented.

Companies that face a moderate degree of company regulation are, in general, less free to act and to respond rapidly to market forces. They take longer to be able to respond. In addition, unlike those facing low levels of regulation, they tend to be able to stretch innovation out over a longer period of time, to find it difficult to change their operations and even overall structure rapidly. Finally, they tend to place more information in the public domain than do the companies facing low levels of company regulation. As a result, the CI most likely to have the greatest bottom-line impact on your competitors are target-oriented and strategy-oriented CI.

Companies that face a high degree of company regulation are, in general, least free to act and to respond to market forces. In addition, as they have the highest levels of regulation, they tend to be able to innovate relatively slowly, to change their operations and even overall structure less rapidly than companies facing less regulation. Finally, they tend to place the greatest amount of information in the public domain. As a result, the CI most likely to have the greatest bottom-line impact on your competitors is strategy-oriented CI.

Barriers to Entry

Companies in a market that has low barriers to entry typically are characterized by higher degrees of flexibility and innovation than are those in other markets. Because of the absence or minimal nature of these barriers, such markets are subject to relatively sudden changes in terms of new participants as well as new products. As a result, the CI likely to have the greatest bottom-line impact on your competitors tends be tactics-oriented CI.

Companies in a market that have moderate barriers to entry typically are characterized by lesser degrees of flexibility and innovation than are those in markets with low entry barriers. Because of these barriers, such markets are not subject to sudden changes in terms of new participants as well as new products. Instead, such changes are more gradual and incremental in nature. As a result, the CI likely to have the greatest bottom-line impact on your competitors tends to be strategy-oriented, target-oriented, and tactics-oriented CI.

Companies in a market that have high barriers to entry typically are characterized by significantly lesser degrees of flexibility and innovation than are those in markets with low entry barriers. Because of these high barriers, such markets are not subject to sudden changes in terms of new participants as well as new products. Instead, such changes are much more gradual and incremental in nature. Companies in such markets do not expect nor often engage in aggressive price competition. As a result, the CI likely to have the greatest bottom-line impact on your competitors tends to be strategy-oriented, target-oriented, and technology-oriented CI.

Barriers to Exit

Companies in a market that has low barriers to exit typically are characterized by higher degrees of flexibility and innovation than are those in other markets. Because of the absence or minimal nature of these barriers, such markets are subject to relatively sudden changes, in terms of participants leaving as well as products being taken off of the market. As a result, the CI likely to have the greatest bottom-line impact on your competitors is tactics-oriented CI.

Companies in a market that have moderate barriers to exit typically are characterized by lesser degrees of flexibility and innovation than are those in markets with low exit barriers. Because of these barriers, such markets are not subject to sudden changes in terms of withdrawing participants as well as withdrawn products. Instead, such changes are more gradual and incremental in nature. As a result, the CI likely to have the greatest bottom-line impact on your competitors tends to be strategy-oriented, target-oriented, and tactics-oriented CI.

Companies in a market that have high barriers to exit typically are characterized by significantly lesser degrees of flexibility and innovation than are those in markets with low exit barriers. Because of these high barriers, such markets are not subject to sudden changes in terms of departing participants as well as products taken off the market. Instead, such changes are much more gradual and incremental in nature. In addition, the high barriers to exit often make those currently in the market more likely to engage in oligopoly-type behaviors. As a result, the CI likely to have the greatest bottom-line impact on your competitors tends to be strategy-oriented and target-oriented.

PRODUCTS AND SERVICES PRODUCED

Here you are looking at the specific products (or services) that your firm provides, as well as those which your competitors provide, and which you all bring to the marketplace where you all are now competing. This is, in turn, divided into four separate areas:

1. Number of direct substitutes
2. Level of regulation of the product or service
3. Lead-time to market
4. Life cycle of the product or service

Number of Direct Substitutes

Companies whose products or services face very few direct substitutes are typically characterized by the fact that they face only a few directly competing organizations, that they are often protected from competition by possessing patents or proprietary processes, and that the marketplace may have significant barriers to entry, to exit, or both. Because of these factors, they tend to be involved in more head-to-head competition, with more emphasis on product differentiation than on price, and with some vulnerability to sudden impacts due to technological changes outside of their marketplace. As a result, the CI likely to have the greatest bottom-line impact on your competitors tends to be target-oriented and technology-oriented CI.

Companies whose products or services face a moderate number of direct substitutes are typically characterized by the fact that they face several directly competing organizations, that they are poorly protected from competition by patents or proprietary processes, and operate in a marketplace that may have only moderate barriers to entry, to exit, or both. Because of these factors, they tend to be involved in more head-to-head competition with competitors as well as product-line competition, with less emphasis on product differentiation and more on price, and with real vulnerability to sudden impacts due to technological changes outside of their marketplace. As a result, the CI likely to have the greatest bottom-line impact on your competitors tends to be target-oriented and tactics-oriented CI.

Companies whose products or services face a large number of direct substitutes are typically characterized by the fact that they face a large number of directly competing organizations, that they are rarely able to rely on any protection from competition by patents or proprietary processes, and operate in a marketplace that may have virtually no barriers to entry, to exit, or both. Because of these factors, they tend to be involved in head-to-head competition with competitors, product-to-product competition, and product-line competition, with very little emphasis on product differentiation and most of the focus on price competition, and with regular impacts due to technological changes outside of their marketplace. As a result, the CI likely to have the greatest bottom-line impact on your competitors tends to be tactics-oriented CI.

Level of Regulation of Product or Service

Companies that are operating in an environment with little or no regulation of the production and sale of their products and services are typically characterized by the fact that they face a market that changes rapidly. New products and services can be introduced with relative ease and frequency; existing products and services can be easily and quickly modified. In addition, often there are multiple, flexible channels of distribution, pricing decisions can be quickly transmitted to the marketplace, and competition is on the basis of perceived differences in product and service characteristics and consumer value. As a result, the CI likely to have the greatest bottom-line impact on your competitors tends to be tactics-oriented and technology-oriented CI.

Companies that are operating in an environment with moderate levels of regulation of the production and sale of their products and services are typically characterized by the fact that they face a market that changes less quickly. While new products and services can be introduced, their introduction is not as easy so they do not appear as often. Similarly, while existing products and services can be modified, that is not done often or quickly. In addition, often there are fewer, less flexible channels of distribution, so that pricing decisions are transmitted to the marketplace less quickly. Competition is typically conducted on the basis of differences in product and service characteristics as well as on brand-name recognition. As a result, the CI likely to have the greatest bottom-line impact on your competitors tends to be target-oriented and technology-oriented CI.

Companies that are operating in an environment with high levels of regulation of the production and sale of their products and services are typically characterized by the fact that they face a market that changes slowly. While new products and services can be introduced, their introduction is not easy so they do not appear with great frequency. Similarly, while existing products and services can be modified, that is not done very often or very quickly. In addition, often there are very few, relatively inflexible channels of distribution. Existing competitors are significantly more important than are potential entrants. Competition is typically conducted on the basis of differences in product and service characteristics as well as on brand-name recognition. As a result, the CI likely to have the greatest bottom-line impact on your competitors tends to be strategy-oriented and technology-oriented CI.

Lead-Time to Market

Companies facing an environment where their competitors, including you, have a long lead-time to market typically see the marketplace occupied by relatively few players. These players are concerned with long-range plans and positioning their product or service portfolios to assure a continuing and growing stream of revenues over time. In addition, such markets are often, but not always, dependant on using existing proprietary technology to make the production and/or distribution more efficient and thus squeeze out additional costs.

The reasons for the long lead-time to market may be related to factors such as the product or service, which is difficult to produce, to the regulatory environment; that is, one rigidly controlling the company and product or service, to low levels of technology, or to operating in a confined environment (limits on exit and/or entry), which permit those in the market to be able to survive with such long lead-times. As a result, the CI likely to have the greatest bottom-line impact on your competitors tends to be strategy-oriented, target-oriented, and technology-oriented CI.

Companies facing an environment where there is a moderate lead-time to market typically see the marketplace occupied by a number of players of varying sizes. These players are concerned with positioning their product or service portfolios to assure a continuing and growing stream of revenues over time, but also are alert to respond to shorter-term changes. In addition, such markets are often developing their own technology to make the production and/or distribution more efficient and thus squeeze out additional costs.

The reasons for the moderate lead-time to market may be related to factors such as the product, which is moderately difficult to produce, to the regulatory environment with limited controls over the company and product or service, or to operating in a market which has moderate limits on exit and/or entry, which all require that those in the market to be able to adapt to survive without long lead-times. As a result, the CI likely to have the greatest bottom-line impact on your competitors tends to be target-oriented, technology-oriented, and tactics-oriented CI.

Companies facing an environment where there is a very short lead-time to market typically see the marketplace occupied by a large number of players of widely varying sizes. These players are less concerned with positioning their product or service portfolios to assure a continuing and growing stream of revenues over time than to assure that they identify and then respond to very short-term changes. In addition, such markets are often using their own technology as well as technology from other sectors to continually force the production and/or distribution to be more efficient and thus squeeze out additional costs.

The reasons for the short lead-time to market may be related to factors such as the product (which is relatively easy to produce), to the regulatory environment (one with few controls over the company and product or service), or to operating in a market which has few, or even no, limits on exit and/or entry, which all require that those in the market be able to adapt quickly to survive. As a result, the CI likely to have the greatest bottom-line impact on your competitors tends to be tactics-oriented CI.

Product or Service Life Cycle

Companies, including yours, that offer a product or service that has a very short life cycle face a market that changes very rapidly, one where prices and costs can take sudden and significant turns. Typically the supporting investment is not relatively significant, but the role of both proprietary and nonproprietary technology is. In addition, the products and services usually cannot be protected by legal regimes such as patent and trademark filings. As a result, the CI likely to have the greatest bottom-line impact on your competitors tends to be tactics-oriented and technology-oriented CI.

Companies that offer a product or service that has a moderate life cycle face a market that changes quickly, but one where prices and costs rarely take sudden and significant turns. Typically the supporting investment is somewhat significant, as is the role of both proprietary and nonproprietary technology. In addition, the products and services usually cannot be completely protected by legal regimes such as patent and trademark filings. As a result, the CI likely to have the greatest bottom-line impact on your competitors tends to be tactics-oriented and technology-oriented CI.

Companies that offer a product or service that has a long life cycle face a market that rarely changes quickly, that is prices and costs rarely take sudden and significant turns. Typically the supporting investment is significant, but the role of both proprietary and nonproprietary technology is less so. In addition, the products and services usually receive significant protection from legal regimes such as patent and trademark filings. As a result, the CI likely to have the greatest bottom-line impact on your competitors tends to be strategy-oriented and technology-oriented CI.

COMPANIES THEY FACE

Here, you are trying to evaluate the firms with which you directly compete in your market or markets, including your own. If your market is one in which there are currently very few competitors, you may want to evaluate it including the first tier of potential entrants.

The way these firms, including your own, are managed and related to each other has a direct impact on which types of CI are best for your competitors. This, in turn, is divided into five separate areas:

1. Centrality of management
2. Level of cooperation
3. Degree of concentration

4. Level of knowledge intensity
5. Reliance on alliances

Centrality of Management

Here, you are taking into consideration how the firms your competitors face, including your own firm, tend to be managed, if there is an overall pattern. While each firm differs from every other firm, experience shows that firms in the same markets tend to have similar degrees of management centrality.

In markets where you or your competitors tend to be centrally managed, you should expect that response time to market and consumer changes will take longer. In addition, decisions, such as those listed previously, will be made only after taking into account the needs and demands of other, nonrelated operations, as well as the need to satisfy a variety of potentially conflicting constituencies, such as employees, unions, governments, owners, and investors. On the other hand, the centrally managed firm should be making its decisions taking into account performance and success as measured over a relatively long time frame, perhaps even several years. As a result, the CI likely to have the greatest bottom-line impact on your competitors tends to be strategy-oriented.

In markets where you or your competitors tend not to be centrally managed, but where some decisions are made at lower, more local levels, you should expect that response time to market and consumer changes will be faster. Decisions, such as those listed previously, will take into account the needs and demands of other, nonrelated operations, as well as the need to satisfy a variety of potentially conflicting constituencies, such as employees, unions, governments, owners, and investors, but will also reflect more immediately local pressures, such as those generated by consumers and local interests. The firm that is making its decisions on this mixed model should be making its decisions taking into account performance and success as measured over a moderately long time frame, running from six months up to two years. As a result, the CI likely to have the greatest bottom-line impact on your competitors tends to be target-oriented as well as strategy-oriented CI.

In markets where you or your competitors tend to be least centrally managed, you should expect that response time to market and consumer changes will be quite fast. Decisions, such as those listed previously, may occasionally take into account the needs and demands of other, nonrelated operations, as well as the need to satisfy a variety of potentially conflicting constituencies, such as employees, unions, governments, owners, and investors. However, they will largely reflect local pressures, such as those generated by consumers and local interests. The firm that is making its decisions on this decentralized model should be making its decisions taking into account performance and success as measured over a relatively short time frame, running from three months up to two years. As a result, the CI likely to have the greatest bottom-line impact on your competitors tends to be tactics-oriented and target-oriented CI.

Level of Cooperation

In markets where the firms are the most highly competitive, there is the lowest levels of cooperation. Such markets tend to be fast moving, and the actions of one firm cannot be a useful predictor of the actions of other firms. As a result, the CI likely to have the greatest bottom-line impact on your competitors tends to be tactics-oriented CI.

In markets where the firms appear to be more cooperative, the overall degree of competition is somewhat less. In these markets, for example, some firms may engage in joint support of research, or of research and development. Others may actually use competitors in other markets as a source of product or service for this market. Such markets tend to be a little slower moving. Given the linkages and other forms of cooperation, there will be situations when the actions of one firm can be a useful predictor of the actions of some other firms. As a result, the CI likely to have the greatest bottom-line impact on your competitors tends to be tactics-oriented and target-oriented CI.

In markets where the firms appear to be cooperating to the greatest degree, they can be said to be operating like a cartel. In those circumstances, the effective levels of competition are even lower. In these markets, for example, most of the firms may engage in joint support of research, or of research and development. Most of them will also be using competitors, in other markets, as a source of product or service for this market. Such markets tend to be much more slow moving. Given a high degree of cooperation, at least tacitly, it will be the usual situation that the actions of one firm can be a useful predictor of the actions of most of the other firms. As a result, the CI likely to have the greatest bottom-line impact on your competitors tends to be target-oriented and strategy-oriented CI.

Degree of Concentration

In a highly concentrated market, the largest firms tend to dominate the competitive landscape. In general, they tend to set and defend prices, and also indirectly control the prices of key inputs, simply because of their size. It is relatively difficult for firms outside of the largest top five to penetrate that tier or to significantly increase market share. Often such radical changes occur only because of major technological shifts.

The competition tends to be at two levels: among the very largest, and among the rest, with little real competition between either group. As a result, the CI likely to have the greatest bottom-line impact on your competitors tends to be target-oriented and strategy-oriented CI.

In a moderately concentrated market, the largest firms tend to heavily influence the competitive landscape. In general, while they tend to set and defend prices, they are vulnerable to competitive initiatives from smaller, more aggressive firms. Also, the very largest firms have less indirect control over the prices of key inputs. While it is difficult for firms outside of the largest top five to penetrate that tier, it is not impossible. The firms outside of the top five can significantly increase market share even without penetrating the top five. Such changes often occur because of major technological shifts, but the development of proprietary technology as well as the deployment in new ways of existing technology is also highly effective.

The competition tends to be among the very largest as a group, and among all firms in the market as well. As a result, the CI likely to have the greatest bottom-line impact on your competitors tends to be technology-oriented, target-oriented, as well as tactics-oriented and strategy-oriented CI.

In a slightly concentrated market, the largest firms tend to have no disproportionate influence on the competitive landscape. They are very vulnerable to competitive initiatives from smaller, more aggressive firms. Also, the very largest firms have very little indirect influence over the prices of key inputs because they do not have significant purchasing leverage. The firms outside of the top five can significantly increase market share and regularly penetrate the tier made up of those in the top five. Such changes can occur because of major technological shifts, through the development of proprietary technology, due to the deployment in new ways of existing technology as well as due to nontechnology drivers.

The competition tends to be among all firms in the market. As a result, the CI likely to have the greatest bottom-line impact on your competitors tends to be target-oriented and tactics-oriented CI.

Knowledge Intensity

In a marketplace where some companies, including your own, are very knowledge intensive, the technology base of the companies, as well as the technology that drives the underlying knowledge management processes, tends to be changing relatively rapidly. This allows the firms that are most knowledge intensive to gain, hold, and exploit competitive advantages, so long as they support that process. As a result, the CI likely to have the greatest bottom-line impact on your competitors tends to be technology-oriented CI.

In a marketplace where companies are only moderately knowledge intensive, the technology base of the companies, as well as the technology that drives the underlying knowledge management processes, tends to be relatively stable. While this allows the firms that are most knowledge intensive to gain, hold, and exploit competitive advantages, other firms can quickly catch up, or even overtake these firms. As a result, the CI likely to have the greatest bottom-line impact on your competitors tends to be technology-oriented CI.

In a marketplace where companies are not knowledge intensive, the technology base of the companies tends to be relatively stable. This provides no individual firm with any permanent competitive advantages, so all other firms can quickly catch up, or even overtake any other firms. As a result, the CI likely to have the greatest bottom-line impact on your competitors tends to be tactics-oriented CI.

Reliance on Alliances

The degree to which you and other firms in your market rely on alliances, whether for research, for manufacturing, for distribution, or for new initiatives, actually changes the nature and number of competitors.

A market in which you or competing firms are relying heavily on alliances is one where the actions of the firm with which you are competing are impacted by the terms of the alliance(s), the resource and time demands of the alliance(s). While absolute freedom of action may be curtailed, each firm moves, in a sense, with an impact including that of its allies. As a result, the CI likely to have the greatest bottom-line impact on your competitors tends to be target-oriented CI.

A market in which you or competing firms rely only moderately heavily on alliances is one where the actions of the firm with which you are competing are only indirectly impacted by the terms of the alliance(s), and the resource and time demands of the alliance(s). While absolute freedom of action may be slightly curtailed, each firm moves with its own impact slightly enhanced by that of its allies. Its own interests and a relatively independent strategy still largely drive its overall actions. As a result, the CI likely to have the greatest bottom-line impact on your competitors tends to be target-oriented and strategy-oriented CI.

A market in which you or competing firms never, or rarely, rely on alliances is one where the actions of the firm with which you are competing are only occasionally, and usually indirectly, impacted by the terms of the alliance(s), and the resource and time demands of the alliance(s). Its own interests and an independent strategy still largely drive its overall actions. As a result, the CI likely to have the greatest bottom-line impact on your competitors tends to be strategy-oriented CI.

PRODUCTION AND SUPPLY CHAIN ISSUES

As companies seek to control and to redefine their own supply chain as well as the way they produce their goods and services, they also change the nature of the firms that you compete with. This, in turn, is divided into four separate areas:

1. Level of technology
2. Number of suppliers
3. Degree of capital intensity
4. Level of innovation

Level of Technology

In a marketplace that is characterized by high levels of production and supply chain technology, we can expect to see competitors able to control and even reduce production and distribution costs on an ongoing basis, the rapid development and deployment of new products and services, as well as relatively low barrier to exit, but not to entry. As a result, the CI likely to have the greatest bottom-line impact on your competitors tends to be technology-oriented CI.

In a marketplace that is characterized by moderate levels of production and supply chain technology, we can expect to see competitors able to control or eliminate increases in production and distribution costs on a short-term basis, the moderately rapid development and deployment of new products and services, as well as relatively low barriers to exit as well as to entry. As a result, the CI likely to have the greatest bottom-line impact on your competitors tends to be technology-oriented CI.

In a marketplace that is characterized by low levels of production and supply chain technology, we can expect to see competitors unable to control or eliminate increases in production and distribution cost, the relatively low development and deployment of new products and services, as well as very low barriers to exit as well as to entry. As a result, the CI likely to have the greatest bottom-line impact on your competitors tends to be tactics-oriented CI.

Number of Suppliers

In a marketplace that is characterized by a relatively small number of suppliers of key ingredients, components or inputs, relative to the number of firms in the market, the suppliers have, potentially, great power.[1] In such markets, the reasons for the number of suppliers are often technological; that is, the technology used by the suppliers is proprietary, or capital—production of the inputs may be very capital intensive. As a result, the CI likely to have the greatest bottom-line impact on your competitors tends to be technology-oriented CI.

In a marketplace that is characterized by a balance between the relative number of suppliers of key ingredients, components or inputs, and the number of firms in the market, the suppliers have potentially much less power. In such markets, the reasons for the number of suppliers are often technological; that is, the technology used by the suppliers is proprietary, or capital—the production of the inputs may be very capital intensive. In addition, firms competing in this niche tend to have developed technological abilities allowing them to move freely from one supplier to another. As a result, the CI likely to have the greatest bottom-line impact on your competitors tends to be technology-oriented CI.

In a marketplace that is characterized by a relatively large number of suppliers of key ingredients, components or inputs, the suppliers have potentially very little power. Firms competing in this niche tend to have developed technological abilities allowing them to move freely from one supplier to another. Regardless of that, they are usually able to play one supplier against another to obtain better terms, including prices. As a result, the CI likely to have the greatest bottom-line impact on your competitors tends to be target-oriented CI.

Degree of Capital Intensity

Firms, including yours, that are very capital intensive tend to have a significant reliance on existing technology, which is imbedded in their investments. In addition, since large capital investments often take time to plan and then implement, these firms will tend to have a long-range view of the market. Their responses to market changes, such as price cuts, will reflect not only current marginal pricing of their output, but the firm's long-term vision of its place in the market, as well as the financial resources available to support the firm's ongoing operations. As a result, the CI likely to have the greatest bottom-line impact on your competitors tends to be strategy-oriented and technology-oriented CI.

Firms, including yours, that are only moderately capital intensive tend to have a less significant reliance on existing technology. That does not mean they do not rely on technology. For example, that technology may be imbedded in strategic partners or suppliers.

Since they are not making large capital investments, these firms will tend to have a short-range view of the market, unlike firms that are very capital intensive. Their responses to market changes, such as price cuts, will tend to reflect current marginal pricing of their output, as well as the financial resources available to support the firm's ongoing operations. As a result, the CI likely to have the greatest bottom-line impact on your competitors tends to be strategy-oriented and target-oriented CI.

Firms, including yours, that are not capital intensive tend to put no significant reliance on their own existing technology. That does not mean they do not rely on technology. For example, that technology may be imbedded in strategic partners or suppliers.

Since they are not making large capital investments, these firms will tend to have a much shorter-range view of the market than do firms that are moderately capital intensive. Their responses to market changes, such as price cuts, will tend to reflect current marginal pricing of their output, as well as the financial resources available to support the firm's ongoing operations. As a result, the CI likely to have the greatest bottom-line impact on your competitors tends to be target-oriented CI.

Level of Innovation

Firms, including yours, that have demonstrated low levels of innovation tend to view the immediate future of a market as an extension of the immediate past. In fact, their time horizon tends to be rather short-term in nature. They are also more often reactive rather than proactive, whether the issue is product improvement or workplace modification. As a result, the CI likely to have the greatest bottom-line impact on your competitors tends to be tactics-oriented CI.

Firms, including yours, that have demonstrated moderate levels of innovation tend to view the immediate future of a market as reflecting the immediate past, but expect that many elements of it can and will change. In fact, their time horizon tends to be medium-term in nature. They are also less reactive than they are proactive, whether the issue is launching a new product or changing their own communications infrastructure. As a result, the CI likely to have the greatest bottom-line impact on your competitors tends to be technology-oriented and target-oriented CI.

Firms, including yours, that have demonstrated high levels of innovation tend to view the immediate future of a market as only a step toward a longer-term, more radically changed future. In many areas, their time horizon tends to be long-term in nature. They are significantly more proactive than they are reactive, whether the issue is terminating a (profitable) line of business or entering into a new strategic partnership. As a result, the CI likely to have the greatest bottom-line impact on your competitors tends to be strategy-oriented and technology-oriented CI.

MARKETPLACE DYNAMICS

The way in which we look at marketplace dynamics is divided into three separate indicators:

1. The number of customers
2. The geographic scope of the market
3. The nature of competition

Number of Customers

In market niches where the firms compete for a relatively small number of customers, these customers individually generally exercise great power over the competitors, and thus should be tracked. Conversely, the change in the relationship between any given competitor and its customer, or customers, can change the dynamics in the marketplace very quickly. As a result, the CI likely to have the greatest bottom-line impact on your competitors tends to be target-oriented CI.

In market niches where the firms compete for a relatively moderate number of customers, these customers individually generally exercise only moderate power over the competitors, and thus should be tracked. But tracking them individually is not necessarily critical. And the change in the relationship between any given competitor and its customer, or customers, will only moderately impact the dynamics in the marketplace quickly. Rather, in such niches, the way in which each firm, and each customer, faces the marketplace and acts in the short-term has a greater impact. As a result, the CI likely to have the greatest bottom-line impact on your competitors tends to be target-oriented and tactics-oriented CI.

In market niches where the firms compete for a percentage from a mass of customers, these customers individually exercise no power over the competitors. Rather, in such niches, the way in which each firm faces the marketplace, acts in the short-term, and responds to the actions of the other firms has the greatest impact. As a result, the CI likely to have the greatest bottom-line impact on your competitors tends to be tactics-oriented CI.

Geographic Scope of the Market

By geographic scope, we mean the area that your competitors, as well as your own firm, serve. Geographic scope impacts performance issues such as logistics, economies of scale in the production of products, and ability to respond quickly to global versus local changes.

Those markets in which firms compete on a global basis tend to have some larger firms with a global portfolio of products or services. To support such scale, these firms typically must develop, or acquire, significant internal support for global operations, plan for, and respond to long-term trends as well as near-terms ones. As a result, the CI likely to have the greatest bottom-line impact on your competitors tends to be strategy-oriented CI.

Those markets in which firms compete on a regional basis, on the other hand, may have some larger firms, but may also see medium-size and small firms in the market. In addition, while the overall strategic goals of the very largest firms will impact the market, the goals and nature of the medium-size firms will also impact the present and future directions of the market. As a result, the CI likely to have the greatest bottom-line impact on your competitors tends to be strategy-oriented and target-oriented CI.

Those markets in which firms compete on a very local level tend to have only medium-size and small firms in the market. The ways in which these firms perceive the market and the ways in which they can and do respond to each other's activities has the greatest impact on the nature of competition in that market. As a result, the CI likely to have the greatest bottom-line impact on your competitors tends to be target-oriented CI.

Nature of Competition

In those markets where competition is based exclusively, or almost exclusively, on price, firms face what is also called a commodity situation. That is the product or service provided by any competitor that is regarded as a satisfactory substitute for that of another, so the sole, or at least dominating, determining factor is price. Commodity markets have historically included fungible products, such as wheat. Today, they can include services, such as group life insurance as well, where price is the single most critical element in making a sale. As a result, the CI likely to have the greatest bottom-line impact on your competitors tends to be tactics-oriented CI, focusing on price-related issues.

In those markets where competition is based on a combination of price and features, firms face a situation of mixed competition. That is, the product or service provided by any competitor is regarded as a satisfactory substitute for that of another competitor, the products or services vary in significant ways of importance to the customer. Thus the customers make decisions based on considering both cost and the benefit to them of features found in one product or service but not in another. It is often the case that the customer is faced with an offering that is actually a mixture of product and service, or where different competitors have adapted or incorporated differing technologies. As a result, the CI likely to have the greatest bottom-line impact on your competitors tends to be tactics-oriented and technology-oriented CI.

In those markets where competition is based largely or exclusively on features, firms face a competition based on customization, where the product is actually made in response to a customer order. That is, the products or services vary in significant ways, ways of importance to the customer. Thus the customers make decisions primarily based on the benefit to them of features found in one product or service, but not in another. Today, this can include products, such as a portrait painted for an anniversary, as well as services, such as writing a computer program. As a result, the CI likely to have the greatest bottom-line impact on your competitors tends to be technology-oriented CI.

SCORING

To determine what type(s) of CI your competitors are or at least should be collecting, use the prior materials to analyze the market or markets they, not you, face. One easy approach is to score your responses. That is, you record your responses to each of these and then total them up.

If your competitors are in several markets, score each of them separately, if you think that they intend to make intelligence gathering available to each separate from the other. If they do not appear to intend to do that, then score the market as it appears to them above the individual market level.

Try using this grid to track their overall score. For each area, check the type or types of CI that are most likely to be collected by your competitors, based on the analysis we have just given you.

Most Likely CI Orientation

Competitive Environment	Strategy	Target	Tactics	Technology
Environment				
Company Regulation	×	×	×	×
Entry Barriers	×	×	×	×
Exit Barriers	×	×	×	
Products and Services				
Substitutes		×	×	×
Regulation	×	×	×	×
Lead-Time	×	×	×	×
Life Cycle	×		×	×
Companies				
Centrality of Management	×	×	×	
Cooperation	×	×	×	
Concentration	×	×	×	×
Knowledge Intensity			×	×
Alliances	×	×		
Production and Supply Chain				
Technology Level			×	×
Number of Suppliers			×	×
Capital Intensity	×	×		×
Innovation	×	×	×	×
Marketplace				
Customers		×	×	
Geographic Scope	×	×		
Type of Competition			×	×

Number of Hits

Strategy-Oriented	_____
Target-Oriented	_____
Tactics-Oriented	_____
Technology-Oriented	_____

Experience shows that if you have indicated one or more types of CI seven times or more, that type of CI is an area in which you should expect your competitors to concentrate.

DO REGULAR AND FORWARD-LOOKING REVIEWS

This analysis deals with the environment, products, services, companies, production, supply, and marketplace as they are now. However, it would be a wise firm that would redo this analysis, seeking to evaluate how each of these would look to competitors in the near term, that is one to three years, and in the long-term, that is two to five years or more. Such an analysis should point your defensive CI program in the directions where your competitors' efforts will gradually move from the present context.

In addition, if your analysis indicates that one or more of these elements are in the process of changing significantly, review your competitors' intelligence needs assessment too. If you think you know when that change will occur, you can be prepared to modify your own defensive CI process and protect the targets that your competitors will be focusing on in the future.

NOTE

1. See Deborah C. Sawyer, "Defining Your Competition: Side Swiped: Supply-Side Competitive Threats," *Competitive Intelligence Magazine* 3, 4 (October–December 2000): 50–51.

─────────────────────────13

What Sources of Data on Your Company Should You First Include in Your Defensive Program?

There are at least two ways to try to determine what kinds of intelligence your competitors are probably collecting on you:

1. Use your own CI program as a basis.
2. Use the analytical framework we have developed as a basis.

From there, you should review these channels to see what they provide on your firm.

YOUR OWN CI PROGRAM

Go to those currently conducting CI on your competitors. From them, get the following information:

- What kinds of competitive intelligence are they currently developing on your competitors?
- What sources of data do they look to in developing that intelligence?
- How effective are these sources in providing the raw data needed?

From this you will then have a first look at where you should be looking to protect your own firm. That is, you should be looking at these same data sources to determine what data are being made available on your firm. Then, you will apply the basic precepts of defensive CI to narrow that task.

ANALYTICAL FRAMEWORK

Take the analysis we have just completed, determine the key types of CI that your competitors are, or at least should be, collecting on you. Then, review Figure 13.1 to determine the channels of data collection that experience shows are best mined for raw data for each type of CI.

WHAT KINDS OF DATA SHOULD YOU BE PROTECTING?

How can you identify the data you need to protect? There are several key elements here:

- Learn what your competitors know about you
- Do a reverse intelligence audit
- Identify what information is really critical

What Do Your Competitors Know about You?

If you were to map outward information flow from your company, you would realize that there are dozens of places to find critical information about you. You have affirmatively released it with the expectation that it would be used for one purpose. Your competitors will collect it for another purpose. In general, assume that if it's been made public, your competitors know it.

How can you find out what your competitors already know about you? Try a reverse intelligence audit. That is, spend a little time, or even hire someone from outside, to develop a profile of your firm. It does not need to be very detailed. Determine what areas are competitively sensitive to you, and then focus on them. The results will probably be very surprising.

What Data Are Really Critical?

What are the steps in identifying the data you should be protecting? First we need to define competitively sensitive information. This is information that is difficult for the competition to obtain without your tacit or active cooperation. It is almost always future oriented, pertaining to intentions, goals, and targets. Today is already history; tomorrow is where you make money in competition.

What do you need to protect? There are several criteria and procedures you can use to identify these kinds of data. The more criteria a particular kind of data meets, the greater the need to protect it;

Figure 13.1
Orientation of CI

Typical Sources of Raw Data	*Strategy*	*Target*	*Tactics*	*Technology*
Secondary				
Trade Journals	♦	♦	♦	♦
Trade associations and chambers of commerce	♦	♦		
Government reports	♦	♦	♦	♦
Government records and files	♦	♦		
Security analyst reports	♦	♦	♦	
Academic case studies	♦			
Research centers	♦	♦		♦
Business information services		♦	♦	
Advertisements		♦	♦	♦
Want ads		♦	♦	♦
Local newspapers and magazines	♦	♦	♦	
Competitive reports	♦	♦	♦	
Competitor news releases	♦	♦	♦	♦
Competitor home page	♦	♦	♦	♦
Directories and reference aids	♦			♦
Technical publications			♦	♦
Catalogs		♦	♦	
General news publications	♦	♦	♦	
Books	♦	♦		♦
Internet aggregators and portals		♦	♦	♦
Primary				
Your own employees	♦	♦	♦	♦
Industry experts	♦	♦	♦	♦
Sales representatives		♦	♦	
Customers		♦	♦	
Security analysts	♦	♦	♦	
Competitors (contacted directly)	♦	♦	♦	
Suppliers	♦	♦	♦	♦
Product and service purchases			♦	♦
Focus groups			♦	
Questionnaires and surveys		♦		
Trade shows		♦	♦	♦
Business conferences	♦	♦		♦
Technical and professional meetings				♦
Facility tours		♦	♦	♦

Figure 13.1 (*continued*)

Retailers and distributors	◆	◆	◆	
Banks	◆	◆		
Advertising agencies	◆	◆	◆	
TV, radio programs, and interviews	◆	◆	◆	◆
Speeches	◆	◆	◆	◆
Internet chat groups		◆	◆	

meeting any one of them should trigger cloaking. Meeting two or three signals a more urgent need for action.

Identifying What to Protect

These are the kinds of information you should be protecting:

- The information that is most difficult for your competitor to obtain or deduce without your tacit or active cooperation. This includes your strategic intentions, tactical goals, and sales by segment or smaller unit.
- Data that would be critical to completing an in-depth profile of your company. For example, if your firm is increasing its market share, there is no reason to tell your competitors, through the press, exactly how fast you are growing. A phrase like "strong growth" is enough to tell people you're doing well without giving away too much.
- Information that is already partially protected. For example, if you have a trade secret, protect information that could allow someone to reverse engineer it.
- Any information that is critical to the core of your business or even its survival.

To identify the information you need to protect, take the following steps:

- Evaluate your information's half-life—the period of time after which it loses half or more of its value. There is no need to protect it for longer than that. Typically the more microlevel and the more future oriented the information, the shorter the half-life.
- Review the CI you are already getting on your competition. What pieces of data are really critical to you when you're trying to analyze their activities? Which data have been very difficult or impossible for you to get? Protect the equivalent data from your competitors.
- Finally, identify the analytical techniques that are likely to be used in your industry. Protect the one or two key bits of information that are vital to completing the analysis.

WHAT TO PROTECT: CAVEATS

Experience shows that there are, and should be, limits on what data you should protect:

- First, accept that *you can't protect everything and you can't stop your competitors from finding out about you.* Trying to protect everything will impair your ability to compete.

- Second, accept that *you can't review everything that goes out the door.* This would be an endless task. You would create a repressive environment, curtail free communication by your employees, and seriously impair your ability to respond quickly in the marketplace or to any crisis.

- Third, *do not waste time cloaking what competitors probably already know.* Assume that your competitors will have at least the intelligence you found in your reverse audit. They have also been doing it longer, and will probably have used sources you did not, so their knowledge will go beyond what your audit revealed.

- Fourth, *if you have other options for protecting critical information, use them* first. Do not rely on cloaking alone. Use a dedicated program to protect trade secrets. Patent, copyright, trademark, and contract protections should also be used. Also, keep in mind that corporate security exists to protect your assets from intrusions, theft, and computer breakins. It does not make sense to make your cloaking system provide that type of protection as well.

14

*Choosing the Right Measurements
for the Defensive CI
Program You Are Managing*

As with the previous chapter, we are applying the basic methodology set out in Part II. However, given the nature of its mission, defensive intelligence is much more difficult to measure than active CI.

- First, the role of the CI professional in defensive CI is one of education and awareness—the job is to teach others to be more careful. So, for the CI professional, it is an indirect process at best.
- Second, the more effective a defensive CI program becomes, the less its competitors can find out competitively sensitive data. So certain knowledge of the effectiveness of a defensive CI program lies outside of the universe that your can survey.
- Third, defensive CI often deals with avoiding the negative—a lost opportunity, lost initiative, and so forth. So those seeking to measure defensive CI may have the unenviable task of quantifying something that did not happen.
- Fourth, defensive CI does not actually use the variety of data source options discussed earlier, and the manner in which it can deliver its message is, as noted in Chapter 10, significantly more limited than the spectrum of options available to active CI professionals.

As a result, of the wide variety of options available for measuring the bottom line impact of active CI of all types, only a limited number are at all useful in working with defensive CI. Figure 14.1 summarizes your options.

Figure 14.1
Potential Defensive CI Metrics

Assignments and Projects	
Meeting objectives	●
Number completed	●
Number completed on time	●
Number requested	●
Number requested - increase by end-users	●
Number of follow-up assignments	□
Number of projects assisted	□
Number of suggestions submitted	□
Budget	
Comparative costs savings	
compared with cost of outsider	●
compared with cost of untrained person	□
Meeting project or function budget constraints	□
Efficiency	
Accuracy of analysis	□
Data quality	□
First time results (no reworking)	□
Meeting project time line	□
Time for research versus time for response	□
End-Users	
Creating compelling reasons to use CI	●
Effectiveness of implementation of findings	□
Meeting needs	●
Number of referrals	□

Figure 14.1 (*continued*)

Number served	●
Feedback	
Written	●
Oral	●
Financial	
Cost avoidance	▫
Cost savings	▫
Goals met	▫
Linking CI to specific investments	▫
Linking CI to investment enhancement	▫
Linking CI to specific savings from unneeded investments	▫
Revenue enhancement	▫
Value creation	▫
Internal Relationships	
Building strong with end-users	●
Formulating relevant strategy or tactics	▫
Quality of relationships with end-users	●
Quality of participation on cross-functional teams	●
New Products and Services	
Number developed due to use of CI	▫
Cost savings/avoidance in development from use of CI	▫
Performance	
Growth, profitable for the unit or firm	●
Impact on strategic direction of unit or firm	▫
Market share gains for unit or firm	●

Figure 14.1 (*continued*)

Reports and Presentations	
Number	□
Number of follow-ups	□
Production of actionable CI	□
Sales effectiveness	
Customer satisfaction	□
Linking to specific customer wins	□
Number of customers retained	□
Number of leads generated	□
Repeat business	□
Improvement in win-loss ratio	□
Surveys	
Written	●
Oral	●
Time	
Gained by CI input	□
Projects delivered on time	□
Saved by CI input	□

Key: Usually relevant   ●

Rarely relevant   □

Glossary

The proper use of terms in CI is an area where CI professionals must now exercise a great deal of care. Why is that the case? Due to unbalanced publicity about the excesses of a few self-described CI "outlaws," CI's image in some business quarters has regressed to the point where some in the business community erroneously equate CI with spying. As a result, it is our belief that all CI professionals must now avoid leaving even the scantest trace that someone can point to that says we think of ourselves as spies and of CI as espionage.

What do we mean by this? We, and others, have for some time been concerned about the direct transfer of military and political terms into CI terms and concepts.[1] That is not the same as rejecting some of the lessons that can be learned from the past and current successes and failures of government intelligence.[2]

For example, we have seen the use of the term "counterintelligence" to describe defensive activities by business firms. But counterintelligence, when used as a military term, actually refers to a process which includes within it active measures to neutralize intelligence collection efforts, as well as hostile efforts toward terrorism and sabotage.[3] Yet these are clearly not efforts that fall within the scope of CI. Why not just use a term like defensive CI?

A similar situation exists with the term "disinformation," a concept that has been transferred bodily from the national intelligence community to the private sector.[4] However, its government roots include activities such as forgery.[5]

Other terms that are in use do not include within them such unfortunate connotations. But there are other terms, again transferred from the military and law enforcement intelligence communities that carry with them, to say the least, undesirable undertones. For example, take the term "surveillance." Don't you feel more comfortable describing your activities watching a competitor at a trade show as "observation?" And using the term "operatives" smacks of law enforcement or government intelligence. In addition, its use unnecessarily blurs the degree of employment relationship. Is an operative on a CI assignment a subcontractor, an employee, what?

An even more troubling one is the use of terms like "war room" and "war college" to describe operational centers established to collect and display CI for use in developing marketing campaigns and corporate strategy. But businesses are not at war. They are competing. The ultimate personal penalty for a failed strategy is not death or enslavement. It is bankruptcy or loss of a job.

"For a short time, the term 'competitive information and analysis' was used. It fell into disuse due to its acronym—CIA."[6]

While CI and related disciplines have and will continue to learn much from the work of the military and civilian intelligence services around the world, all too often CI professionals, most of whom do not come from those backgrounds, have become overwhelmed with terms originating in that world.[7]

While these terms may sometimes be the best we have, we must always keep in mind, and reiterate, the clear difference between the way these terms are understood in CI, just as there is a very clear difference between business competition and national conflicts. In one case, we win or lose a market; in the other we are dealing with national and personal survival. While government-sanctioned economic espionage directed at the private sector seems to blur this separation, for most of our readers there is still a clear demarcation. The Economic Espionage Act of 1996 draws a clear line that CI professionals respect.

It is with an eye to maintaining and even enhancing that demarcation that we have always tried to limit the excessive use of such terms. And fortunately we are not alone. A former president of SCIP has cautioned CI professionals against inappropriate skill transfers from government intelligence. These include

- Recruitment and control, motivated by financial regard, revenge, hatred or excitement
- Use of covers (false identification)
- Technical surveillance [i.e., wiretapping]
- 'Active' measures [i.e., assault and assassination]
- Destabilization [i.e., undermining the ability of an organization to manage or govern]."[8]

One way to even prevent thinking about such inappropriate action is to control what we call what we do. That is more important than ever. For that reason, we now suggest that CI professionals completely eliminate the warfare analogies and use others, perhaps from sports, nature, or disciplines such as anthropology.[9] While the military and war analogies are superficially attractive, they are not only carrying unnecessary baggage for CI, they are also intellectually flawed.

The goal of being competitive is much closer to winning (sports) or growing and surviving (nature) than it is to killing people and breaking things (military) or war through other means (diplomacy).

DEFINITIONS

Active CI: Competitive intelligence operated by and for the benefit of a particular unit, firm, or organization.

Analysis: In competitive intelligence, evaluating and interpreting the facts and raw data to provide finished intelligence to support effective decision making.

APQC: American Productivity and Quality Center.

Benchmarking: Analyzing what you do, quantifying it, and then finding ways that other firms do it better, or better and differently, or not at all. Then, you adapt (not adopt) what you have learned to your own firm.

Benchmarks: Refers to processes and results that represent the best practices and performance for similar activities, inside or outside of an organization's industry.

Business Intelligence (BI): An old term for CI. Also used in Knowledge Management (KM) to describe the product of KM activities.

CI Cycle: The process of establishing CI needs, collecting raw data, processing it into finished CI, distributing it to the end-users who then use it. It also includes feedback among the various phases.

Competitive Intelligence (CI): Competitive intelligence consists of two overall activities. First is the use of public sources to develop data (raw facts) on competition, competitors, and the market environment. Second is the transformation, by analysis, of those data into information (usable results).

Competitive Scenario: An analysis of what one or more competitors can be expected to do in response to changes in market and other conditions affecting their activities. The analysis is based on a profile of the competitor, including estimations of its intentions and capabilities, stemming from a study of its past actions, and of the perceptions, style, and behavior of its present and future management. Each competitor's actions are studied against the same set of expected market conditions and changes.

Competitive Technical Intelligence (CTI): Those intelligence activities that allow a firm to respond to threats from and/or to identify and exploit opportunities resulting from technical and scientific change.

Corporate Security: A process that is aimed primarily at protecting and preserving all corporate assets, both tangible and intangible. Typically it operates to set up protections (such as of databases or automobiles) to determine potential threats and to provide a barrier. In some corporate security operations, a special focus is on the identification and protection of trade secrets. This is also one of the units (IT being the other) involved with hacking.

Counterintelligence: A military term, the process of identifying and then foiling intelligence activities. It can involve measures such as military assaults on opposing spies. In the business context, it should be called defensive CI, as it refers to intelligence activities aimed at your firm.

Crisis Management Program (CMP): A formal method of developing, updating, and implementing crisis management plans.

Current Data: Facts that deal with a relatively short period of time, centered on the present. Examples of this might be a competitor's sales figures for the past three-month period.

Customer: A person or organization, internal or external, which receives or uses outputs from one group or division. These outputs may be products, services, or information.

Cycle Time: The time required to fulfill commitments or to complete tasks.

Data: Raw, unevaluated material. Data may be numeric or textual. Data are the ultimate source of information, but becomes usable information only after they have been processed and analyzed. See also Current Data, Historic Data, Macrolevel Data, and Microlevel Data.

Data Mining: The process of sifting through massive amounts of data (in computer-readable form) to reveal intelligence, hidden trends, and relationships between customers and products.

Data Warehousing: The ability to store large amounts of data by specific categories, so that it can easily be retrieved, interpreted, and sorted (Data Mining) to provide useful information, typically about customers and products.

Defensive Competitive Intelligence (DI): The process of monitoring and analyzing your own business's activities as your competitors and other outsiders see them. You can then protect your firm's competitively sensitive information from being accessible to your competitors.

Disinformation: Incomplete or inaccurate information designed to mislead others about your intentions or abilities. When used in the arena of international politics, espionage, or intelligence, the term also means the deliberate production and dissemination of falsehoods, fabrications, and forgeries aimed at misleading an opponent or those supporting an opponent.

Economic Espionage Act of 1996 (EEA): A U.S. (federal) criminal statute, P.L. 104-294 of October 11, 1996, which criminalizes, at the federal level, the misappropriation of trade secrets. It provides additional penalties if such misappropriation is conducted by foreign entities.

End-Users: Persons or organizations that request and use information obtained from an on-line search or other source of CI.

Espionage: Either the collection of information by illegal means or the illegal collection of information. If the information has been collected from a government, this is a serious crime, such as treason. If it is from a business, it may be a theft offense.

Fraud: An act that involves distributing erroneous or false information with intent to mislead or to take advantage of someone relying on that information.

Gaming: An exercise that has people acting either as themselves or playing roles in an environment that can be real or simulated. Games can be repeated, but cannot be replicated, as is the case with simulations and models.

Historic Data: Data that cover a long period of time. They are designed to show long-term trends, such as gross sales in an industry over a five-year period. These may include projections made covering a long period of time.

IBC: International Benchmarking Clearinghouse, a division of APQC.

Inductive Methods: Problem-solving methods that involve reasoning from particular facts or individual cases to a general conclusion.

Information: The material resulting from analyzing and evaluating raw data, reflecting both data and judgments. Information is an input to a finished CI evaluation.

Intelligence: Knowledge achieved by a logical analysis and integration of available information data on competitors or the competitive environment.

Intranet: An internal or limited-access Internet.

IT: Information technology.

Key Intelligence Questions (KIQ): These are developed from KITs when the KITs are very broad.

Key Intelligence Topics (KIT): A process, adapted from the government process model of National Intelligence Topics, to identify and then prioritize senior management's key intelligence needs.

Knowledge Management (KM): The combination of Data Warehousing and Data Mining, aimed at exploiting all data in a company's possession.

Macrolevel Data: Data of a high level of aggregation, such as the size of a particular market or the overall rate of growth of the nation's economy.

Market Intelligence: Intelligence developed on the very current activities in the marketplace.

Metrics: Measurements.

Microlevel Data: Data of a low level of aggregation or even unaggregated data. These might be data, for example, on a competing company or division's sales of a particular product line.

Modeling: Representing an entity, such as a competitor, or a situation, such as a particular market's dynamics, in such a way that it has the relevant features or properties of the original. Usually used to help predict future actions.

Profiling: Process of developing personality and psychological profiles of key individuals to help an analyst predict future behavior.

Qualitative: In measures, it refers to evaluating the basic nature or attributes of a process or event.

Quantitative: In measures, it refers to the accurate measurement of the components or consequences of a process or event.

Reverse Engineering: This involves acquiring (usually buying) and then dismantling a product to identify how it was designed and constructed. This process enables an investigator to estimate costs and evaluate the quality of the product. In the case of nonpatentable processes and devices, it can also provide direct information on how to produce a competitive, compatible, or substitute product.

ROCE: Return on capital expenditures.

ROI: Return on investment.

Scenarios: See Competitive Scenarios.

SCIP: Society of Competitive Intelligence Professionals.

Shadowing: A process of closely following a defined activity of a competitor. It has four differing aspects: shadowing of specific markets; developing a shadow market plan; shadow planning, as an ongoing process; and shadow benchmarking.

Simulation: Representing a system or an organism, such as a business firm, by use of another system or model that is designed to have a relevant behavioral similarity to the original. Very often this involves a computerized model. Often used to generate complex financial responses to changes in underlying forces.

Strategic Business Unit (SBU): One of several operating entities making up an enterprise.

Strategic Intelligence: Competitive intelligence provided in support of strategic, as distinguished from tactical, decision making.

Supplier: A company or person that provides inputs to tasks or jobs, whether inside or outside of the company.

Target: A specific competitor, or one or more of its facilities, SBUs, or other units.

Total Quality Management (TQM): A process of organizing and managing all operations to stress the delivery of products and services of the highest quality to consumers.

Trade Secret Protection: This is the use of contracts, civil litigation, and even criminal prosecution, under both state and federal law, to prevent trade secrets from being used by competitors. Trade secrets are a very narrowly defined type of information. For example, trade secret protection is available only if the firm treats specific information differently from all other information, and may be lost if the information becomes public, even if by accident.

Uniform Trade Secrets Act (UTSA): A model law, drafted by the National Conference of Commissioners on Uniform State Laws, dealing with the civil penalties for misappropriation of trade secrets. Last amended in 1985, it has been passed, in one form or another, in forty-one states.

War Game: A simulated military operation using gaming techniques. See Gaming.

NOTES

1. McGonagle and Vella, *Protecting Your Company*, viii–ix; and John J. McGonagle and Carolyn M. Vella, "Selling CI: Negatives Are Not Positive," *Competitive Intelligence Magazine* 4, 5 (September–October 2001): 37–38. See also Constance Thomas Ward, "Real Life CI: CI-AOK; But CIA—No Way," *Competitive Intelligence Magazine* 2, 3 (July–September 1999): 35.

2. See, for example, Stanley A. Feder, "Overcoming 'Mindsets': What Corporations Can Learn from Government Intelligence Failures," *Competitive Intelligence Review* 11, 3 (Third Quarter 2000): 28–36.

3. See, for example, U.S. Marine Corps, *Counterintelligence*, FMFM 2–4, December 3, 1983.

4. See, for example, Paul Dishman, "Red Herrings and Disinformation: A Strategic Component of Counterintelligence," *Competitive Intelligence Magazine* 2, 4 (October–December 1999): 11–14.

5. See U.S. Department of State, *Active Measures: A Report on the Substance and Process of Anti–U.S. Disinformation and Propaganda Campaigns* (Washington, D.C.: U.S. Department of State, 1986).

6. McGonagle and Vella, *A New Archetype*, 40.

7. See, for example, an analysis of this in Scott Savitz, "Wolf, Eagle, and Bear: CI Lessons from the Cold War," *Competitive Intelligence Review* 10, 3 (Third Quarter 1999): 79–83.

8. Stephen H. Miller, "Special Report: Learning from the Government Intelligence Community," *Competitive Intelligence Magazine* 4, 4 (July–August 2001): 9, 10.

9. On the use of anthropological terms, see Jonathan Calof, "Opportunity Intelligence: The Missing CI Tribe," *Competitive Intelligence Magazine* 3, 3 (July–September 2000): 35–37.

Bibliography

BOOKS AND REPORTS

APQC International Benchmarking Clearinghouse. *Competitive and Business Intelligence: Leveraging Information for Action*. Houston, Tex.: American Productivity & Quality Center, 1997.

APQC International Benchmarking Clearinghouse. *Developing a Successful Competitive Intelligence Program: Enabling Action, Realizing Results*. Houston, Tex.: American Productivity & Quality Center, 2000.

APQC International Benchmarking Clearinghouse. *Managing Competitive Intelligence Knowledge in a Global Economy*. Houston, Tex.: American Productivity & Quality Center, 1998.

APQC International Benchmarking Clearinghouse. *Strategic and Tactical Competitive Intelligence for Sales and Marketing*. Houston, Tex.: American Productivity & Quality Center, 1999.

APQC International Benchmarking Clearinghouse. *Using Science and Technology Intelligence to Drive Business Results*. Houston, Tex.: American Productivity & Quality Center, 2001.

Baldrige National Quality Program. *2001 Criteria for Performance Excellence*. Milwaukee, Wisc.: American Society for Quality, 2000.

Barndt, Walter D., Jr. *User-Directed Competitive Intelligence: Closing the Gap Between Supply and Demand*. Westport, Conn.: Quorum Books, 1994.

Davis, Julie L., and Suzanne S. Harrison. *Edison in the Boardroom*. New York: John Wiley & Sons, 2001.

Fahey, Liam. *Competitors: Outwitting, Outmaneuvering, and Outperforming*. New York: John Wiley & Sons, 1999.

Fleisher, Craig S., and David L. Blenkhorn, eds. *Managing Frontiers in Competitive Intelligence*. Westport, Conn.: Quorum Books, 2001.

Geisler, Eliezer. *The Metrics of Science and Technology.* Westport, Conn.: Quorum Books, 2000.

Gilad, Ben, and Jan P. Herring, eds. *Advances in Applied Business Strategy, Supplement 2A.* Greenwich, Conn.: JAI Press, 1996.

Gilad, Ben, and Jan P. Herring, eds. *Advances in Applied Business Strategy, Supplement 2B.* Greenwich, Conn.: JAI Press, 1996.

Godson, Roy, ed. *Intelligence Requirements for the 1980's: Analysis and Estimates.* Washington, D.C.: National Strategy Information Center, 1986.

Graef, Jean L. *Executive Briefing: CFO's Guide to Intellectual Capital.* Montague, Mass.: Limited Edition Publishing, 1997.

Herring, Jan P. *Measuring the Effectiveness of Competitive Intelligence— Assessing & Communicating CI's Value to Your Organization.* Alexandria, Va.: Society of Competitive Intelligence Professionals, 1996.

Jaworski, Bernard, and Liang Chee Wee. *Competitive Intelligence: Creating Value for the Organization—Final Report on SCIP Sponsored Research.* Vienna, Va.: Society of Competitive Intelligence Professionals, 1993.

Kent Ridge Digital Labs. *Charting Your Course in the Digital Age—An IT Perspective.* Singapore: Kent Ridge Digital Labs, 1999.

McGonagle, John J., and Carolyn M. Vella. *How to Use a Consultant in Your Company: A Managers' and Executives' Guide.* New York: John Wiley & Sons, 2001.

McGonagle, John J., and Carolyn M. Vella. *The Internet Age of Competitive Intelligence.* Westport, Conn.: Quorum Books, 1999.

McGonagle, John J., and Carolyn M. Vella. *A New Archetype of Competitive Intelligence.* Westport, Conn.: Quorum Books, 1998.

McGonagle, John J., and Carolyn M. Vella. *Outsmarting the Competition: Practical Approaches to Finding and Using Competitive Information.* Naperville, Ill.: Sourcebooks, 1990.

Meyer, Herbert E. *Real World Intelligence.* Friday Harbor, Wash.: Storm King Press, 1991.

Miller, Jerry, and the Business Intelligence Braintrust. *Millennium Intelligence: Understanding and Conducting Competitive Intelligence in the Digital Age.* Medford, N.J.: CyberAge Books, 2000.

Nolan, John. *Confidential: Uncover Your Competitors' Top Business Secrets Legally and Quickly—and Protect Your Own.* New York: HarperBusiness, 1999.

Porter, Michael E. *Competitive Advantage: Creating and Sustaining Superior Performance.* New York: The Free Press, 1985.

Porter, Michael E. *Competitive Strategy: Techniques for Analyzing Industries and Competitors.* New York: The Free Press, 1980.

Prescott, John E., ed. *Advances in Competitive Intelligence.* Vienna, Va.: Society of Competitive Intelligence Professionals, 1989.

Prescott, John E., and Stephen H. Miller, eds. *Proven Strategies in Competitive Intelligence: Lessons from the Trenches.* New York: John Wiley & Sons, 2001.

Society of Competitive Intelligence Professionals. *CI Team Excellence Award: 2001 SCIP World-Class Competitive Intelligence Award—Application and Instruction Booklet.* Alexandria, Va.: Society of Competitive Intelligence Professionals, 2000.

Society of Competitive Intelligence Professionals. *2000/'01 Competitive Intelligence Professionals Salary Survey Report and Reference Guide on Analyst Job Descriptions.* Alexandria, Va.: Society of Competitive Intelligence Professionals, 2001.

Telofski, Richard. *Dangerous Competition: Critical Issues in eCompetitive Intelligence Analysis.* New York: Writers Club Press, 2001.

Tyson, Kirk W. M. *Business Intelligence: Putting It All Together.* Lombard, Ill.: Leading Edge Publications, 1986.

Vella, Carolyn M., and John J. McGonagle. *Improved Business Planning Using Competitive Intelligence.* Westport, Conn.: Quorum Books, 1988.

Vibert, Conor. *Web-Based Analysis for Competitive Intelligence.* Westport, Conn.: Quorum Books, 2000.

Walle, Alf H., III. *Qualitative Research in Intelligence and Marketing: The New Strategic Convergence.* Westport, Conn.: Quorum Books, 2001.

ARTICLES AND PRESENTATIONS

Barndt, Walter D., Jr. "New to Competitive Intelligence? 10 Tips for Survival and Success." *Competitive Intelligence Magazine* 2, 3 (July–September 1999): 23–24.

Barron, Anne. "Three Easy Steps for Gathering Intelligence at Trade Shows." *Competitive Intelligence Magazine* 3, 3 (July–September 2000): 19–21.

Belkine, Michael, ed. "Corporate CI—Tactical or Strategic?" *Competitive Intelligence Magazine* 4, 5 (September–October 2001): 27–31.

"Beware Rival's Web Subterfuge." *Competitive Intelligence Magazine* 3, 1 (January–March 2000): 8.

Breacher, Sarah. "Tools for Predicting Alternative Futures." *Competitive Intelligence Magazine* 2, 3 (July–September 1999): 19–22.

Brenner, Merrill S. "Technology Intelligence and Technology Scouting." *Competitive Intelligence Review* 7, 3 (Fall 1996): 20–27.

Budd, Tim. "Competitive Technical Intelligence at Applied Biosystems: Attracting, Monitoring, and Exploiting Technology-Based Opportunities." *Competitive Intelligence Review* 11, 4 (Fourth Quarter 2000): 5–11.

Cain, John. "Supporting Field Force Sales with Competitive Intelligence." *Competitive Intelligence Magazine* 1, 1 (April–June 1998): 16–18.

Calof, Jonathan. "Opportunity Intelligence: The Missing CI Tribe." *Competitive Intelligence Magazine* 3, 3 (July–September 2000): 35–37.

Calof, Jonathan, and Bill Skinner. "Government's Role in Competitive Intelligence: What's Happening in Canada?" *Competitive Intelligence Magazine* 2, 2 (April–June 1999): 20–23.

Cappel, James J., and Jeffrey P. Boone. "A Look at the Link between Competitive Intelligence and Performance." *Competitive Intelligence Review* 6, 2 (Summer 1995): 15–23.

Carr, Laurence A. "Front-Line CI: Actionable Intelligence for the Business Infantry." *Competitive Intelligence Magazine* 4, 2 (March–April 2001): 11–15.

"CI at Avnet: A Bottom-Line Impact." *Competitive Intelligence Magazine* 3, 3 (July–September 2000): 5–8.

"CI at Cisco Systems: An Acquisitions Success Story." *Competitive Intelligence Magazine* 4, 1 (January–February 2001): 5–6.

Codogno, Enrico. "Getting CI from Internal Sources." *Competitive Intelligence Magazine* 2, 1 (January–March 1999): 21–23.

Cook, Michelle, and Curtis Cook. "Anticipating Unconventional M&As: The Case of DaimlerChrysler." *Competitive Intelligence Magazine* 4, 1 (January–February 2001): 19–22.

"CTI = M&A Success of DuPont." *Competitive Intelligence Magazine* 4, 1 (January–February 2001): 7.

Cullen, Susan E. "Communicating Complex Issues to Decision Makers." *Competitive Intelligence Magazine* 3, 3 (July–September 2000): 23–30.

Darveau, Louis-Jacques. "Forecasting an Acquisition: 5 Steps to Help You See It Coming." *Competitive Intelligence Magazine* 4, 1 (January–February 2001): 13–17.

Davison, Leigh. "Measuring CI Effectiveness: Insights from the Advertising Industry." In *Proceedings—2001 Annual International Conference and Exhibit* (pp. 387–391). Alexandria, Va.: Society of Competitive Intelligence Professionals, 2000.

Dishman, Paul. "Red Herrings and Disinformation: A Strategic Component of Counterintelligence." *Competitive Intelligence Magazine* 2, 4 (October–December 1999): 11–14.

Dishman, Paul. "Two Tools for M&A Analysis." *Competitive Intelligence Magazine* 4, 1 (January–February 2001): 23–26.

Feder, Stanley A. "Overcoming 'Mindsets': What Corporations Can Learn from Government Intelligence Failures." *Competitive Intelligence Review* 11, 3 (Third Quarter 2000): 28–36.

Fehringer, Dale. "Hot Off the Wires! Improve the Effectiveness of Your CI Newsletter." *Competitive Intelligence Magazine* 4, 3 (May–June 2001): 11, 14.

Fink, Alexander, and Oliver Schlake. "Scenario Management—An Approach for Strategic Foresight." *Competitive Intelligence Review* 11, 1 (First Quarter 2000): 37–45.

Fiora, Bill, and Paul Houston. "Recruiting for CI Positions." *Competitive Intelligence Magazine* 4, 5 (September–October 2001): 32–36.

Fleisher, Craig S. "A Farout Way to Manage CI Analysis." *Competitive Intelligence Magazine* 3, 2 (April–June 2000): 37–40.

Fleisher, Craig S. "Public Policy Competitive Intelligence." *Competitive Intelligence Review* 10, 2 (Second Quarter 1999): 23–36.

Flynn, Robert. "NutraSweet Faces Competition: The Critical Role of Competitive Intelligence." *Competitive Intelligence Review* 5, 4 (Winter 1994): 4–7.

Francis, David B., and Jan P. Herring. "Key Intelligence Topics: A Window on the Corporate Competitive Psyche." *Competitive Intelligence Review* 10, 4 (Second Quarter 1999): 10–19.

Gilad, Ben. "Industry Risk Management: CI's Next Step." *Competitive Intelligence Magazine* 4, 3 (May–June 2000): 21–27.

Gilbert, A. Lee. "Using Multiple Scenario Analysis to Map the Competitive Landscape: A Practice-Based Perspective." *Competitive Intelligence Review* 11, 2 (Second Quarter 2000): 12–19.

Glitman, Erik. "Comprehending 'Irrational' Competitor Actions through Futures-Based Analysis." *Competitive Intelligence Magazine* 3, 4 (October–December 2000): 29–32.

Holder, Bob J. "Scouting: A Process for Discovering, Creating and Acting on Knowledge." *Competitive Intelligence Magazine* 4, 2 (March–April 2001): 17–21.

House, Douglas. "Getting Inside Your Competitor's Head: A Roadmap for Understanding Goals and Assumptions." *Competitive Intelligence Magazine* 3, 4 (October–December 2000): 22–28.

Hovis, John H. "CI at Avnet: A Bottom-Line Impact." *Competitive Intelligence Review* 11, 3 (Third Quarter 2000): 5–15.

Hruby, F. Michael. "Scramble Competition: New Tools for Confronting New Competitors." *Competitive Intelligence Magazine* 2, 3 (July–September 1999): 15–18.

Kennedy, Kevyn. "Doing Business Globally? Focus CI on Suppliers." *Competitive Intelligence Magazine* 3, 1 (January–March 2000): 11–13.

Kennedy, Kevyn. "Minding the Supply Chain: Gray-Market Goods, Production 'Leakage', and Global CI." *Competitive Intelligence Magazine* 3, 3 (July–September 2000): 20–22.

Kennedy, Robert J. "Benchmarking and Its Myths." *Competitive Intelligence Magazine* 3, 2 (April–June 2000): 28–33.

Kerr, Roger Q. "Are Your CI Skills Valued?" *Competitive Intelligence Review* 6, 3 (Fall 1995): 61–63.

Kilmetz, S. David, and R. Sean Bridge. "Gauging the Returns on Investments in Competitive Intelligence: A Three-Step Analysis for Executive Decision Makers." *Competitive Intelligence Review* 10, 1 (First Quarter 1999): 4–11.

Klavans, Dick. "So, What Is the Value of Technical Intelligence? *Actionable Intelligence* (December 1997): 4.

Klein, Chuck. "The 7 Gates of Export Marketing Intelligence." *Competitive Intelligence Magazine* 3, 2 (April–June 2000): 34–36.

Laalo, Allan T. "Intranets and Competitive Intelligence: Creating Access to Knowledge." *Competitive Intelligence Review* 9, 4 (Fourth Quarter 2000): 63–72.

Langabeer, James A. "Exploring the CI Value Equation." *Competitive Intelligence Review* 10, 3 (Third Quarter 1999): 27–32.

Lisse, Bill. "Should U.S. Intelligence Agencies Provide CI?" *Competitive Intelligence Magazine* 2, 2 (April–June 1999): 25–26.

Margulies, Robert A., and Andre G. Gib. "Making Competitive Intelligence Relevant to the User: A Case Example." *The Competitive Intelligencer* 3, 1 (Spring 1988): 9.

McGonagle, John J. "Patterns of Development In CI Units." *Competitive Intelligence Review* 3, 1 (Spring 1992): 11–12.

McGonagle, John J., and Carolyn M. Vella. "Selling CI: Negatives Are Not Positive." *Competitive Intelligence Magazine* 4, 5 (September–October 2001): 37–38.

Miller, Jerry P. "The Education of Intelligence Professionals: A Surmountable Challenge." *Competitive Intelligence Review* 6, 3 (Fall 1995): 20–28.

Miller, Stephen H. "Special Report: Learning from the Government Intelligence Community." *Competitive Intelligence Magazine* 4, 4 (July–August 2001): 9–10.

Naylor, Ellen. "Capturing Competitive Intelligence From Your Sales Force." *Competitive Intelligence Magazine* 3, 1 (January–March 2000): 24–28.

Powell, Tim. "Tech Knowledge: Spotting Lemons on the Web." *Competitive Intelligence Magazine* 4, 2 (March–April 2001): 45.

Price, John. "Competitive Intelligence in Latin America: New Science Meets Old Practice." *Competitive Intelligence Magazine* 3, 4 (October–December 2000): 16–18.

Reibstein, David J., and Mark J. Chussil. "Putting the Lesson Before the Test: Using Simulation to Analyze and Develop Competitive Strategies." *Competitive Intelligence Review* 10, 1 (First Quarter 1999): 34–48.

Rice, Steve. "Public Environmental Records: A Treasure Chest of Competitive Information." *Competitive Intelligence Magazine* 3, 3 (July–September 2000): 13–19.

Robinson, Mark. "Competitive Information Security: Lessons from Los Alamos." *Competitive Intelligence Magazine* 4, 4 (July–August 2001): 14–16.

Rosen, Linda. "Capturing and Sharing Competitive Intelligence: Microsoft's Intranet." *Competitive Intelligence Magazine* 1, 2 (July–September 1998): 9–12.

Rothberg, Helen N. "Fortifying Strategic Decisions with Shadow Teams: A Glance at Product Development." *Competitive Intelligence Magazine* 2, 2 (April–June 1999): 9–11.

Russell, James. "Measuring the Value of Competitive Intelligence (CI) Activities: A Pilot Study." In *Conference Proceedings—2000 Annual International Conference and Exhibit* (p. 263). Alexandria, Va.: Society of Competitive Intelligence Professionals, 2000.

Savitz, Scott. "Wolf, Eagle, and Bear: CI Lessons from the Cold War." *Competitive Intelligence Review* 10, 3 (Third Quarter 1999): 79–83.

Sawka, Kenneth. "The Analyst's Corner: Are We Strategic?" *Competitive Intelligence Magazine* 3, 3 (July–September 2000): 57–58.

Sawka, Kenneth. "The Analyst's Corner: Are We Valuable?" *Competitive Intelligence Magazine* 3, 2 (April–June 2000): 53–54.

Sawka, Kenneth. "The Analyst's Corner: Drills and Holes." *Competitive Intelligence Magazine* 4, 1 (January–March 2000): 36–37.

Sawka, Kenneth. "The Analyst's Corner: Finding Intelligence Analysts." *Competitive Intelligence Magazine* 2, 1 (January–March 1999): 41–42.

Sawka, Kenneth. "The Analyst's Corner: Keep Your Message Short and Sweet." *Competitive Intelligence Magazine* 3, 1 (January–March 2000): 54–55.

Sawka, Kenneth. "The Analyst's Corner: Scenario Analysis: Alternative Worlds." *Competitive Intelligence Magazine* 4, 5 (September–October 2001): 41–42.

Sawka, Kenneth. "Competitive Intelligence Analysis: Filling the Corporate Analytic Void." *Competitive Intelligence Review* 8, 1 (Spring 1997): 87–89.

Sawyer, Deborah C. "Defining Your Competition: Are You Blunting Your Own Strategic Weapons?" *Competitive Intelligence Magazine* 3, 1 (January–March 2000): 44–45.

Sawyer, Deborah C. "Defining Your Competition: Balance of Power: When Suppliers Are Your Main Threat." *Competitive Intelligence Magazine* 3, 3 (July–September 2000): 51–52.

Sawyer, Deborah C. "Defining Your Competition: Inside Job: Organizational Structure as Competitive Saboteur." *Competitive Intelligence Magazine* 2, 1 (January–March 1999): 45–46.

Sawyer, Deborah C. "Defining Your Competition: One Step Forward, Two Steps Back." *Competitive Intelligence Magazine* 4, 4 (July–August 2001): 43–44.

Sawyer, Deborah C. "Defining Your Competition: Side Swiped: Supply-side Competitive Threats." *Competitive Intelligence Magazine* 3, 4 (October–December 2000): 50–51.

Sawyer, Deborah C. "Defining Your Competition: The Forest or the Trees?" *Competitive Intelligence Magazine* 4, 3 (May–June 2001): 43–44.

Sawyer, Deborah C. "Defining Your Competition: Trojan Horses, Fifth Columns, and Other Threats." *Competitive Intelligence Magazine* 3, 2 (April–June 2000): 45–46.

Sawyer, Deborah C. "Defining Your Competition: Turmoil Inside = Disadvantage Outside." *Competitive Intelligence Magazine* 2, 3 (July–September 1999): 47–48.

Shaker, Steven, and Mark P. Gembicki. "Competitive Intelligence: A Futurist's Perspective." *Competitive Intelligence Magazine* 2, 1 (January–March 1999): 24–27.

Sharp, Sheena. "Substitutes: Your Next Marketing Headache." *Competitive Intelligence Magazine* 1, 1 (April–June 1998): 44–46.

Sharp, Sheena. "Truth or Consequences: 10 Myths that Cripple Competitive Intelligence." *Competitive Intelligence Magazine* 3, 1 (January–March 2000): 37–40.

"Shedding Light on Science & Technology." *Competitive Intelligence Magazine* 3, 4 (October–December 2000): 12–13.

Simon, Neil. "Managing the CI Department." *Competitive Intelligence Magazine* 3, 2 (April–June 2000): 47–50.

Simon, Neil J. "Managing the CI Department: CI Teams Must Keep Pace as Companies Grow." *Competitive Intelligence Magazine* 1, 1 (April–June 1998): 47–49.

Simon, Neil J. "Managing the CI Department: Determining Measures of Success." *Competitive Intelligence Magazine* 1, 2 (July–September 1998): 45–47.

Solomon, Marc. "The Intelligence Asset-Building Process." *Competitive Intelligence Review* 7, 4 (Winter 1996): 69–76.

Stover, Peggy R. "Shoestring Intelligence: Preventative Medicine Against CI Attacks." *Competitive Intelligence Magazine* 2, 2 (April–June 1999): 37.

Stover, Peggy R. "Shoestring Intelligence: The Want Ads." *Competitive Intelligence Magazine* 1, 2 (July–September 1998): 43–44.

Stover, Peggy R. "Shoestring Intelligence: When the Press Interviews Your Competitors." *Competitive Intelligence Magazine* 2, 1 (January–March 1999): 37.

Thomas, Cody. "Surviving Deregulation: Using Field Reps for CI in the Electric Utility Industry." *Competitive Intelligence Magazine* 3, 1 (January–March 2000): 30–31.

Vella, Carolyn M., and John J. McGonagle. "Profiling in Competitive Analysis." *Competitive Intelligence Review* 11, 2 (Second Quarter 2000): 20–30.

Ward, Constance Thomas. "Real Life CI: Alphabet Soup for Lunch, Anyone?" *Competitive Intelligence Magazine* 2, 4 (October–December 1999): 42.

Ward, Constance Thomas. "Real Life CI: CI-AOK; But CIA—No Way." *Competitive Intelligence Magazine* 2, 3 (July–September 1999): 35.

Wells, Cheryl Ann. "Analyzing Corporate Personalities: A New Method for Your CI Toolkit." *Competitive Intelligence Magazine* 4, 4 (July–August 2001): 17–20.

Werther, Guntram F. A. "Beyond the Blocking Tree: Improving Performance in Future-Oriented Analysis." *Competitive Intelligence Magazine* 3, 4 (October–December 2000): 40–44.

Werther, Guntram F. A. "Profiling 'Change Processes' as a Strategic Analysis Tool." *Competitive Intelligence Magazine* 3, 1 (January–March 2000): 19–22.

Williams, Phil. "Criminal Risk Assessment: A New Dimension of Competitive Intelligence." *Competitive Intelligence Review* 10, 2 (Second Quarter 1999): 37–45.

Wreden, Nick. "Business Intelligence—Turning on Success." *Beyond Computing* (September 1997): 19, 24.

Yake, Thomas. "Why Retailers Fail: Discovering the Telltale Signs." *Competitive Intelligence Magazine* 4, 3 (May–June 2001): 15–19.

Index